The Legacy of Erich Fromm

The Legacy of
Erich Fromm

Daniel Burston

Harvard University Press
Cambridge, Massachusetts
London, England
1991

Library of Congress Cataloging-in-Publication Data

Burston, Daniel, 1954–
    The legacy of Erich Fromm / Daniel Burston.
        p.   cm.
    Includes bibliographical references (p.   ) and index.
    ISBN 0-674-52168-4 (acid-free paper)
    1. Fromm, Erich, 1900–1980.   2. Psychoanalysis.   I. Title.
BF109.F76B87   1991   90-5348
150.19′57′092—dc20   CIP

To my father and mother

Preface

When I first resolved to write this book, I was concerned that the work of Erich Fromm had been subject to excessive or misinformed criticism from many quarters. To form an accurate critical understanding of Fromm's ideas and to help rescue him from relative obscurity, it seemed necessary to debunk some widespread misconceptions of Fromm as a naive utopian, a naive environmentalist, or an accomplice in the so-called Americanization or trivialization of psychoanalysis. It soon became apparent that, to do this effectively, I would have to periodize Fromm's work and explore a variety of topics that are commonly ignored or treated in relative isolation in the extant literature. This burgeoning list of topics eventually came to include: (1) Fromm's "Freud piety" and his differences with Karen Horney and Harry Stack Sullivan; (2) Fromm's synthesis of Marx, Freud, and Weber in his studies of fascism, authoritarianism, and contemporary social character; (3) his relationship to Marx and to his older contemporary Wilhelm Reich; (4) Fromm's use of the matriarchal theory of J. J. Bachofen; (5) his affinities and differences with non-Marxist proponents of matriarchal theory such as Carl Jung, Otto Rank, and Ian Suttie and with object-relations theorist Ronald Fairbairn; (6) his affinities and differences with existential psychoanalysts and philosophers such as Martin Buber, Max Scheler, Martin Heidegger, Ludwig Binswanger, and Viktor Frankl; and (7) the lingering influence on Fromm of German Enlightenment and neo-Kantian thought, which were submerged during his first, Freudo-Marxist phase but surfaced in midlife in his existentialism and political theory.

As my research progressed, I realized how shortsighted it is to classify Fromm as a neo-Freudian. By emphasizing Fromm's resemblance to Horney, Sullivan, and Clara Thompson, historians of psychology, psychiatry, and psychoanalysis inadvertently overlook some of the most dynamic and multifaceted dimensions of Fromm's ideas. By situating him in a midcentury "post-Freudian" climate of opinion, particularly an American one, friends and critics alike overlook Fromm's profound indebtedness to nineteenth-century German thought. At the same time, I found that the radically dehistoricized and frequently uncharitable assessments of Fromm that pervade the literature conceal the real tensions and contradictions in his thought. By early middle age, Fromm saw himself as Freud's pupil and translator, intent on transposing Freud's insights out of his mechanistic and biologistic language and into the idiom of radical or existential humanism. Unfortunately, Fromm did not see that his brand of Marxist or existential humanism was simply not equipped to grapple in a rigorous and methodical way with the developmental dimension that Freud had introduced to the study of clinical psychopathology. As a result, most of his writings on psychoanalytic characterology place more emphasis on the dialectic between innate constitution (temperament) and socioeconomic conditions than on the idea of "arrested development." Indeed, most of Fromm's formulations on symptom and character after 1939 unequivocally reject Freud's attempt to situate neurotic and psychotic character traits at specific points along a hypothetical psychosexual continuum. Nevertheless—and inconsistently—Fromm invoked the ontogenetic schemata developed by Freud, Sandor Ferenczi, and Karl Abraham when it suited his purpose, expounding on them with great skill, sensitivity, and obvious appreciation.

Fromm's dual posture toward the developmental dimension in Freudian theory had one unfortunate repercussion in his theory of "necrophilia." In the late 1940s and the 1950s, Fromm had described gratuitous violence as the result of "unlived life," or a kind of negative transcendence that results from an individual's characterological inability to engender or promote life actively. He contended that sadism and destructiveness are distinctively human phenomena; they result from the frustration of existential needs that arise from the human condition and are rooted in abortive attempts to transcend our condition of "thrownness" (Heidegger's *Geworfenheit*) and to achieve genuine relatedness to other human beings. These ideas, though by no means original to Fromm, constituted a cogent and persuasive rebuttal to the orthodox Freudian position that sadism and destructiveness are irrevocably inscribed in our instinctual being. They remained a stabilizing plank in Fromm's humanist platform. But in 1973 Fromm speculated that necrophilia represents a morbid intensification of anal trends, issuing in a regressive reactivation of a previous phyletic stage, the so-called anal-olfactory-hating orientation supposedly characteristic of four-legged mammals. Having staked his reputation on redeeming Freud's essential discoveries from the mechanistic and biologistic limitations of the libido theories, Fromm was now conjuring with the most dubious feature of Freud's psychobiology, Ernst Haeckel's biogenetic principle, which regards ontogenetic development as a straightforward recapitulation of our entire history as a species.

Fromm's belated excursion into speculative biology played a peripheral role in his work as a whole. However, this apparent lapse of logic and judgment seems emblematic of his whole posture toward Freud and the psychoanalytic movement. It represents a desperate, last-minute attempt to authenticate his claim to be following in Freud's footsteps, and an oblique admission that perhaps Freud was at least partly right and that his own reflections on sadism and destructiveness—though intriguing and persuasive on many levels—lacked an adequate biological foundation.

The question then arises: were Fromm's claims to be following in Freud's footsteps based in fact? My answer is an emphatic but still qualified yes. I disagree with the pundits who regard Fromm's work after 1941 as a simple capitulation to American cultural anthropology or as a descent into idealism, pragmatism, or mere "positive thinking." Although Fromm's style did become increasingly homiletic as the years passed, his philosophical outlook was a thoughtful blend of humanism, existentialism, and Marxism, mediated through the prism of German Enlightenment and neo-Kantian thought and infused with traces of prophecy and mysticism. It is also, admittedly, a revisionist system of psychoanalysis, as Fromm himself insisted. But it is neither as glib nor as inconsistent with Fromm's earlier work as many of his critics allege.

I owe a profound debt to many people for their help or inspiration over many years.

My first thanks must go to Professor Henri Ellenberger, whose *Discovery of the Unconscious* remains the single most valuable resource in the history of psychoanalysis. Ellenberger is the only author save Fromm to reckon J. J. Bachofen's importance to psychoanalytic theory at something like its real worth, and the first to situate the history of psychoanalysis within the broader history of ideas. Next, I must thank Professor Paul Roazen, who alerted me early on to the many pitfalls of Freud piety, while keeping a balanced appreciation for Freud's accomplishments. His many publications are filled with searching characterizations of Freud and his circle, and a wealth of information and reflection that are well-nigh indispensable for the fledgling historian of psychoanalysis.

Next, I must thank Professor Kurt Danziger, who supervised my doctoral dissertation, for alerting me to the ethnocentric bias in American theorists' attempts to grasp, formulate, or criticize Fromm's ideas, for deepening my grasp of nineteenth-century German thought, and for making me lastingly and profoundly distrustful of "textbook history." I am also grateful to him for many thoughtful suggestions—both substantive and stylistic—that are incorporated in this book.

Doctors Mark Kanzer, Eric T. Carlson, Doris Nagel Baker, Lawrence Freeman, Cornelius Clark, and Jacques Quen at the History of Psychiatry Section at the Payne Whitney Clinic, Cornell Medical Center, New York Hospital, provided moral, technical, and financial support while I was a predoctoral fellow there. In that stimulating atmosphere I shared the excitement and perplexities engendered by my research in ongoing dialogues with Dr. Carlson, Dr. Nathan Kravis, and Dr. Lenny Groopman. Warm thanks to them all, and to the friends and associates of the History of Psychiatry Section who read or remarked on some aspect of this book, including Dr. John Kerr, Dr. Paul Stepansky, Kitty Moore, Professor Jeffrey Wollock, and Professor Barbara Leavy.

Solomon Asch commented in generous detail on the chapters concerning Fromm's psychology of conformity. The warmth and interest of Professor Asch and his wife, Florence, strengthened my faith that my project was worthwhile.

I thank my friends at the Mexican Institute of Psychoanalysis, which invited me to the First National Congress of Humanistic Psychoanalysis in March 1990 to learn more about Fromm's sojourn in Mexico. Warm thanks also to Dr. Rolando Weissmann, Dr. Ivan Illich,

Dr. Alejandro Cordova, Martha Ortiz-Monasterio, Martha Ortiz-Monasterio (the younger), and Mr. and Mrs. Frederico Lachica.

Many informants and interlocutors gave me their time either in person or by letter. I owe a special debt of gratitude to Dr. Rainer Funk, Dr. Michael Maccoby, and Professor David Riesman for their candor, cooperation, and support over the years. Dr. Funk, executor of the Erich Fromm Literary Estate, Tübingen, kindly gave me permission to quote from Fromm's texts and to use the photographs included in this volume. Thanks also to Professor Ashley Montagu, Dr. Douglas Carmichael, Dr. Marianne Ekhart, Dr. Bernard Landis, Dr. Anna Antonovsky, Dr. Herbert Spiegel, Professor Robert Rieber, Dr. Maurice Green, and Dr. Paul Wachtel.

I thank Professors Christian Lenhart and Neal Wood of the Department of Political Science at York University for thorough and thoughtful readings of the manuscript and for many valuable suggestions. Thanks also to Doctors Morris Eagle and Ray Fancher of the Psychology Department at York University for their kindness and support, and to Michael Aronson and Angela von der Lippe of Harvard University Press for their solid, supportive encouragement and their help in ensuring that this book was published.

Finally, I am deeply grateful to the Social Science and Humanities Research Council of Canada for its many years of unfailing support, which allowed me to complete this project.

Contents

Illustrations

All photographs are from the Erich Fromm Archives, Tübingen.

The Legacy of Erich Fromm

1 *The Man and His Work*

Of the psychoanalysts who have contributed both to clinical and social psychology and to the psychoanalytic movement, Erich Fromm was, for a time, among the most popular and prolific. His books *Escape from Freedom* (1941), *The Sane Society* (1955b), *The Art of Loving* (1956a), and *Zen Buddhism and Psychoanalysis* (1960d) were bestsellers, commanding a wide and attentive audience. Since Fromm's death, however, they have had little impact on scholarship, and Fromm himself has fallen into obscurity. This intellectual biography aims to rescue Fromm from that undeserved fate and to put his contributions into critical and historical perspective, enabling us to dispense with banal stereotypes of the man as a towering genius or as a vague, homiletic popularizer who was secretly impervious, if not actually hostile, to the deeper implications of Freud's thought.

Apart from Fromm's intrinsic merits as a clinician, social psychologist, and existential humanist, there are several reasons why his work is of interest in the history of psychology and psychoanalysis. Fromm's reflections on social psychology were unique in attempting a synthesis of the spirit and sophistication of various proponents of the nineteenth-century *Geisteswissenschaften* with an empirical research program on the social and historical determinants of obedience and conformity in contemporary society, uniting past and present in social psychology with elements from Karl Marx and Sigmund Freud. Moreover, Fromm's ideas on the history of the psychoanalytic movement are extremely thought-provoking, and his life and his dealings with colleagues provide an illuminating example of what I term "Freud piety." The texture, content, and underlying determinants of this attitude of reverence toward the master are among the most neglected topics in psychoanalytic historiography. On close inspection Fromm's life and thought are replete with examples of this phenomenon. Admonishing some of his contemporaries in the introduction to Patrick Mullahy's *Oedipus: Myth and Complex,* for example, Fromm wrote: "The credulous public often fails to distinguish between a genius, whose name will be remembered centuries from now . . . and those who add to, revise and correct his findings. Indeed, to stand on a giant's shoulders makes some people think they are taller than the giant and that they have reason for looking down on him" (Mullahy, 1948, p. iv).

On another occasion, in conversation with Richard Evans, Fromm differentiated himself from Karen Horney and Harry Stack Sullivan by saying, "I feel . . . like a pupil and translator of Freud who is attempting to bring out his most important discoveries in order to enrich them and to deepen them by liberating them from the somewhat narrow libido theory" (Evans, 1966, p. 59).

In other words, although he never actually met him, Fromm's relationship to Freud was pivotal to his sense of identity, and a distinctive property of his evolving life's work was how it reflected his sustained attempts to reconcile his loyalty to Freud with other influences and ideas. This was not his unique destiny, of course. It was shared by all of Freud's "loyal opposition"—those analysts whose loyalties to Freud prompted them to stay within the organizational framework of psychoanalysis despite their disagreements with him on important issues and despite the diminished trust, esteem, and credibility they often suffered among their colleagues as a consequence.[1] This group included independent analysts such as Ludwig Binswanger, Georg Groddeck, Sandor Ferenczi, Karen Horney early in her career, and others who were subsequently identified with a discernible aim or tendency, among them Freudo-Marxists such as Wilhelm Reich, Fromm, Otto Fenichel, and object-relations theorists such as W. R. D. Fairbairn and Harry Guntrip. Of these, the Freudo-Marxists were the most fractious, the most prone to argue among themselves about which features of Freud's work were essential and which were expendable or wrong.

The loyal opposition, which included many gifted thinkers, found itself in occasional conflict with the "dissident fringe" of the psychoanalytic movement, a varied lot including Alfred Adler, Carl Jung,

Otto Rank, and Horney in her later years, who, after a period of apprenticeship, languished briefly in opposition but were either expelled or felt constrained to leave or start their own schools. Here also belong influential figures such as Ian Suttie and Charles Rycroft, who had no personal dealings with Freud and no desire to start a school but counted themselves as crusaders in Freud's cause until a personal and intellectual crisis intervened, and their revised clinical orientation precipitated a forthright critique of the master (for example, Rycroft, 1985, introduction). Harry Stack Sullivan belongs in their midst, if only because of his utter *lack* of Freud piety, which probably annoyed Fromm no end.

A third group, the "crypto-revisionists," resembled the orthodox and the loyal opposition in stressing their fidelity to Freud. But instead of an open avowal of their revisionist agendas, they made what are actually major departures from orthodoxy appear as logical extensions or developments of the master's own thought. They did this by their seeming acceptance of the traditional Freudian emphasis on sex and aggression—while developing ideas at a tangent to them—or by taking ideas that originate on the dissident fringe and rearticulating them in terms of the libido theories without acknowledging their dissident forebears. This is the most heterogeneous classification of all, including people such as Erik Erikson, Heinz Hartmann, Edith Jacobson, Melanie Klein, Heinz Kohut, Margaret Mahler, Donald Winnicott, and, in a curious way, even Jacques Lacan, who, unlike the others, courted expulsion from orthodox circles in the interests of fidelity to Freud—or Freud as he understood him—rather than staying in the mainstream.

Still, all three groups—the loyal opposition, the dissident fringe, and the crypto-revisionists—are distinguished more by their attitudes toward Freud and their posture toward "orthodoxy" and "outgroups" than by the actual content of their ideas. For with the appropriate rites of passage, ideas originating among the dissident fringe eventually make their way into the mainstream, where struggles to authenticate one's loyalties to Freud by dismissing or denouncing the early heretics continue in earnest. Thus the conceptual distance between Jung and Rank (dissident fringe), Fromm and Fairbairn (loyal opposition), and Mahler and Jacobson (crypto-revisionists) on the importance of individuating from the intrauterine or symbiotic matrix is comparatively small in comparison with the substantive differences between Hartmann and Lacan (crypto-revisionists) on the nature and function of the ego.

Contemporary psychoanalysis is the product of the murderous antipathies and inevitable confluences among these three groups, and the urgent need of the orthodox and the crypto-revisionists to assimilate into the mainstream—covertly, if possible—insights into the etiology and treatment of neuroses that originate outside their circle, to offset the incipient theoretical ossification that would otherwise paralyze the movement. Though seldom thought of in this connection, Fromm was an important player in this process. As a left-wing member of Freud's loyal opposition, with affinities to the dissident fringe, he helped mediate the transfer of ideas from the periphery to the center of the psychoanalytic movement. And because he played this mediating function, many ideas that actually originated with him were espoused by (and attributed to) other, more respectable pundits somewhat later.

In classifying Fromm with the loyal opposition, I implicitly reject the orthodox and crypto-revisionist consensus that places him on the dissident fringe. By his own estimation—and mine—a salient difference between him, Horney, and Sullivan was his sense of kinship with and loyalty to Freud. Moreover, strong elements of Freud piety suffuse his polemics against Adler, Jung, and Rank despite his outspoken critique of Freud's intolerance toward dissidents. I suspect that Fromm's diatribes against the medicalization and bureaucratization of psychoanalysis contributed greatly to his being classified with the dissident fringe: his frank and outspoken stand on these issues put him in de facto opposition to those who constitute the mainstream in North America, who lump Freud's loyal opposition and the dissident fringe together indiscriminately for their own convenience.

Periodizing Fromm's Work

Although any attempt to periodize a thinker's output can be misleading, it helps to situate him among contemporaries and to contextualize his development in a changing intellectual environment. From this standpoint, it makes sense to characterize the period 1929–1935 as Fromm's Freudo-Marxist phase. Although Fromm continued to ponder a Freud-Marx synthesis thereafter, this project dominated his early career, while other interests—such as Bachofen and matriarchal theory—were tied to this superordinate objective (Funk, 1984). These years witnessed Fromm's publication of remarkable studies on psychoanalysis and historical materialism, matriarchal theory, and the psychology of fascism and a growing dissatisfaction with orthodox Freudianism, culminating in an article titled "The Social Limitations of Psychoanalytic Theory" (Fromm, 1935a: Jay, 1973).

The middle period, from 1936 to 1960, began with a sketch for *Escape from Freedom* titled "Selfishness and Self-Love" (Fromm, 1939a) and was characterized by an increasing preoccupation with religious and theological topics. It witnessed the emergence of a distinctive philosophical anthropology rooted in existential philosophy, Spinoza, Marx, the Old Testament, Zen Buddhism, and Renaissance humanism, leavened with references to Christian and Islamic mystics. It was also a period of political activism and of Fromm's greatest popularity worldwide. During this time Fromm published numerous best-sellers, including *Escape from Freedom, The Sane Society,* and *The Art of Loving*. He established a psychoanalytic institute in Mexico, where he resided most of the time after 1950 but continued to lecture in the United States and Europe, including nations in the Eastern bloc, notably Yugoslavia and Poland, where his influence on dissident Marxists was profound.

Fromm's final years, from 1960 to 1980, began with a kind of return to Freud and an intriguing (if problematic) attempt to transpose Freud's life and death instincts into an entirely new key. They were also a period of review, consolidation, and, from a scholarly standpoint, much needless repetition, although Fromm's writing continued to be punctuated by fresh and provocative insights. *The Anatomy of Human Destructiveness* (1973) was an instant best-seller because of its topical subject matter and Fromm's worldwide reputation. *To Have or to Be?* (1976) had little tangible impact in North America but was widely read and cited among the ecologically minded, radically decentralized political party that has sprung up in West Germany and elsewhere, called "the Greens." Together with *Greatness and Limitations of Freud's Thought* (1980), published shortly before his death, it represented a kind of synthesis and summing up, combining material from earlier books with new and probing variations on old themes, including the negligible role of instinct in regulating human behavior, socially patterned defects, existential needs, and Freud's patriarchalism and incorrigible sexism.

This way of periodizing Fromm's output focuses on vagaries of style, subject matter, and the public's response to his work. Another way of periodizing Fromm's work is to see it as a series of responses to crises. The first crisis to absorb Fromm's attention was the protracted period of cognitive dissonance that seized western Marxism as the revolution that Marx had predicted in Western Europe failed to materialize and as fascism gathered ominous momentum. Many central European intellectuals (such as Karl Popper, Arthur Koestler, and Simone Weil) regarded the proletariat's evident inability to deliver the death-blow to capitalism as a resounding refutation of historical materialism and turned elsewhere for enlightenment and emancipation. Left-wing Freudians, including Paul Federn, Siegfried Bernfeld, Reich, Fenichel, and Fromm, took up the challenge posed by the failure of Marx's predictions. Rather than reject Marxism completely, they attempted, with the aid of psychoanalytic theory, to fathom the "subjective factor" that engendered proletarian inertia. The prevailing consensus in this group was that Freud's attempt to explain the irrationality and compliance of the masses on the basis of an "archaic inheritance," or putative events in remote prehistory, was misleading. According to them, widespread patterns of compliance and guilt originate in interlocking levels of socialization characteristic of the authoritarian family, church, and educational systems. Although Federn, Bernfeld, and Reich preceded him somewhat, Fromm developed an original point of view and, with the support of the Frankfurt Institute for Social Research, first studied these trends empirically, setting the stage, methodologically speaking, for *The Authoritarian Personality,* by Theodor Adorno and his associates (Adorno et al., 1950).

From the 1940s through the 1960s Fromm continued to write on the psychology of authoritarianism and attempted to reconcile Freud and Marx. But through most of this period he focused preeminently on the spiritual malaise of postwar industrial capitalism, the crisis of reason embodied in the Cold War and nuclear arms race, and the looming ecological crisis. Like Max Horkheimer and Adorno, C. Wright Mills, R. D. Laing, and others, Fromm saw the problems of consensus, conformity, and false consciousness taking on new and disturbing dimensions in the context of a nominally democratic and "open" society characterized by alienation, consumerism, and a "mass culture" unlike any existing before. Fromm emphasized the need for spiritual rediscovery and renewal, for a conscious and deliberate renunciation of the acquisitive, consumeristic, and materialistic orientation of contemporary culture. This stance contributed to his popularity among the young and prompted him to extend enthusiastic support to the antinuclear and anti–Vietnam War movements, and somewhat more qualified support to other aspects of student activism and the counterculture that rejected middle-class mores and material aspirations.[2]

After 1970 Fromm continued to decry the materialism of Western society, as in *To Have or to Be?* (1976). But the crisis that now occupied him most was the crisis of psychoanalysis (Fromm, 1970a). Fromm thought that declining enrollments at analytic institutes and the waning popularity of psychoanalysis as a treatment modality were symptomatic of a deeper problem. According to Fromm, psychoanalysis had become a bureaucratic organizational apparatus, not unlike a church, which stifled independent thought and promoted conformist values. To be sure, this was not the first time Fromm had said so (for example, 1935a, 1959b). But by his current reckoning, the crisis had reached unprecedented proportions and could deepen in the decades ahead unless psychoanalysis gave up its desire for respectability and forthrightly addressed what he termed "the pathology of normalcy." Fromm was not alone. Indeed, he was part of a growing chorus who uttered dire prognostications for psychoanalysis. Sadly and ironically, the majority of people who seemed to share his misgivings on some level also charged Fromm with embodying the conformist trends he so deplored. From 1955 to the end of his life, Fromm was repeatedly reproached for reviving all the trite nostrums of conventional morality; of fashioning a theory remote from the depths of human experience (for example, Marcuse, 1955; Jacoby, 1975; Robinson, 1976). With one or two exceptions, these withering indictments echoed the polemics of the Frankfurt School that had dogged Fromm's career since his departure in 1938 (Roazen, 1973; Jay, 1973).

The problem with this periodization, as with any other, is that it tends to emphasize change and difference at the expense of continuity. Even if we eschew discrete stages and think in terms of phases that blend into one another, we are simply describing Fromm's career, as viewed from the outside, and not the internal development of his thought. In so doing, we may lose sight of the structural and thematic continuity that unites his earliest reflections on psychoanalysis and sociology (1929) with his final reflections on Freud (1980). Once we do that, we are susceptible to developing a distorted picture of Fromm's theoretical development or an arbitrary preference for a specific period, like Fenichel and Marcuse, who contrasted the "good" Freudian Fromm of the late 1920s and early 1930s with the "bad," "revisionist" Fromm thereafter (Fenichel, 1944; Marcuse, 1955). Careful study of Fromm's work suggests that it underwent gradual and harmonious evolution, with later positions clearly foreshadowed in the earliest material. If there is a definitive transition, as his critics allege, it is discernible chiefly as a significant *shift in focus* that occurred partway through the "middle period," marked by Fromm's increasing concern with what he variously termed "automaton conformity" (1941), the "marketing character" (1947), obedience to "anonymous authority" (1955b), and correspondingly less emphasis on fascism and the problems of old-fashioned authoritarianism, which had brought him widespread recognition in *Escape from Freedom*. This change of emphasis was prompted by Fromm's visceral response to features of American social character that he found alarming and distasteful, rather than by a change in theoretical orientation.

Childhood, Education, Role Models

Erich Pinchas Fromm was born March 23, 1900, in Frankfurt, Germany. He was the only child of Rosa and Naphtali Fromm. Theirs was not a happy marriage, and in later life Fromm did not hesitate to characterize his mother as overprotective, his father as distant, and himself as an "unbearable, neurotic child" (Funk, 1982, p. 1). Rosa Fromm, née Krause, often said that every good trait of character young Erich possessed sprang from his Krause ancestry; everything bad, from the Fromm line. Apart from the antipathy Rosa bore Erich's father, she was apparently more concerned for secondhand fame and recognition than for Erich's personal happiness, and tried to live vicariously through her offspring. Rosa dreamed that young Erich would be a famous pianist and composer, and became deeply depressed as Fromm abandoned music in favor of Talmud study under the influence of a great-uncle, Ludwig Krause, one of Erich's earliest role models (ibid., p. 14).

Though close to his father in early childhood, Fromm felt that

Fromm with his mother, Rosa, née Krause

Naphtali lost interest in him as he matured. However, when he was twenty-one Naphtali came to be with him during final exams at Heidelberg University, apparently anxious that his son might fail and contemplate suicide, although he did nothing of the kind (Funk, 1984, p. 21). At the very least, this episode suggests that Naphtali was prone to projecting his own fears of failure and inadequacy onto his son. Perhaps beneath this anxious display of parental solicitude lurked the *wish* that young Erich might fail. Naphtali, too, had hoped to be a scholar or rabbi, as his son was becoming, and he deeply regretted the missed opportunity.

Young Erich, for his part, may have fueled the ambivalence his father felt toward him by his choice of career. Naphtali was a small wine merchant, descended (like Erich's mother) from a long line of rabbis. He was unhappy with his vocation but extremely active in the Jewish community; among other things, he was a cofounder and president of the Hermann Cohen Lodge in their community (Funk, 1984, p. 21). Rainer Funk, citing interviews with Fromm, notes that as a child Fromm felt shame and embarrassment in the presence of any adult who identified himself as a businessman, since presumably this indicated that the person spent his life in pursuit of material prosperity and profit, rather than spiritual development (ibid., p. 8). Funk takes this attitude as evidence of Erich Fromm's spiritual precocity. Perhaps it was. But it may also have reflected Erich's feelings toward his father. Holding to "spiritual values" that disregard the practical necessity of making money, or taking other men besides one's father as role models, might be culturally acceptable ways for sublimating Oedipal rivalry. Then again, Erich may only have identified with his father's feelings of inferiority vis-à-vis his failure to become a rabbi, his modest income, his inability to make the marriage work, and so on.

From Fromm's published reminiscences we know of two adolescent experiences that shaped his later intellectual development. At age twelve, Fromm was shocked by the suicide of a friend of the family, who took her life after her father died. She was twenty-four, a gifted painter, extremely attractive, and presumably had a great deal to live for. Fromm had been very fond of this woman and was stunned by the irrationality of the act, puzzling over its meaning for years afterward (Fromm, 1962, chap. 1). The second experience was the First World War. Fromm's antipathy to Jewish nationalism, and indeed to all kinds of nationalist fervor, was rooted in this experience of collective madness (ibid.). Indeed, it is tempting to speculate that *The Anatomy of Human Destructiveness* (1973), written while Fromm was in his seventies, was conceived in response to questions that germinated in the anguish and confusion felt by a sensitive, gifted, and insecure adolescent discovering himself in midst of the carnage, deception, and the deep sense of helplessness he experienced during wartime. In his own words: "When the war ended in 1918, I was a

Fromm with his father, Naphtali

deeply troubled young man who was obsessed with the question of how war was possible, by the wish to understand the irrationality of human mass behavior, by a passionate desire for peace and international understanding. More, I had become deeply suspicious of all official ideologies and declarations, and filled with the conviction that 'of all one must doubt' " (1962, p. 9).

As he grew older, Fromm's distrust of all official ideologies expressed itself in his attraction to psychoanalysis and Marxism, and
soon thereafter in his forthright challenges to the prevailing ortho-
doxies within these schools of thought. Fromm's adolescence was not
all *Sturm und Drang*, however. Despite family estrangement and the
fears and perplexities engendered by the war, there was intellectual
stimulation and conviviality in his milieu. In keeping with his name
(Fromm means "pious"), as a child Erich had received an intense
religious education, with a view to becoming a Talmudist (Funk,
1984, chap. 2). He was taught by noted scholars and friends of the
family, but during adolescence he cultivated particularly close ties
with R. Nehemia Nobel, a mystic and Goethe enthusiast who had a
profound influence on Franz Rosenzweig, the noted Jewish philosopher.

According to Leo Lowenthal, another of Nobel's students and Erich
Fromm's childhood friend, Nehemia Nobel mixed conventional Talmud instruction with mysticism, philosophy, socialism, and psychoanalysis, all in conjunction with conservative Judaism (Lowenthal,
1987, pp. 19–21). Despite his traditionalism in religious observance,
Nobel was deeply immersed in the legacy of the German Enlightenment and was a student and friend of Hermann Cohen, the celebrated
neo-Kantian philosopher and biblical scholar of Marburg who was
mentor to Ernst Cassirer. Cohen was a liberal in terms of religious
observance and biblical exegesis but espoused a variety of socialist
humanism similar to that of Moses Hess, the left-wing Hegelian who
had converted Engels, and then Marx, to socialism in 1840 (Schulman, 1963; Avineri, 1981, chap. 3). The philosophical parallels between Hess and Cohen would not be noteworthy had Hess not thematized the "being" and "having" modes of existence in 1842, and it
is through his mediation that these ideas entered into Marx's work
(Schulman, 1963, chap. 2) and, from there, into Fromm's thought
(Fromm, 1961b, 1976). Hess influenced the kibbutz movement,
which practiced a brand of communitarian socialism not unlike that
which Fromm espoused in *The Sane Society* (1955b). Yet mention of
Hess is conspicuously absent from most of Fromm's books—perhaps
because Hess, having despaired of international socialism, became a
Zionist and a mentor to Theodor Herzl (Avineri, 1981, chap. 9).

Although Fromm was for a brief time an ardent Zionist—evidently
under Nobel's influence—he repudiated Zionism in 1927, the same

year he commenced clinical practice, and one year after he abandoned religious observances. Gershom Scholem, who knew Fromm peripherally, remembered 1927 as the year Fromm became a committed Trotskyist (Bonss, 1984, p. 20n). Rainer Funk dismisses this claim as "nonsensical" (1984, p. 35). But it may contain a germ of truth. Politically, Fromm was being radicalized by his contact with Rabbi Salman Baruch Rabinkow, whose pupil Isaak Steinberg had taken an active part in both the first and second Russian revolutions, and left the U.S.S.R. only in 1923, when the Bolsheviks repressed all opposition (ibid., p. 37). According to David Riesman, in later life Fromm expressed a deep admiration for Trotsky "as revolutionary thinker, as general, as exile" (personal communication, July 9, 1985). Consequently, it is possible that Trotsky's views on "the Jewish question," which paralleled Marx's, influenced Fromm. Dr. Anna Antonovsky—among others whom Fromm supervised at the William Alanson White Institute—recalls Fromm's passionate denunciations of the injustices perpetrated by Israeli settlers on Palestinian Arabs (personal communication, March 1988).

But if Trotsky's influence went deep, Hermann Cohen's went deeper. Like Trotsky—but for different reasons—Cohen opposed Jewish nationalism, charging that the universalism and humanism of the prophets precluded loyalty to a state—even a "Jewish" one (Funk, 1984). Although he never mentioned Cohen in connection with politics, in *You Shall Be as Gods* (1966), Fromm's book on the Old Testament, he paid homage to Cohen's universalist humanism, citing him repeatedly in the opening passages and marginalia (for example, p. 9).

While studying sociology in Heidelberg, at age eighteen, under the instruction of Alfred Weber, Fromm became acquainted with Habad Hassidism through R. Salman Baruch Rabinkow (Funk, 1984, chap. 3), who was a mystic and a socialist. Hassidism, which germinated in Eastern Europe in the middle to late eighteenth century, was a populist reaction against the excessive legalism and rationalism of mainstream rabbinic orthodoxy. It dignified the piety of peasants and tradesmen not versed in Torah by investing the rituals of daily life with religious significance and by making the joy and sincerity of the worshiper, rather than his knowledge of scripture, the criterion of faith and the path to redemption. Habad Hassidism differed from most varieties of Hassidism by reinvesting study with great significance, although its interpretation of scripture was in a mystical, Kabbalistic vein popular with the common people. Indeed, study acquired such exalted stature among the Habadniks that it became the preeminent form of worship, elevated, in many cases, above actual religious observance.

Fromm's exposure to Habad Hassidism was probably too brief to qualify him as a real Habadnik. But it had an enduring influence; although Fromm renounced his belief in God, he never tired of singing the many Hassidic songs he had learned in Rabinkow's company, and he meditated on scripture throughout his life. In an unpublished fragment entitled "Memories of Rabbi Salman Baruch Rabinkow" summarized in Rainer Funk's biography, Fromm praised his former teacher for his powerful and deeply felt synthesis of the politics of protest with traditional Jewish piety. He did this, according to Fromm, by interpreting the Jewish tradition in the spirit of "radical humanism," the same spirit in which Fromm himself approached the Old Testament (Funk, 1984, pp. 39–45).

Although Fromm was chiefly attracted to conservative and orthodox teachers, he also had contact with more "modern" Jews. Georg Salzberger, a liberal rabbi from Frankfurt, remembered talking with Fromm immediately after World War I about ways of fostering Jewish awareness through education. As a result of these deliberations, Salzberger and this eager adolescent founded the Gesellschaft für jüdische Volksbildung im Frankfurt am Main (Frankfurt Association for Jewish Studies) in February 1920. With the arrival of Franz Rosenzweig in Frankfurt that summer, and the influx of Rosenzweig's friends and pupils, these associates jointly founded a new society, the Freie Jüdische Lehrhaus (Free Jewish Study House), devoted to the secular study of Judaica. The influx of more experienced personnel and Fromm's youth seem to have kept his teaching opportunities there minimal. Nevertheless, the experience afforded him the opportunity to meet Martin Buber, Gerschom Scholem, and S. I. Agnon (Funk, 1984).

Although he is often characterized as some sort of Pollyanna, Fromm's assessment of contemporary life could be scathing, and we need only reflect on Fromm's early role models to appreciate why his alienation from contemporary capitalism was so profound. The uniquely Jewish synthesis of mysticism and rationalism, of soulful spontaneity and love of learning, of profound loneliness and a love of community, of radical protest and a love of tradition—these antinomies were combined in Fromm's character in more or less the same proportion as they existed in his cultural surround. Significantly, Fromm's adolescent role models opposed assimilation, stressing the necessity for Jews to consecrate themselves to their special destiny; but they distinguished themselves as individuals by their openness, originality, and syncretism. Like them, in their diverse ways, Fromm was one of a kind. This emphasis on being different from the compact majority, and the deep distrust of official ideologies engendered by the First World War, had lasting reverberations in Fromm's character and life's work.

Adult Life and Development

From the ages of eighteen to twenty-two, Fromm obtained a doctorate in sociology from the University of Heidelberg with a dissertation on three Jewish communities—the Karaites, the Hassidim, and Reform Jewry—under the supervision of Alfred Weber. Among his teachers at the time were Karl Jaspers and Heinrich Rickert, who had a profound influence on Fromm's classmate Leo Lowenthal (Lowenthal, 1987, pp. 47–48). Neither Rickert nor Jaspers seems to have had much effect on Fromm; their ideas are not mentioned anywhere in his published work in the form of either defense or critique (Funk, 1984, p. 47). Clearly, if the interpersonal chemistry and the direction of Fromm's own interests allowed, he could learn a great deal. Otherwise, he was too headstrong or indifferent to make much use of what he was exposed to (ibid., pp. 46–48).

At twenty-three, his education complete, Fromm returned to Frankfurt to become editor of a small Jewish newspaper. At twenty-four, through Golde Ginsburg (later Mrs. Leo Lowenthal), he met Frieda Reichmann, his first analyst (and later, his wife), who had established a small sanatorium in Frankfurt. At twenty-five, Fromm commenced a new analysis with Wilhelm Wittenberg, a zealous Freudian, in Munich. After a year with Wittenberg, Fromm spent a more productive period under Karl Landauer's supervision in Frankfurt, which had a major effect on his clinical and scientific outlook (Funk, 1984, pp. 49–50).

In 1927 Fromm commenced analytic training with Hans Sachs and

Theodor Reik in Berlin. Sachs and Reik were lay analysts, like himself, who had not found secure footholds in Vienna. Although Reik encouraged Fromm's interest in the psychology of religion, Fromm criticized Reik's psychology of religion on methodological grounds (1930b) and seems never to have praised Reik publicly on any subject. According to later recollections (Funk, 1984, pp. 56–57), Fromm found Sachs a sad and pathetic figure, whose abject loyalty to Freud was poorly repaid.[3]

Although Freud loyalists such as Sachs, Reik, and Karl Abraham were leading figures at the Berlin Psychoanalytic Institute—Abraham having administrative and theoretical seniority—the organization as a whole was tolerant and progressive and fostered a creative intellectual ferment that is without parallel in the history of the psychoanalytic movement (Jacoby, 1983, chap. 3). Lay analysts held senior positions, and there was a free polyclinic open to the working classes, the first of its kind. It was in Berlin that Otto Fenichel conducted his celebrated *Kinderseminar,* a study group organized on behalf of younger, left-leaning analysts (Rubins, 1978, chap. 10; Jacoby, 1983, chap. 2). It was here that Karen Horney took issue with Freud on feminine psychology, and Wilhelm Reich alerted a generation of analytic clinicians—Fromm among them—to social and political conditions and their bearing on the clinical situation. During this brief period, the golden age of analytic theory, psychoanalysis was an integral part of Weimar culture at its most exhilarating and unconventional (Gay, 1968, pp. 34–37). Conversations in cafés and clubs between analysts or between analysts and candidates in training on psychology, philosophy, politics, and art often lasted long into the night; something unimaginable in the American context.

From 1927 to 1932 Fromm was instrumental in organizing a group of south German analysts, including Karl Landauer, Georg Groddeck, Heinrich Meinong, and Ernst Schneider, to form the Frankfurt Psychoanalytic Institute. This was only the first of such efforts: later Fromm would help cofound the William Alanson White Institute in New York City (Funk, 1984) and would be the driving force behind the Sociedad Mexicana de Psicoanalisis (Mexican Institute of Psychoanalysis) in Mexico City.

After 1929, his training complete, Fromm divided his time between private practice, lecturing, and writing in Berlin, and the Frankfurt Institute for Social Research, where he deepened his familiarity with

Fromm around 1922

Marxist social science through his association with Horkheimer and Marcuse. Fromm's friend Lowenthal introduced him to the Frankfurt Institute, and Fromm promptly became the head of the section on social psychology.

Fromm came to the United States in 1933 after separating from his first wife, Frieda Reichmann, and a year spent in Davos, Switzerland, recovering from a bout of tuberculosis. A life-threatening illness following a marital separation often gives rise to great anxiety and existential reflection, and possibly a new outlook on life, but there is no documentary evidence as to what was on Fromm's mind in 1932.

At Horney's invitation, Fromm went to Chicago to assist her and Franz Alexander at the recently organized Chicago Psychoanalytic Institute. But a clash between Horney and Alexander in their attitudes to orthodoxy soon scuttled the arrangement, and Fromm came to New York to start a private practice and to resume his role as director of social psychology at the Frankfurt Institute for Social Research in 1934, which had recently relocated at Columbia University (Jay, 1973).

Fromm's ties to the Frankfurt Institute eroded after the latter's relocation in America, ending bitterly a few years later. Several issues were involved. Fromm, who had done pioneering research in matriarchal theory and its application to psychoanalysis, became an outspoken critic of the patriarchal underpinnings of Freudian theory (Fromm, 1935a). Although Horkheimer and Walter Benjamin had endorsed Fromm's earlier research on social psychology, Fromm's Freud critique caused serious problems. In an interview with Martin Jay, Fromm recalled that Horkheimer and Adorno had discovered a more "radical" Freud shortly before his departure for America (Jay, 1973, p. 101). Then again, Fromm, together with Ernst Schachtel, had conducted a landmark study of authoritarianism among German workers in 1930, which Horkheimer had refused to publish under Institute auspices. There were also strong antipathies between Fromm and Adorno (Bonss, 1984, p. 2) and between Fromm and Marcuse (Funk, 1984, chap. 6). Accordingly, Fromm left the Institute for Social Research in 1938, just before Adorno's arrival at Columbia University.

Fromm was one of many German-speaking émigrés seeking refuge in America. Before the European exodus, psychoanalysis in the United States had been a small and informal affair. Americans made pilgrimages to Vienna for training when possible, and Freud would occasionally intervene in the Americans' organizational affairs by favoring one man over another for administrative seniority (Kardiner, 1977). The most flagrant example of this was Freud's appointment of Horace Frink, a relative newcomer, over long-standing loyalist A. A. Brill as the administrative head of the American organization. The result, predictably enough, was dissension and discord in the small but growing American Psychoanalytic Association, which contributed to the growing resistance to training "lay analysts" or nonmedical people; an instance of noncompliance with the master's wishes that angered Freud deeply (Millet, 1966, p. 553; Roazen, 1974, pp. 378–381).

As the ranks of native American psychoanalysts were thinned by wartime service, and European émigrés came to America in increasing numbers, the old status quo was reversed. Formerly, Americans had gone to Vienna, Berlin, or Budapest for analytic training. Now, central Europe came to them. By the early 1940s, the language spoken and heard on the floor at psychoanalytic seminars and conventions in New York City was chiefly German, although papers were presented and discussed in English (Millet, 1966). As New York City became saturated with psychoanalysts, new associations were formed in Baltimore, Boston, Chicago, Detroit, Los Angeles, Philadelphia, and San Francisco to accommodate the influx of Europeans. Thus when American psychiatrists returned from service, they could now converse and train with people who had enjoyed a somewhat fabled, fairy-tale status in their minds, as Freud's intimates or trainees.

Not all the émigrés fared well, however. Indeed, Freud's advocacy of lay analysis and his appointment of Frink had lasting repercussions. Theodor Reik, Freud's prize pupil and Fromm's former teacher, was refused admission to the American Psychoanalytic Association despite his international reputation and, after years of struggle in undeserved obscurity, founded his own National Psychological Association for Psychoanalysis in 1948 (Natterson, 1966). Otto Fenichel died tragically of overwork, laboring fiercely to refurbish his medical credentials (Jacoby, 1983). Even those who prospered economically had to deal with culture shock, which often led to an intensified parochialism. Martin Grotjahn, who arrived in 1936, recalls:

> I had moved from the psychoanalytic coffeehouses of Europe to the big American institutes of psychoanalysis. For most Europeans psychoanalysis was research directed; for the Americans it was therapy or patient directed. This difference caused fateful confusions; it led many immigrant analytic scholars to become dogmatic Freudians who taught the canon but not always the spirit of psychoanalysis. For them, psychoanalysis symbolized the spirit of the old country that had to be transplanted into the fruitful soil of the new country. For them, analytic training became a kind of indoctrination instead of a learning experience. Their kind of analysis formed a bodyguard which kept therapeutic psychoanalytic technique almost unchanged . . . (1968, p. 53)

Fromm came to the United States at the age of thirty-three. As a lay analyst, like Reik, Fromm would have been vulnerable professionally had it not been for the help of Karen Horney and her associates and for his tenured position at the Frankfurt Institute. But these connections soon dissolved. In the meantime, however, Fromm was developing. His services as a teacher were greatly in demand. Like Ferenczi, Groddeck, Horney, and Fromm-Reichmann, Fromm in his approach to therapy was oriented more to patient care than to research, so that he probably found it easier to relate to his American students than did many of his older or more orthodox contemporaries. Fromm was also becoming a successful author. *Escape from Freedom,* published in 1941, garnered considerable attention, esteem, and envy from a variety of quarters. Financial considerations aside, the popularity of this work must have been a great morale booster for a man entering middle age.

Fromm's success as an author stemmed from several factors. Because the United States is a land of émigrés and their children, Americans are understandably interested in the problems of alienation and uprootedness in the modern psyche, which Fromm first thematized for psychoanalytic theory (1941). Fromm had a ready-made audience. Martin Grotjahn describes the reception accorded European psychoanalysts in these terms: "The alienated man in modern America welcomed the alien from Europe in whom he saw the expert in the art of dealing with the problems of existence" (1968, p. 52). Fromm played this role to the hilt—far too much, in the opinion of some. This change in approach was reflected in the audience Fromm reached. In Europe, Fromm's audience had been a specialized sector of the intelligentsia interested in psychoanalysis, sociology, politics, and matriarchal theory; all scholarly, and most of them German speaking. Fromm's American audience included people from all walks of life, and they, of course, spoke English.

Stylistic transitions within a language are easy to identify, but in Fromm's gradual shift from German to English in the late 1930s it is difficult to pinpoint any specific stylistic changes. Fromm's English was direct and elegant, very much like his German style. But Fromm reached out to his audience in a number of ways. He cited indigenous thinkers such as Emerson, Thoreau, and Dewey whenever a suitable occasion arose; and, unlike his more mainstream colleagues, he referred to American anthropologists, sociologists, and others whose thoughts on character and culture were convergent with his own. Then again, the combination of skepticism, humanism, and eclecticism Fromm brought to bear on the study of religion appealed to something deep in the American character that, for historical reasons, has no precise counterpart in Europe, where it offends both high-brow and low-brow sensibilities.[4]

In other words, Fromm infused the role of the alien "expert in the art of dealing with the problems of existence" with an element of accessibility and respect for American thought that his audience was unlikely to find among many other émigrés. Fromm's former associates at the Frankfurt Institute for Social Research are a case in point. Apart from their contributions to the psychology of anti-Semitism and authoritarianism, which had an enormous influence on American social science, they labored in deliberate obscurity (Jay, 1973). By contrast, Fromm always strove to be accessible. As a consequence, even émigrés who won acclaim and prosperity in analytic circles could seldom command an audience as big, as varied, or as enthusiastic as Fromm's was among the general public, Erik Erikson being a possible exception.

Despite Fromm's strivings for accessibility and his dalliance with American intellectual life, however, he was always essentially European in outlook, and many of his own sensibilities were associated in his own mind with Europe's feudal legacy. In his own words,

> The feudal heritage has, aside from its obvious negative qualities, many human traits which, compared with the attitude produced by pure Capitalism, are exceedingly attractive. European criticism of the United States is based essentially on the older human values of feudalism, inasmuch as they are still alive . . . It is a criticism of the present in the name of a past which is rapidly disappearing in Europe itself. The difference between Europe and the United States in this respect is only the difference between an older and a newer phase of Capitalism, between a Capitalism still blended with feudal remnants and a pure form of it. (1955b, p. 97)

Despite his persistently European bias, Fromm's success in America prompted many critics to charge him with being an accomplice to "the Americanization of psychoanalysis" (compare, for example, Sykes, 1962; Jacoby, 1983; Fuller, 1986). There are problems with this claim that are seldom sufficiently appreciated. If by the Americanization of psychoanalysis we mean the transformation of the clinical situation to chiefly therapeutic rather than research-oriented endeavor, Fromm is guilty as charged. As Grotjahn, among others, points out, the tendency to exploit the clinical situation for its research possibilities was a concomitant to a growing therapeutic pessimism in Freud's circle that Fromm evidently did not share. However, Fromm's views here, like those of Fromm-Reichmann, Horney, and Clara Thompson, followed those of the German Groddeck and the Hungarian Ferenczi (Fromm, 1935a).

If by Americanization we mean the increasing medicalization and bureaucratization of psychoanalysis (Jacoby, 1983), Fromm had no part in it. In fact no other person of his stature opposed these trends as vigorously over the years; a fact that cost him credibility in the analytic mainstream in the United States.

On the other hand, if by Americanization we mean the attempt to *democratize* psychoanalysis, by demedicalizing it and introducing it into other spheres of life and human interaction, there is justice in the attribution. Fromm hoped to disseminate psychoanalytic insight among teachers, nurses, and social workers and labored actively to do so in the early and mid-1940s at the William Alanson White Institute, although this effort was interrupted by his second wife's illness and their consequent move to Mexico.[5]

Finally, when speaking of Americanization Fromm's critics often imply a substantive alteration in Fromm's basic outlook that coincided with (or resulted from) his emigration, changing him from a radical scholar to a fashioner of platitudes that he glibly dispensed to an idolatrous public (for example, Jacoby, 1975). These indictments would not be so sharp or mean-spirited had he not abandoned the libido theories or challenged Freud's incorrigible sexism so often and openly.

Unfortunately, in abandoning the libido theories, Fromm *did* neglect to give sexual desire its due both as a formative and disruptive force in human development, and as a reality in the clinical setting. But contrary to prevailing opinion, Fromm experienced no radical change in outlook somewhere in the mid-Atlantic or after his arrival in the United States. Granted, Fromm learned how to reach an audience, and as a consequence of his rapid success he became narcissistically invested in his role as an "expert in the art of living." Still, a careful analysis of Fromm's *intellectual* development shows that most of his later, "revisionist" ideas are clearly prefigured in his earlier work. And despite unfortunate lapses into a homiletic style, Fromm was capable of astute and penetrating reflections on numerous topics throughout his life. To ignore these is to lose the baby with the bathwater.

So far, I have discussed Fromm's life and times in a somewhat artificial way, as if his parents and teachers were his only "significant others." In fact, however, Fromm's early career was profoundly affected by his love life, and vice versa. His first analysis was with Frieda Reichmann, who was ten years his senior. Perhaps her legendary perceptiveness, dedication, and empathic ability made the precocious young Fromm cherish the mature companionship he found with her. From 1918 to 1920 Reichmann was Kurt Goldstein's laboratory assistant, and in 1922–23 she did a psychiatric internship with Emil Kraepelin before her own analysis with Sachs in 1924. In the United States, Frieda Fromm-Reichmann became famous in her own right for her pioneering therapy of schizophrenia, training numerous researchers in this field, including Harold F. Searles. On the advice of Georg Groddeck, Erich and Frieda had an amicable separation four years after their marriage but maintained close personal and professional contact thereafter. She and Fromm were formally divorced in 1940. Fromm's fondness for her persisted, however. According to Rose Spiegel, Fromm was immersed in grief and prayer when she died in April 1957 (Spiegel, 1981).

Another of Fromm's loves was Karen Horney. Like Reichmann, Horney was a devoted friend of Georg Groddeck, the only man besides D. T. Suzuki, the noted Zen scholar, who elicited the same intensity of personal admiration that Fromm first felt toward R. Rabinkow in late adolescence and early adulthood. Horney was fifteen years Fromm's senior, and a prominent member of the Berlin Psychoanalytic Institute when they met. Fromm probably admired Horney's direct, earthy quality and her straightforward and courageous dealings with Freud. His reflections on the psychology of the sexes were influenced by her essays from the late 1920s and early 1930s, while her reflections on neurosis as a manifestation of widespread cultural tendencies owe much to Fromm's influence (Rubins, 1978, chap. 18). Despite Fromm's youth, Horney may have looked to him as a father figure whom she admired ambivalently. To her great embarrassment, she once introduced Fromm to an American audience as "Dr. Freud" (Quinn, 1987, p. 366). In view of Horney's ambivalence toward Freud, this parapraxis was probably loaded with a multiplicity of meanings. Among them, I suspect, was an unarticulated wish to stress both Fromm's loyalty to Freud and the way this differentiated his work from her own.

Fromm's break with Horney, ostensibly on the issue of lay analysis

(Funk, 1984, pp. 103–105), had manifold determinants. According to Susan Quinn, it was fueled by the disintegration of their romantic liaison over several years, and complicated by crisscrossing personal loyalties and professional rivalry (Quinn, 1987, p. 366). According to Janet Rioch, an intimate observer of these proceedings, Harry Stack Sullivan subtly abetted their falling out, as the burgeoning Fromm-Thompson-Rioch group provided him with the personnel and students to start a New York branch of the Washington School of Psychiatry and, later, the William Alanson White Institute for Psychiatry, Psychology and Psychoanalysis (Eckardt, 1976, p. 149). Horney was deeply wounded by Fromm's ultimate unwillingness to commit himself (Quinn, 1987, chap. 18). The hurt was not one-sided, however. Despite the many opportunities he had to acknowledge her work and influence on him, Fromm was sparing in praise of Horney in later life. His reticence suggests that whatever gratitude he felt was blighted by more powerful sentiments of a less positive nature and by a desire to distance his theories from hers. It is probably no coincidence that neither Fromm's second or third wife was a psychoanalyst or appreciably older than he.

There is little information about Fromm himself after his emigration to the United States in 1933, but two biographies of Horney (Rubins, 1978; Quinn, 1987) tell us much about the social and intellectual milieu in which he moved during the 1930s and 1940s. Of particular interest is the so-called Zodiac Club, an informal discussion group that met regularly and included Harry Stack Sullivan, Karen Horney, Clara Thompson, William Silverberg, and, somewhat later, Fromm, who was a frequent participant though never an official member. The entire group developed ties with Abram Kardiner and with anthropologists Ralph Linton, Margaret Mead, and Ruth Benedict, among others. Although we have no way of knowing what was discussed, since minutes of the gatherings were not kept, these friendly, informal get-togethers must have had a substantial impact on psychiatry, anthropology, and other social sciences in the following two decades (Rubins, 1978, p. 236; Eckardt, 1976, p. 146). And it was through this network of acquaintances that Fromm met Ralph Linton, with whom he taught at Yale in 1948–49 (Fromm, 1973, p. 193n).

On July 24, 1944, Fromm married Henny Gurland (née Schonstadt), a left-leaning Jewish woman from Mannheim who had fled

Fromm in 1946

the Nazis to Paris. Her marriage was already disintegrating in 1940 when her husband was incarcerated by the occupation forces. She fled to Walter Benjamin in Marseilles with her seventeen-year-old son, Joseph, and accompanied Benjamin on his flight from France, which ended in his suicide at the Spanish frontier on September 26, 1940. It was she who arranged for his burial (Funk, 1984, pp. 109–110). Fromm had deep respect and affection for Henny and undertook to finance Joseph's education immediately on their arrival in the United States later that year.

In 1946 Fromm was made director of clinical training at the William Alanson White, a post he held formally till 1950. However, as a result of Henny's deteriorating health from rheumatoid arthritis, she and Fromm moved to Mexico late in 1949, where Fromm soon founded the Mexican Institute of Psychoanalysis under the auspices of the National Autonomous University of Mexico. Fromm taught

Fromm in 1946

there till 1965, when he became a professor emeritus. Henny died in 1952, but Fromm maintained a residence in Mexico until 1974, when he moved to Locarno, Switzerland, with his third wife, Anis Freeman, an Alabaman, whom he married on December 18, 1953 (Derbez, 1981; Funk, 1984, chap. 6).

A remarkable though much-neglected feature of Fromm's life from the late 1940s till the 1960s was his seemingly magical immunity from the ravages of McCarthyism. Despite his outspoken opposition to the Cold War, nuclear arms, and the Vietnam War, there is no public record of Fromm's having suffered from the kind of official harassment, persecution, and character assassination that became the commonplaces of other people's lives during the McCarthy era and its aftermath. Nor is there any evidence that he did anything to combat it. His conduct contrasts markedly with that of his friend Leo Lowenthal, who energetically joined the fight against McCarthyism (Lowenthal, 1987, pp. 86–91). According to informants in Washington and New York, Fromm never seemed to give his remarkably safe and secure situation much thought.

Although Fromm spent more than half of every year in Mexico, he continued to teach in American universities and played an active role in American public life. In the company of his friend and former analysand, American sociologist David Riesman, Fromm frequently conferred with prominent public figures such as J. William Fulbright and Philip Hart on the problems of Cold War politics in the 1950s (Riesman, personal communication, July 9, 1985), and as late as 1974 Fromm delivered a paper to a Senate committee hearing on the problems and possibilities of détente (Funk, 1982, chap. 1). In 1960, after the worst excesses of McCarthyism had abated, Fromm joined the American Socialist party and penned their party platform for that election year (Fromm, 1960b). During the 1960s Fromm traveled in Eastern Europe and developed close ties with Yugoslav, Czech, and Polish Marxists, who evinced a keen appreciation of Fromm's brand of Marxist humanism. *Socialist Humanism: An International Symposium* (Fromm, 1965) testifies to their collaboration and joint interests. In addition to these activities in America and Eastern Europe, Fromm lent enthusiastic support to A. S. Neill's controversial school Summerhill (Fromm, 1960a) and befriended two renowned Latin American pedagogues, Ivan Illich and Paolo Friere, who had considerable influence on educational thinking in those heady and remarkable times.

In 1969 Fromm was made president of the International Forum of Psychoanalysis, an organization he had helped found, but was unable to deliver his presidential address because he was recuperating in Switzerland from a severe heart attack. As a result of this experience, from 1969 to 1973 Erich and Anis Fromm spent their summers in Locarno and moved there the following year (Funk, 1984, pp. 118, 119). Although Fromm's influence was waning slightly in North America, his *To Have or to Be?* (1976) was a big best-seller in Germany. Fromm stopped all clinical activities in 1974 and devoted himself to

Fromm in 1974

writing, with an occasional interview for radio or television. He died of a heart attack on March 18, 1980 (ibid., pp. 109–110). Anis Fromm died in 1985. Their devoted friend, Ivan Illich, helped bury them both.

To the naive observer, Fromm may seem to be a contradictory character. A man who cherished an abiding love for the values of humanistic religion and the Jewish tradition in which he was raised, Fromm was nonetheless a committed atheist who regarded belief in a personal creator God as a historical anachronism. Yet despite his lack of personal faith, Fromm denounced much of modern-day religiosity as idolatrous and inauthentic with all the passionate conviction of a sincere believer. In a similar way, he took exception to Freudian orthodoxy but was loyal to Freud, in his fashion, and reproached those who parroted Freud's views as gospel but lacked his courage, originality, or faith in the emancipatory power of reason.

Friends and admirers have remarked widely on Fromm's deep and spontaneous generosity, his sympathy for the outsider and the underdog, and his uncompromising dislike of sham and pretense. His critics are less charitable, of course, and have often charged him with being doctrinaire and fostering a cliquish and sycophantic group of followers in New York City. Both perspectives contain a measure of truth. The alleged inconsistencies between Fromm's humanistic theory and his actual conduct, reflected in the less flattering anecdotes about him, need not be particularly disturbing. Few people achieve an unfailing congruence in their lives between theory and practice. The man who emerges in the following pages was, if nothing else, a probing, creative and sometimes visionary thinker whose life's work merits study.

2 Freudo-Marxism and Matriarchal Theory: Early Methodological Perspectives

Fromm's Early Papers

Many of Fromm's early papers can best be understood as installments in a concerted response of left-wing intellectuals to the crisis faced by Western Marxism in the 1920s and 1930s. Marx had predicted a decisive revolutionary struggle under the conditions that obtained at the time, but despite urgent exhortations from the left, the working class failed to rise to the occasion. Freud, a shrewd critic of historical materialism, rebuked Marxism for its disregard of the irrational in social or "mass" psychology. In his *New Introductory Lectures on Psychoanalysis,* for example, Freud observed that

> what are known as materialistic views of history sin in underestimating this factor. They brush it aside with the remark that human ideologies are nothing other than the product and superstructure of their contemporary economic conditions. This is true, but very probably not the whole truth. Mankind never lives entirely in the present. The past, the tradition of the race and the people, lives on in the ideologies of the super-ego, and yields only slowly to the influences of the present. (1932, p. 67)

Elsewhere Freud was less magnanimous in his assessment of Marxist theory. Although he occasionally acknowledged the truth-value of some Marxist formulations (ibid., chap. 35), most of his work contradicted the Marxist interpretation of social and historical processes. Although Freud did not deny the manifold injustices and privations endemic in class society (Freud, 1927, secs. 1 and 2), their causal underpinnings had a different significance for him and were of decidedly secondary importance to the "civilizing" function of class rule. In his "Autobiographical Study" Freud observed that "the events of human history, the interactions of human nature, cultural development and the precipitates of primeval experience (the most prominent of which is religion), are no more than a reflection of the dynamic conflicts between the ego, id and super-ego—are the very same processes repeated on a wider stage" (1925, p. 72).

Freud was not the first to suggest that social development and class conflict can be understood by analogy with intrapsychic processes and structures. The idea goes back to Plato, and had had a more recent advocate in the person of J. F. Herbart, who attempted to model social conflict and cooperation along the lines of mutual facilitation, conflict, and inhibition among aggregates of ideas striving for "dominance" or access to consciousness (Danziger, 1983, p. 306). Likewise, the emphasis on the specifically irrational dimension of "mass psychology," along with reliance on charismatic leaders, had been articulated by Freud's older contemporaries Gabriel Tarde and Gustave Le Bon, with whom Freud was intimately familiar (Moscovici, 1985), and whose ideological agenda was frankly reactionary.

Unlike the many doctrinaire leftists who ridiculed Freud, however, the Freudo-Marxists were alive to the magnitude and seriousness of Freud's challenge and to the practical and theoretical problems caused by Marxism's disregard of the irrational in human psychology. What united Reich, Fromm, Fenichel, and Horkheimer, among others, was their outspoken opposition to Freud's penchant for modeling sociohistorical processes, structures, and conflicts on analogues from the intrapsychic domain. As Marxists they were committed to the thesis that individual psychology is derived from social structure, not vice versa. In exploring the roots of social irrationality, they evolved a keen appreciation of the role of the family, education, and religion in inculcating the attitudes and inhibitions that foster widespread compliance to class rule and apathy or hostility toward social change. Of all the early Freudo-Marxist offerings, Fromm's first papers remain outstanding as sensitive and penetrating applications of Freudian theory to social and historical questions. Though deviating from Freud in several minute particulars—and indeed, on methodological premises as well—they sought to expunge the speculative and quasi-mythological character of Freud's more extravagant conjectures, lending psychoanalytic social psychology the rigor and dignity of genuine historical inquiry.

Fromm's first major paper was "The Dogma of Christ: A Psychoanalytic Study of the Social Psychological Function of Religion" ([1930a] 1963a). Like Karl Kautsky and Friedrich Engels, Fromm saw Christianity as an incipiently revolutionary movement of the enslaved and dispossessed. But whereas Freud and his followers had contrived elaborate comparisons between religious belief and obsessional neurosis (Freud, 1913), Fromm noted that what were interpreted retrospectively as symbols of Oedipal ambivalence in Christian mythology actually represent the amalgamation of doctrines originating in diverse periods and social strata, expressing differing aims and world views rather than the conflicted impulses of a unitary psychological subject (Fromm, 1963a, p. 84; Wallace, 1983, pp. 187–188). Fromm's analysis of the way in which the gradual development of Christian dogma mediated the repression and "secondary revision" of sharp class antagonisms in the interests of Roman hegemony lends this essay its special charm and persuasiveness. Judged by contemporary standards, Fromm's scholarship is dated, and his conclusions are therefore erroneous in some instances. But this was an important document and has rightly been cited by many (for example, Kardiner, 1946; Riesman, 1949; Wallace, 1984) as a pioneering study in psychology, religion, and historical sociology.

In "The Method and Function of an Analytic Social Psychology: Notes on Psychoanalysis and Historical Materialism" ([1932a] 1970a), Fromm made the methodological premises underlying "The Dogma of Christ" more explicit. Fromm charged that the Freudian analogies between obsessional neurosis and religious ideation were really deviations from the "authentic" analytic method, and that Freud had engaged in an unwarranted (albeit unconscious) transposition of the patricentric psychology of his own milieu onto all humanity. In a move to reestablish the primacy of economic conditions as the main determinants in social psychology, Fromm now declared that

> the phenomena of social psychology are to be understood as processes involving the active and passive adaptation of the instinctual apparatus to the socio-economic situation. In certain fundamental respects, the instinctual apparatus is a biological given; but it is highly modifiable. The role of primary formative factors goes to the economic conditions. The family is the essential medium through which the economic situation exerts its formative influence on the individual's psyche. The task of social psychology is to explain the shared, socially relevant, psychic

attitudes and ideologies—and their unconscious roots in particular—in terms of economic conditions on libido strivings.   (1970a, p. 149)

Having asserted the primacy of economic conditions, however, Fromm avoided the sterile economic reductionism that was so prevalent in the Marxism of his day. By invoking the notorious plasticity of the sexual instincts, Fromm lent credence to aspects of Freudian theory that explained the "ideological hegemony" of the ruling class in ways that are *humanly* convincing, and without recourse to either the dry, rationalistic pedantry of old-fashioned vulgar Marxism or the quasi-explanatory, labyrinthine complexities of contemporary structuralist Marxism. With respect to the origins and persistence of ethical ideals—an area in which Marxism can be incredibly glib—the young Fromm asserted:

Psychoanalysis can show how these seemingly ideal motives are actually the rationalized expression of the instinctual, libidinous needs and that the content and scope of the dominant needs at any given moment are to be explained in terms of the socio-economic situation on the instinctual structure of the group that produces the ideology. Hence it is possible for psychoanalysis to reduce the loftiest motives to their earthly, libidinal nucleus, without having to consider economic needs as the only important ones.   (1970a, pp. 156–157)

Like Freud, Fromm contended that object-relationships of an early, childlike character constitute the "social cement" that consolidates the ties between rulers and ruled. And although the idealization of parental imagos described by Freud does not originate in the economic sphere, it is manipulated in its interest, as are "certain moral principles which entice the poor to suffer rather than do wrong, and which lead them to believe that the purpose of their life is to obey their rulers and do their duty. These ethical conceptions, which are so important for social stability, are the products of certain affective and emotional relations even to those who create and represent such norms" (ibid., p. 159).

In another essay published the same year, "Psychoanalytic Characterology and Its Relevance for Social Psychology" ([1932b] 1970a), Fromm endeavored to show how the conditions of early capitalism and the industrial revolution had fostered the proliferation and intensification of anal character traits, with a concomitant atrophy and suppression of genitality. Though undoubtedly of interest on historical grounds, this paper is significant for at least two other reasons. Like Reich, Fromm took economic developments and structures to have an origin and momentum of their own. Rather than derive the psychology of capitalism from a mysterious and otherwise unaccountable upsurge of anality, like Ferenczi (1914) and, somewhat later, Norman O. Brown (1959, 1966), Fromm regarded the traits of industry, sobriety, self-denial, and the miserly pleasures of hoarding as environmentally adaptive, and destined to prevail as long as the dominant methods and relations of production and exchange remained unchanged. Fromm argued, in effect, that although capitalism is rooted in objective economic conditions, it taps and intensifies different instinctual energies of a pregenital variety, converting them into productive forces that fuel the engines of economic development. Echoing Max Weber's concept of "inner worldly asceticism," Fromm argued that the intensification of anality characteristic of early industrial capitalism robbed the goal of earthly, sensuous happiness of its hitherto self-evident validity (Fromm, 1970a, p. 180).[1]

Although Fromm never said so in so many words, we can infer that inasmuch as anality constitutes a barrier to the expression and development of genital trends, he was already concerned with what he would later term the "pathology of normalcy" (see Chapter 6, below). Fromm's emphasis on the vicissitudes of genitality and the heightened anality of capitalist society was indebted to the theories of his older contemporary Wilhelm Reich, who thought that the suppression of genital sexuality invariably prompted a heightened libidinal cathexis of pregenital orientations, sadism and anal eroticism being the most frequent substitutes. Like Reich, Fromm cautioned that prolonged nonsatisfaction of "normal" genitality results in the intensification of sadistic trends (ibid.), and is therefore undesirable from a sociological standpoint. In words that echo Reich's, Fromm observed:

> Sexuality offers one of the most elementary and powerful opportunities for satisfaction and happiness. If it were permitted to the full extent required for the productive development of the personality, rather than limited by the need to maintain control over the masses, the fulfillment of this important opportunity for happiness would necessarily lead to intensified demands for satisfaction . . . in other areas of life. Since the satisfaction of these demands would have to be achieved through material means, these demands of themselves would lead to the breakup of the existing order. Closely allied to this is another social function of

restrictions put on sexual satisfaction. Insofar as sexual pleasure as such is deemed sinful, while sexual desires remain perpetually operative in every human being, moral prohibitions always become a source of production for guilt feelings, which are often unconscious, or transferred to other matters.

These guilt feelings are of great social importance. They account for the fact that punishment is experienced as just punishment for one's own guilt, rather than blamed on the effects of social organization. They eventually cause emotional intimidation, limiting people's intellectual, and especially their critical capacities, while developing an emotional attachment to the representatives of social morality. ([1934] 1970a, p. 126)

Another indication of Fromm's affinities with Reich is the fact that he reviewed the latter's *The Invasion of Compulsory Sex Morality* ([1932a] 1976) with obvious enthusiasm in *Zietschrift für Sozialforschung* (Fromm, 1933b). This fraternal gesture was not reciprocated, however. Reich unleashed a storm of abuse at Fromm in a chapter titled "The Use of Psychoanalysis in Historical Research," appended to the 1934 version of "Dialectical Materialism and Psychoanalysis." The specific occasion for this polemic was "The Method and Function of an Analytic Social Psychology" ([1932a] 1970a), in which Fromm, though praising Reich, had contrasted Reich's thinking with his own, intimating that Reich's work had undergone a welcome change that heralded possibly more convergent perspectives in the future.

Reich disregarded Fromm's highly favorable review and angrily refuted the suggestion that there was any change in his methodological assumptions. He likened Fromm to "scientific jugglers of a certain well known type" (Reich, 1934, p. 69), implying, in effect, that Fromm was a charlatan. Reich noted that Fromm saw analytic social psychology as liable to all kinds of fanciful and erroneous constructions and inferences because it failed to apply the methods of analytic individual psychology with rigorous consistency. However, Reich charged, the representatives of orthodoxy had in fact already done that. Society, noted Reich, has no id, ego, or superego—that is, is not a unified psychological subject—so that analyzing the "latent content" of mass phenomena like strikes is a pointless and misleading exercise.

In fact Fromm never suggested that society has an id, ego, or superego or that its structure is analogous to the structure of the

psyche, as had Herbart and Freud. He never minimized the importance of objective conditions, nor was he interested in episodic instances of ostensibly irrational mass behavior, such as a general strike.
By contrast, this had been the focal point of sociological interest for Le
Bon and for Freud and his followers. By coupling Fromm with this
tradition, Reich was slyly and subtly impugning Fromm's Marxist
credentials.

In fairness to Reich, Fromm *did* labor under the misconception that
Freud had done away with the myth of the collective subject once and
for all, and used this claim to buttress his assertion that a more
rigorous application of the methods of individual psychology could
yield valid scientific results (1932a). This polemical and methodological stance furnished a useful platform from which to scold the orthodox and to launch his reputation as a credible spokesman for Freud's
loyal opposition, intent on rescuing Freud from his disciples—and
indeed, from himself. In fact, however, Fromm's assertions along
these lines flew in the face of an explicit statement to the contrary in
Totem and Taboo, in which Freud argued that without the assumption
of a collective psyche, social psychology in general is not possible
(1913, pp. 157–158).[2]

The more important point, however, is that Fromm and Reich
agreed fundamentally on the ideologically freighted character of orthodox Freudian social psychology and the unreality of the "collective subject." Reading Reich's polemic, one searches in vain for any
real, substantive disagreement that would warrant the length or urgency of his diatribe. In light of their conjoint emphasis on prevailing
economic and political conditions, the role of the family in shaping
character in conformity with social requirements, and so on, the issue
of whether or not a "correct" application of the "authentic" method
of individual psychology to social phenomena was valid was a secondary one, a breeding ground for grandstanding and sectarian ob-
fuscation. So what prompted Reich to accord it such momentous
significance?

Perhaps Reich's egocentric investment in leading—or indeed, in
being—Freud's loyal opposition on the left dictated the nature of his
response. Fromm's review of Reich's *The Invasion of Compulsory Sex
Morality* had been as enthusiastic as it was because Reich, inspired
by Bronislaw Malinowski (1927), had attempted an integration of
matriarchal theory with psychoanalysis and historical materialism.

Leaning on the much earlier work of J. J. Bachofen, Fromm was embarked on a parallel trajectory, with brilliant though not identical results (1933a, 1934). Had Fromm merely written a derivative treatment instead of attempting to stake out his own intellectual ground, Reich would never have attacked him in this way. Instead, Fromm ventured an independent view, and Reich was apprehensive lest Fromm steal his thunder—either then, or for posterity. Accordingly, he interpreted what was a mild rebuke coupled with great praise as a hostile attack—a typical gesture for this brilliant, courageous, but vain and competitive man.

In retrospect, this situation had both sad and comic dimensions. But it should not be taken lightly. More was at stake than individual egos jockeying for position; more than the assertion of priority or individual identity. Apart from their intellectual differences and whatever competitive instincts they cherished, Reich and Fromm were also competing, indirectly, to express the gratitude, admiration, and love that they felt for Freud—feelings that ran deep, notwithstanding their outspoken criticism—and their desire to correct the master. In Reich's case, as we shall see presently, this attitude of Freud piety took the form of focusing on the "actual neuroses," which he took for the revolutionary core of Freud's system. In Fromm's case, it took the form of claiming to have discovered the methodologically correct application of the authentic analytic method.

In any case, Reich's mania for establishing his own priority and for discrediting alternative formulations on social psychology caused Fromm to be very reticent thereafter in acknowledging the parallels between them (Jacoby, 1983, p. 109). Fromm's reflections on the sadomasochistic character (1936, 1941), which he later termed the "authoritarian character," were influenced by Reich, though articulated increasingly within a framework that deemphasized the primacy of sexual needs over other dimensions of human character and motivation.[3]

Bachofen and Freud

Among Fromm's early papers, one outstanding effort, "The Theory of Mother Right and Its Relevance for Social Psychology" ([1934] 1970a), was devoted to the work of J. J. Bachofen and to the reception accorded matriarchal theory in the late nineteenth and early twentieth centuries. Fromm's self-chosen tasks here were to explain the attraction this colorful conservative thinker had for both left- and right-wing ideologues and to explore Bachofen's relevance to psychoanalytic theory.

An eminent Swiss jurist, a friend and mentor to the young Friedrich Nietzsche, J. J. Bachofen (1815–1881) was an avid classicist and mythographer. Though a scholar by preference, Bachofen was heir to an immense fortune. As one of Basel's foremost citizens, he was probably acquainted with C. G. Jung (1794–1864), Basel's leading physician, who, like himself, was an outspoken and colorful proponent of Romantic philosophy (Ellenberger, 1970, pp. 660–661), and whose grandson would figure prominently in the annals of psychoanalytic historiography. In old age, Freud's erstwhile disciple Carl Jung had a vivid childhood recollection of seeing Jacob Burkhardt accompanying J. J. Bachofen through the old city's streets (Jung, 1963, p. 111). This memory—if it was a genuine memory—was not accidental. Although he seldom cited him in print, Jung did much to ensure that Bachofen's spirit lived on (Hogenson, 1983).

In his youth Bachofen was a devoted friend and student of Friedrich Carl von Savigny, a leading spokesman for the Historical School of Law. The Historical School attacked the rationalist character of theories of natural law, which posited the existence of laws binding on all humanity derived from reason alone. In contrast with Enlightenment thought, it maintained that the idiosyncrasies and seeming irrationalities of a given people's juridical system reflect the vicissitudes of their cultural evolution and were therefore uniquely suited to their needs. Accordingly, this scholarly, antiquarian, and deeply conservative enclave fostered comparative and historical research on the development of legal codes (Bloch, 1961; Gossman, 1983).

In keeping with the spirit of the Historical School, Bachofen originated the theory of mother right to account for certain peculiarities of Etruscan funerary symbolism and for archaic vestiges in Roman law that circumvented the characteristic *patria potestas*.[4] According to Bachofen in his book *Mother Right* ([1861] 1973), social organization in remote prehistory hinged not on patriarchal authority or brute force, as many contemporaries believed, but on the mother-child bond and the mysteries of birth, death, and regeneration. Before the discovery of paternity and the shift to patriarchal modes of life, social life was characterized by community of goods, a kind of primitive democracy, and group marriage. With the passage of time, Bachofen speculated, women's allegedly innate conservatism and good sense prompted them to invent monogamous marriage, to spare themselves the indignities of consorting with multiple sexual partners (Ellenberger, 1970, pp. 218–223). However, the most important feature of the matriarchate (for the purposes of this discussion) was the spirit of sociability and the lack of constraint that supposedly infused all social relations at the earliest phase of social development. In Bachofen's words,

> The relationship which stands at the origin of all culture, of every virtue, of ever nobler aspect of existence, is that between mother and child; it operates in a world of violence as a divine principle of love, of union, of peace . . .
> The matriarchal cultures present many expressions and . . . juridical formulations of this . . . maternal principle. It is the basis of the universal freedom and equality so frequent among matriarchal peoples, of their hospitality, and of their aversion to restrictions of all sorts. It accounts for the broad significance of the Roman paricidium (parricide, or murder of a relative), which only later exchanged its natural, universal meaning for an individual, restricted one. And in it is rooted the admirable sense of kinship . . . which knows no barriers . . . and embraces all members of a nation alike. Matriarchal states were particularly famed for their freedom from intestine strife and conflict. The great festivals where all sections of a nation delighted in a sense of brotherhood and a common sense of nationality were first introduced among these peoples . . . The matriarchal peoples—and this is no less characteristic—assigned special culpability to the physical injury of one's fellow men or even of animals . . . An air of tender humanity, discernible even in the facial expression of Egyptian statuary, permeates the culture of the matriarchal world. (1973, pp. 79–81)

Paradoxically, although Bachofen praised the matriarchate for its tender sociability and fellow feeling, he also regarded the *lex talionis,* the principle of retribution or the blood feud, as a legacy of the matriarchal world, and accordingly regarded the advent of patriarchal social organization, which introduced more elevated juridical principles, as an advance in the overall level of spiritual development (Bloch, 1961). In Bachofen's view, both the unfettered sociability and the spirit of vengeance associated with matriarchal law arise from the fact that the maternal principle is bound to matter and the spirit of equality (democracy), while the paternal-spiritual principle—a kind of disembodied spirituality—rises above material ties and constraints and is explicitly hierarchical in character (Fromm, [1934] 1970a, pp. 114–119). As a staunch Lutheran, Bachofen regarded the Sermon on the Mount, which expressly repudiates the principle of retribution, as the consummate expression of patriarchal spirituality. But as a reactionary aristocrat, he opposed any movement toward economic and political democracy as a historically regressive step, because it supposedly seeks to reinstate matriarchal social relations (Fromm, 1934; Bloch, 1961).

In any case, Bachofen's theory of matriarchy drew heavily on myth and the accounts of ancient historians (for example, Herodotus, Polybius, Caesar, and Tacitus). It seemed to make sense of otherwise unintelligible aspects of Greek art and letters, particularly the *Oresteia* of Aeschylus (Fromm, 1951, pp. 206–207). Before its drift into relative obscurity, it commanded respect among historians, classicists, and anthropologists, including luminaries such as J. F. McLellan, Lewis Henry Morgan, Bronislaw Malinowski, Robert Briffault, Gordon Childe, Jane Ellen Harrison, F. M. Cornford, and Robert Graves. A salient feature of Bachofen's *Weltanschauung* was his emphasis on the role of religion in cultural development. According to Bachofen, religion is the vehicle for the expression of what another pupil of Savigny's, Emile Durkheim, termed the *conscience collectif*, those beliefs and moral sentiments that animate and govern a people. The historian's task, thought Bachofen, was to infer the core process (or *Geist*) of a civilization from its myriad and seemingly disconnected manifestations in the laws, folklore, and religious observances of a people—something not possible for those who compile facts in an additive fashion, without setting aside the spirit and preconceptions of their own society (Gossman, 1983).

Freud's relationship to Bachofen is exceedingly difficult to analyze because of Freud's deliberate policy of minimizing or altogether denying its existence. These attempts were ultimately unsuccessful, however. Toward the end of his life, in *Moses and Monotheism*, Freud declared:

> Under the influence of external conditions—which we need not follow up here and which in part are also not sufficiently known—it happened that the matriarchal structure of society was replaced by a patriarchal

one. This naturally brought with it a revolution in the existing state of the law. An echo of this revolution can still be heard, I think, in the *Oresteia* of Aeschylus. This turning from the mother to the father, however, signifies above all a victory of intellect [*Geist*] over the senses—that is to say, a step forward in culture, since maternity is proved by the evidence of the senses whereas paternity is a surmize based on a deduction and a premiss. This declaration in favor of the thought-process, thereby raising it above sense-perception, has proved to be a step charged with serious consequences. (1939, pp. 145–146)

Still, although Freud was conversant with Bachofen and did him the dubious honor of paraphrasing him without due citation, he also contradicted Bachofen's contention that the tie to the mother is primordial, and the relationship to the father a product of later historical development. In May 1912, in a rejoinder to Jung's objections to his theory of the incest complex—where Bachofen's influence on Jung is patent, incidentally—Freud declared: "It seems likely that there have been father's sons at all times. A father is one who possesses the mother sexually [and the children as property]" (McGuire, 1971, p. 504).

Freud's striking assertion here is merely a brief intimation of what was to follow in *Totem and Taboo* a year later. Leaning on some conjectures of Darwin's, Freud speculated that our remote ancestors lived in "primal hordes" dominated by tyrannical "fathers" who monopolized the available women and terrorized younger males through brute force. The brutal, selfish father figure was loved and hated, feared and idealized. The younger males rebelled, killed him, and devoured his body as an expression of their admiration, identification, and hatred. The immediate effect of this oft-repeated occurrence was a new kind of social organization entailing a more equitable distribution of sexual chattels, and a kind of civil law or social contract entailing equal amounts of instinctual renunciation by all the associated antagonists in return for the (unspoken) guarantee that they would not try to usurp the primal father's unrestricted access to women and his monopoly on coercive force. This (unspoken) social contract, and the anguished ambivalence that gave rise to it, were celebrated in the annual totem feast, when an animal representing the primal father—whose killing and consumption were normally proscribed—was killed and eaten, with a concomitant relaxation of most social constraints for a brief period.

Had cultural development stopped here, thought Freud, humanity would have remained in the tribal stage. But the strong positive feelings that the sons still cherished toward the old despot, expressed archaically in their cannibalistic incorporation of his body, and its symbolic reenactment in the totem feast, accompanied by guilt, fear of punishment, and a yearning for forgiveness from their idealized forebear—all these persisted and colored the unconscious milieus of subsequent generations. In this way, the hatred of and longing for the primal father formed the nucleus of dynamic conflict around which religion, law, and moral feeling find increasingly refined and complex expression.

For Freud, Christianity was the last and most ambitious attempt in a series of mystery-cult religions that try to resolve the hateful, affectionate, and guilty impulses transmitted from one generation to the next. Christ, the son figure par excellence, atones for the sins of the collective—that is, incestuous and parricidal impulses—with his own death. His resurrection and subsequent unification with the father express the positive valence of the Oedipal drama with vivid clarity, and the exoneration he achieves is shared vicariously by all through the medium of the eucharist. However, on closer inspection, according to Freud, the eucharist is merely a refined and elaborated version of the primitive totem feast, and Christ's paradoxical identity with the father, ostensibly a guarantee of redemption, really means that the father has been slain and eaten once more. And so the endless cycle of guilt and atonement, like the wheel of Ixion, rolls on.

A striking feature of Freud's philosophy of history was the absence of women as agents or actors in the historical process. By Freud's reckoning, even the transition to matriarchy was decided collectively by men, not women, and as a consequence of their troubled relationship to the primal father, rather than a primordial maternal imago. In the march toward civilization, women presumably intervened as objects of lust but remained incapable of inspiring the uncanny combination of reverence and dread that Jung, following Rudolph Otto, termed the "numinous." Moreover, by virtue of their biological endowment, or lack thereof, women were deemed less capable of the sublimation of impulse on which the development of culture presumably depends.

Freud's desire to rob women of any active role in the history of culture found parallel expression in his tendency to devalue women's role in biological reproduction. In a poem honoring the birth of

Wilhelm Fliess's first son, composed December 29, 1899, Freud unselfconsciously declared:

> Hail,
> To the valiant son who at the behest of his father appeared at the
>   right time,
> To be his assistant . . . ,
> But hail to the father, too, who just prior to the event found in his
>   calculations
> The key to restraining the power of the female sex
> And to shouldering his burden of lawful succession;
> No longer relying on sensory appearances, as does the mother,
> He calls upon the higher powers to claim his right, conclusion,
>   belief and doubt;
> Thus, at the beginning, there stands, hale and hearty, equal to
>   the exigency of error, the father, in his infinitely mature
>   development,
> May the calculation be correct and, as the legacy of labor, be
>   transferred from father to son and beyond the parting of
>   centuries
> Unite in the mind what the vicissitudes of life tear apart.
>
> (Masson, 1985, pp. 393–394)

Arguably this poem, which was penned for a sentimental occasion on the eve of a new century, is not really representative of Freud's theoretical views. After all, it is exquisitely designed to flatter Fliess, who spent many hours trying to calculate the precise birth time and sex of his new offspring on the basis of his theory of biological periodicity. What it does establish beyond a shadow of reasonable doubt, however, is that Freud was conversant with Bachofen as early as 1899, while composing *The Interpretation of Dreams* (1900). That said, it is tempting to speculate that this poem presages Freud's later ambivalence toward Bachofen's matriarchal hypothesis. On the one hand, as in *Moses and Monotheism* (1939), Freud shows himself to be an enthusiastic exponent of the patriarchal revolution, which, like Bachofen, he construes as a movement away from the maternal powers that are reliant on sensory appearance toward the liberating powers of intellect. On the other hand, as in *Totem and Taboo* (1913), he refuses to grant the mother any priority in the male infant's emotional life, having subtly denigrated the mother's biological role in carrying the child, and exalted Fliess's calculations—which were probably off a day or two. Freud then declared that "at the beginning, there stands, hale and hearty, equal to the exigency of error, the father . . ." (ibid., p. 394).

Although it was not on his public agenda at the time, Freud would labor to make the law of the father a culture-constitutive phenomenon and would ignore the role of pre-Oedipal processes in the development of culture. Another striking feature of Freud's utterances throughout is his insistent juxtaposition of the themes of fatherhood and property. In his rebuttal to Jung, he states that the father is one who possesses the mother sexually, and possesses the children as property. In his earlier letter to Fliess, the theme of the male "shouldering his burden of lawful succession" and his use of intellectual or "higher powers" are linked to the imperative of "restraining the power of the female sex" (1913, p. 394). Clearly, for Freud fatherhood implies not merely intellect or abstract thought but also rights of ownership and use in people and, secondarily, perhaps, in things. To the extent that "there have been fathers' sons at all times," as Freud declared to Jung, it would follow that property relations have suffused the collective life of the human species for time immemorial.

For Bachofen, by contrast, our remote prehistory was characterized by community of goods and group marriage, till women's innate conservatism and good sense prompted them to invent monogamy. During this phase, in which property relations were not yet determined by patrilineal descent, women were either dominant or on an equal footing with men, and goddesses held sway in the pagan pantheons. The continual conflict that in Freud's theory characterizes the transition from our early hominid ancestors to civilization was deferred by Bachofen to the later, warlike patriarchal period. And although Bachofen welcomed patriarchy as a progressive step, women were anything but passive nonentities in the first phases of human evolution. On the contrary, they were the standard-bearers. As Fromm would later point out (1934), this feature of Bachofen's theorizing caught the imagination of Friedrich Engels and August Bebel, who brought a modified and specifically socialist interpretation of Bachofen's theory to a much wider audience. Thus, Alfred Adler was following established precedent on the left when he cited Bachofen's theory to prove that women are potentially equal partners to men, and that certain features of feminine psychopathology are directly attributable to their historic subordination, which should be abolished (Adler, 1927). Although Adler's sentiments were commendable, his use of Bachofen *psychologically* was rather trite and literal-minded. The deeper implications of Bachofen for a theory of human development were left to others to explore.

Jung, Rank, Fromm, and Suttie

In contrast to Freud and Adler, Jung emphasized the clinical significance of the mother early on. The first intimation of Bachofen's influence, ironically, is Jung's essay "The Significance of the Father in the Destiny of the Individual" (1909), in which he drew some startling parallels between neurotic father-syndromes and historical trends, which Freud later exploited to his own advantage. But Jung, unlike Freud, qualified his remarks on the role of the father in psychic development by observing that the preeminence of the father was a recent historical phenomenon, not a culture-constitutive one.

Soon afterward some striking convergences between schizophrenic ideation and mythic motifs prompted Jung to posit the existence of a primary regressive urge in *Symbols of Transformation* (1913). Jung termed this regressive tendency "incestuous libido." But whereas Freud's libido—incestuous or otherwise—sought for tension reduction on the program of the pleasure principle, Jung's incestuous libido *seeks to reinstate intrauterine existence,* that is, reunion with the mother, which is experienced as a threat to the symbiotic ego, so that counter-vailing fantasies of matricide arise to halt a further descent into madness, to promote individuation and a return to external reality.

The existence of a primordial force promoting a return to the womb and, from the standpoint of consciousness, an undifferentiated or adualistic cosmos was a mainstay of Romantic, and particularly late Romantic, philosophy. Nietzsche borrowed the term *Dionysian* from Bachofen to describe this phenomenon, and the term *Apollonian* for the countervailing tendency to individuation (Nietzsche, 1871; Ellenberger, 1970, pp. 218–223). For Bachofen and Jung, the struggle to emancipate oneself from the regressive lure of symbiotic fusion with the mother is the first and in some sense most momentous problem of all human development, in which the father figures more as a positive ally than as a hostile competitor (Hogenson, 1983, pp. 59, 85). Jung merely transposed the idea from the philosophy of history to the clinical setting.

By the mid 1920s another of Freud's prodigal sons, Otto Rank, evinced a parallel appreciation for the process of individuation. *The Trauma of Birth* (1924) was the first psychoanalytic treatise to be an explicit philosophy of history. This fact makes it all the more significant that Rank's indebtedness to Bachofen is plain throughout the book: Bachofen is cited as often as Freud. Moreover, in Rank's new historical perspective the chief engine of the neuroses, and of cultural and historical development, is no longer Oedipal rivalry, but the trauma of separation from the mother and its manifold repercussions. In 1924 Rank was unprepared for the magnitude of his emerging differences with Freud and his circle and argued, for a time, that his work was merely a consistent application of Freud's own insights. Years later, however, Rank would write:

> To the unique work of the Swiss scholar, Bachofen, we owe our knowledge of the . . . once widespread [form of social organization] in which the father role was not yet acknowledged and the mother, supported by her brother as the masculine head of the family, ruled the clan. This custom is still in practice among some primitive islanders . . . and the social organization of which it was an essential feature has been designated by Bachofen as the matriarchal system. From all this it follows that the family, as we know it, emerged at a very late date in the history of mankind. (1941, p. 120)

However, Rank continued,

> anthropologists and sociologists, indeed, even our modern psychologists . . . tacitly assume that the family unit existed from the very beginning . . . and, since they could not find such a pleasing "tableau" in the history of the past, they naively projected their own conception into it. Freud, when he had to supplement his psychology of the individual by the social aspects of personality development, even went so far as to reinterpret primitive anthropological material in the light of our present-day family organization. In his sensational interpretation of the Greek Oedipus-saga we find the social significance of a collective myth explained in terms of the highly individualized psychology of modern neurotics. (Ibid., pp. 121–122)

Although Rank's thinking on the birth trauma became increasingly metaphorical, he continued to interpret the totemistic rituals that Freud construed in light of the obsessional neuroses as dramatizations of *pre-Oedipal* or symbiotic conflicts. As his battle against Freud's Oedipal monism escalated, Rank's reliance on Bachofen developed apace. In *Beyond Psychology,* for example, Rank ventured to suggest:

At the height of the patriarchal rule in ancient Rome, the father became invested with a power derived from the magic self of the hero in whose image civic fatherhood was created as a social type. Paradoxically enough, it seems that Freud's "primitive dominance of the father" who ruled tyrannically over the "herd of brothers" only existed politically in the highly organized Roman state at the peak of its power. In this light, psychoanalysis, centered around the father psychology, appears as the last stand of the crumbling patriarchal ideology which collapsed together with imperialism in the [first] World War. For a while, the outlived father-principle found refuge in an individualistic psychology which explained the father-son relation on the basis of a personal, more specifically sexual rivalry between two individuals within the same family. On the basis of its patriarchal ideology, psychoanalysis had to explain the Oedipus saga in terms of the Decalogue and thus appears as the last bulwark against the decadence of bourgeois family structure as it grew from socialized fatherhood in Roman law. (Ibid., pp. 126–127)

Although Bachofen is not cited explicitly here, the sentiments are entirely his. He, too, had seen Roman society as the epitome of the patriarchal spirit in antiquity, and might have responded to Freud this way himself. In a similar vein, Rank now reproached Freud for deriving social psychology from individual psychology, rather than vice versa, and for not respecting the concrete historicity of myths and fables. But Rank was not alone or even first in the field in this regard. The first critique along these lines came from the Freudo-Marxists, who were also conversant with matriarchal theory. Voicing sentiments that reflected an emerging consensus on the left in analytic circles, Fromm complained in 1932:

Psychoanalysis has focused on the structure of bourgeois society and its patriarchal family as the normal situation . . . This necessarily led to a renunciation of the authentic analytic method. Since they did not concern themselves with the variety of life experience, the socio-economic structure of other kinds of society, and therefore did not try to explain psychic structure as determined by social structure, they necessarily began to analogize instead of analysing. They treated mankind or a given society as an individual, transposed the specific mechanisms found in contemporary individuals to every possible type of society, and "explained" the psychic structure of these societies by analogy with certain phenomena (usually of a neurotic sort) typical of human beings in their own society.

In doing this, they overlooked a point of view that is fundamental even to psychoanalytic individual psychology. They forgot the fact that

neurosis . . . results from the abnormal individual's faulty adaptation . . . to the reality around him; most people in a society, i.e., the
"healthy" people, do possess this ability to adapt. Thus phenomena
studied in social (or mass) psychology cannot be explained by analogy
with neurotic phenomena. They should be understood as the result of
the adaptation of the instinctual apparatus to the social reality.

The most striking example of this procedure is the absolutization of
the Oedipus complex, which was made into a universal human mechanism . . . The absolutization of the Oedipus complex led Freud to base
the whole development of mankind on the mechanisms of father-
hatred and the resultant reactions, without any regard for the material
conditions of the group under study.   (1970a, pp. 146–147)

Though influenced by Bachofen in the 1930s, however, Fromm
differed from Jung and Rank in that he still considered himself a
Freudian, and did not yet give evidence of appreciating the pathogenic potential of the primary regressive urge. But Fromm's study of
Bachofen did prompt him to distinguish two psychological types,
with elective affinities to certain religious and political ideologies
historically. The patricentric, or father-centered, type is one in which
the relationship to the father is more strongly cathected than other
emotional involvements. It is characterized by dependence on fa-
therly authority, involving a mixture of guilt, anxiety, love and hate,
identification with the aggressor, and a superego whose principle is
that duty takes precedence over happiness. In contrast stands the
matricentric type, in which the relationship to the mother takes
precedence, typically with a mood of greater optimism about life,
fewer guilt feelings, a weaker superego, and a less impaired capacity
for intimacy and sensual pleasure. Along with these traits, Fromm
added, there develop democratic tendencies and an ego ideal of
motherly compassion for the weak and helpless (1970a, pp. 125–
135). Not surprisingly, Fromm concluded that the psychic basis of the
Marxist social program was matricentric.

At something of a remove from Fromm, geographically speaking,
was Ian Suttie, a Scottish psychiatrist at the Tavistock Clinic in London (1935). Suttie's book *The Origins of Love and Hate* leaned on the
work of Robert Briffault, a renowned British anthropologist and
exponent of matriarchal theory of whom Fromm was also quite fond
(Fromm, 1933a). Like Fromm, Suttie chafed at Freud's misogyny and
advocated modifications in technique along lines proposed by Sandor

Ferenczi (Suttie, 1935, chap. 14; Fromm, 1935a). Although these parallels are impressive, others are almost uncanny. Like Fromm, Suttie interpreted the theological and political history of Western Europe from the dawn of Christianity down to early modern times in terms of a clash between "matrist" and "patrist" sensibilities, terms that coincide with Fromm's matricentric and patricentric orientations (compare Fromm, [1934] 1970a, pp. 131–135; Suttie, 1935, chap. 9). Like Fromm somewhat later (1943, 1951), Suttie contended that feminine "penis envy" is a cultural artifact, and that a deep exploration of the patriarchal psyche discloses that "the fundamental jealousy is that of man for woman's reproductive and lactational powers. Indeed, patriarchal culture and character are themselves largely expressions of this envy and not that of natural superiority" (1935, p. 180).

The concepts of breast and womb envy did not originate with Suttie, however. In "The Flight from Womanhood" ([1926] 1967), Karen Horney had already remarked on the frequency of breast and womb envy clinically and had speculated that the creative urge in men is often the sublimated expression of a compensation for unconscious feelings of this nature. Horney expressed astonishment at the sexist character of the penis-envy theory, which neglects to accord any intrinsically enviable properties to female reproductive biology. In words now justly famous, she declared:

> At this point, I, as a woman, ask in amazement, and what about motherhood? And the blissful consciousness of bearing new life within oneself? And the ineffable happiness of the increasing expectation of the appearance of this new being? And the joy when it finally makes its appearance and one holds it in one's arms? And the deep pleasurable feeling of satisfaction in suckling it and the happiness of the whole period when the infant needs her care?   (Horney, 1967, p. 60)

Like Melanie Klein and Joan Rivière subsequently, however, Horney saw penis envy and womb envy as biological givens, the logical extension of our innately bisexual disposition (Klein and Rivière, 1937, pp. 30–36). What makes Suttie and Fromm remarkable is that instead of invoking bisexuality to restore balance and symmetry to the discussion of gender and culture, they adopted the more radical position, making womb envy primary, and penis envy secondary or artifactual. The fact that they—and not their female counterparts—

adopted this perspective on the psychology of patriarchy makes their intellectual kinship all the more intriguing.

Given the extensive parallels between Fromm and Suttie, it is puzzling to discover that neither knew of the other's work. Ashley Montagu, a friend and disciple of Briffault's and an admirer of Ian Suttie's, assured me that during Fromm's lectures on psychoanalytic anthropology at the Wenner-Gren Foundation in New York, and warm but sporadic contact between them thereafter, Fromm never mentioned Suttie; moreover, Montagu was surprised to learn that Fromm had accorded Briffault's work a very warm reception in *Zeitschrift für Sozialforschung* (Fromm, 1933a), because Briffault had never surfaced in conversation either (personal communication, April 23, 1983). Suttie published and died in 1935, while Fromm was settling in America, so it is possible, though unlikely, that Fromm knew of Suttie's work but chose not to discuss it. A more plausible supposition is that this was an instance of the historian's *Zeitgeist* phenomenon, whereby different theorists arrive at parallel formulations simultaneously as a result of their immersion in the same subject matter.

However, the same cannot be said of Fromm's relationship to Jung and Rank. He knew their work well and, over time, offered some corroborating testimony in favor of their ideas. But in 1934 Fromm did not seem to grasp the regressive lure of symbiotic fusion as a salient clinical phenomenon. This changed with *Escape from Freedom* (1941), when Fromm first discussed the problems of symbiotic attachment and individuation, albeit with amazingly few explicit references to fantasies concerning the maternal imago such as are found in Jung, Rank, and Klein. However, Fromm's next remarks on Bachofen, in *The Sane Society* (1955a, pp. 47–51), credited Bachofen with a deeper understanding of the "incest complex" than Freud had attained, but did not mention Jung or Rank, who had arrived at similar conclusions some years previously. It is hard to imagine that this oversight was not deliberate.

The next reference to Bachofen was in *The Forgotten Language* (Fromm, 1957, pp. 196–231). Here again, Fromm took issue with Freud's rendering of the incest complex and interpreted the Oedipus myth in light of Bachofen's rendering of the *Oresteia*. Once again, references to Jung and Rank were conspicuous by their absence. And by now, of course, Fromm had delivered some devastating criticisms of both Jung and Rank, comparing them unfavorably with Freud on a variety of issues. Even if we credit Fromm's criticisms of the sweeping subjectivism of Jung and Rank (1939a; 1947, introduction), it is unclear why Fromm was so reluctant until much later (for example, 1964, p. 100n) to acknowledge the parallels that *did* exist between them. Like Fromm, both Jung and Rank rejected the Freudian premise that religion is necessarily symptomatic of unresolved parricidal guilt. For them, spiritual aspirations and values had a legitimate existence in their own right. As offshoots of Freudian depth psychology, the schools of Jung and Rank were critical toward the contents of consciousness but rejoined the older, pre-Darwinian philosophical anthropology by stressing the synthetic, self-actualizing aspects of the psyche, the role of ethical considerations in clinical psychopathology, and the pervasive influence of culture and history on human character and motivation. And so, in time, did Fromm's, Freudo-Marxism notwithstanding.

Finally, as Dieter Wyss has observed, Fromm resembled Jung and Rank in seeing neurosis, fundamentally, as a failure of individuation (Wyss, 1973, p. 273). To this, we can only add that his concept of the incest complex and of development generally was transposed to the clinical domain from Bachofen's philosophy of cultural and historical development, as his remarks in *The Sane Society* make plain (1955a, chaps. 2 and 3). This fact differentiates Fromm from Horney, Sullivan, and the other neo-Freudians, for whom Bachofen is an altogether minor figure. Consequently, it is interesting to note that, in conversation with Richard Evans, Fromm sought to differentiate his own position not by reference to Bachofen, Jung, or Rank, but to Freud himself: "Perhaps the distinguishing factor is that I feel much closer to Freud than Horney or Sullivan felt, and I have attempted throughout the years to translate Freud into philosophical categories which seem to me to correspond more with recent philosophical and sociological thought patterns" (Evans, 1966, p. 59).

Apparently Fromm felt constrained to distance himself from Jung and Rank—whether consciously or otherwise—because of the distinctive kind of Freud piety shared by all the Freudo-Marxists, who, unlike Adler, Jung, and Rank, claimed to have gone beyond Freud and to have transcended his frame of reference completely.

Consequently, it is both sad and strange that Fromm is frequently construed as a kind of neo-Adlerian (for example, Wittels, 1939; Jacoby, 1975). It is strange because, in most respects, Adler was insensible to the deeper psychological implications of Bachofen's theory, and is accordingly the "dissident" whom Fromm resembled least. It is also sad, because in advancing this charge, Fromm's wish to be classed among Freud's loyal opposition, among his pupils and "translators," has been violated, often on specious or inflated grounds. Besides, Adler was, if nothing else, a gifted and well-meaning individual, whose sympathies on feminist issues, though anachronistic by contemporary standards, were generally in the right direction, and quite commendable for his day. The use of his name as a term of derogation and abuse is merely one more example of the kind of sectarian mudslinging characteristic of Freud zealots, which conscientious historians will not take too seriously.

3 Fromm's Clinical Contributions

Any synoptic overview of Fromm's clinical orientation based solely on his published output soon runs into difficulty. Many of Fromm's finest clinical formulations are dispersed amid rambling, discursive analyses of social, historical, philosophical, and theological topics, whose relevance to the average clinician is not immediately apparent. Fromm never disentangled his operative clinical assumptions and methods from the humanistic scholarship that made up so much of his life's work, and the book on analytic technique that he promised in 1970 never materialized. Moreover, with the widespread dissemination of object-relations theory and self-psychology in North America today, the idea that the need for relatedness and an integrated self takes precedence over the obstacles to drive reduction in the etiology of neurosis sounds almost commonplace. It is easy to forget how original these ideas were when Fromm first propounded them, much less to wonder why his name is seldom associated with them and why they entered the mainstream through different channels.

Although Fromm is traditionally classed among the neo-Freudians—a designation he evidently disliked—it is more useful to contrast Fromm's clinical orientation with those of Freud, Reich, and object-relations theorists. The Fromm-Horney-Sullivan-Thompson comparisons that abound in the psychoanalytic literature are now stale and overrehearsed, promising little fresh insight. Moreover, the comparisons themselves are not always as apt or illuminating as is sometimes imagined, for reasons that will become apparent in the following pages.

Freud in Historical Context

Like the French philosopher Paul Ricoeur somewhat later, Fromm traced the beginning of modern depth psychology to the philosophy of Spinoza (Fromm, 1964, chap. 6; Fromm and Xirau, 1968, pp. 140–151; Ricoeur, 1970, pp. 452–458). However, although Spinoza's thoughts on irrational passions lend themselves to interpretation in terms of unconscious motivation, an explicit concept of unconscious mental processes begins with Spinoza's younger contemporary Leibniz. Leibniz took issue with Locke's view of human knowledge as something that emerges chiefly through the passive registration of external stimuli impinging on the organism. In fact, argued Leibniz, conscious thought and perception are shaped by memory, habit, and attention, as well as by the novelty and intensity of the incoming stimulus, so that many sensory stimuli that act upon the organism— his *petites perceptions*—are never consciously apprehended (Fromm and Xirau, 1968, pp. 155–158; Burston, 1986a). More important, Leibniz had an enormous influence on the German educator J. F. Herbart, a contemporary of Kant, Fichte, and Hegel whose later expositor, Gustav Lindner, Freud studied as a *Gymnasium* student (Ricoeur, 1970, pp. 72–73, 452–458).

In other words, Freudian mythology notwithstanding, the psychology of the unconscious was already quite advanced in Freud's day. In the early nineteenth century, many decades before *Studies on Hysteria* (Freud, 1895), Herbart suggested that the reciprocal interaction of ideas bearing varying energic charges may promote or inhibit one another in their struggle to cross the threshold of consciousness; that the bulk of mental "contents" are excluded or repressed (*Verdrangungen*) at any given time. Herbart, however, was more interested in the principles of correct instruction than in the mysteries of the disordered psyche, to which he gave very little attention. As a result, he addressed the mechanisms but not the *motives* for repression, and sidestepped the phenomenon of motivated ignorance or *false consciousness,* whose undoing, presumably, lies at the heart of the analytic process.

By the 1890s the idea of the repressed pathogenic memories as a factor in hysteria had been advanced by Jean Martin Charcot, Pierre Janet, and others, while the sexual etiology of hysteria was advanced independently and before Freud by the Viennese physician Moritz

Benedickt (Ellenberger, 1976, chap. 5). Moreover, there was the lingering influence of Arthur Schopenhauer. In the mid-nineteenth century, Schopenhauer had devoted many pages of reflection to the role of sexuality in human affairs, where, in his estimation,

> it is really the central invisible point of all action and conduct, and peeps out everywhere in spite of all the veils thrown over it. It is the cause of war and the end of peace, the basis of what is serious, and the aim of jest, the inexhaustible source of wit, the key to allusions, and the meaning of all mysterious hints, of all unspoken offers and glances, the daily meditations of the young, and often also of the old, the hourly thought of the unchaste, and even against their will the constantly recurring imagination of the chaste . . .   (1844, pp. 106–107)

In this cultural and intellectual climate, Freud's claim to originality lay in his theories regarding the motives for repression, and the specific character and complexity of the symptoms through which the conflicting needs and intentions of the suffering person are embodied or expressed. Freud's etiological hypotheses regarding hysterical and obsessional symptomatology were soon joined to a new theory of psychosexual development, in which adult psychopathology was construed as a regressive reactivation of older conflicts and libidinal positions as a result of sexual stasis or life's inevitable misfortunes. These theories, in turn, were coordinated into a psychology of religion, a social psychology, and a whole father-centered philosophy of history; an immensely ambitious undertaking. Here, however, the clinical domain is our sole concern.

In Freudian theory, symptom formation is a complex affair, and no brief presentation can capture the depth and subtlety of Freud's formulations. Suffice it to say that for Freud, a hysterical or obsessional symptom is a compromise formation between the repressed impulses and the forces that strive to keep them out of awareness. Moreover, it represents a partial and substitutive gratification of the repressed impulse, and a kind of code or communication that enables the sufferer to communicate to others, without fear of reprisal or the experience of guilt and shame, the feelings and emotions that are socially tabooed (for example, Freud, 1895, 1901, 1905). And much as the patient suffers, there are hidden benefits. People with a mysterious ailment, for example, may compel deference and attentiveness they might not otherwise command, compensating them for an otherwise unbearable sense of powerlessness or deprivation, gratifying an unconscious will to power.[1]

According to Freud, a routine obstacle to the resolution of analysis—the decoding of the symptom—is a particular kind of resistance called transference. In transference phenomena, the patient acts out unresolved and unconscious feelings toward significant others with the analyst while experiencing this peculiar displacement as something grounded in present-day reality (Freud, 1915). In most transferences, and particularly in cases involving the obsessional disorders, Freud discovered a strong measure of ambivalence toward the analyst. Though initially deemed Oedipal in origin (Freud, 1913, chap. 4) and ascribed to a phylogenetic or "archaic inheritance," this primary ambivalence was thought by Karl Abraham to be rooted in the vicissitudes of the oral libido. In the course of normal development, presumably, the internalization of parental imagos and guilt over tabooed impulses give rise to the superego, which observes those manifestations of the id that escape the ego's waking scrutiny, judging or condemning them in accordance with standards linked to the parental ideals and admonitions.

Even in normal circumstances and in the absence of manifest disturbance, Freud insisted that the superego we supposedly inherit from remote prehistory is important. In the orthodox literature this recurrent emphasis on the superego becomes intelligible in light of Freud's conviction that our sociability and goodwill, our fondness for work, love of truth, and so on are the secondary transformations of other, more refractory impulses; a kind of *second nature* superimposed on an antisocial core. The deep, spontaneous sense of solidarity, the relative absence of constraint, that Bachofen attributed to matriarchal societies has no place in Freud's psychology. To this day, the essentially antisocial character of our instinctual endowment is a tenet of analytic orthodoxy, separating "true believers" from those fallen into apostasy.

Reich's Clinical Orientation

Among the first to challenge Freud's model of human nature was Wilhelm Reich. Like Fromm, Reich came to matriarchal theory via Engels and August Bebel, but he ignored Bachofen and Briffault, relying on the more recent work of Bronislaw Malinowski (Cattier, 1971). Like the younger Freud of "Civilized Sexual Morality and Modern Nervousness" (1908), Reich was struck with how the lack of reliable contraception and prevailing sexual mores contributed to the prevalence of mental disturbance. Among his demands, which distressed even his Communist colleagues, was the sexual emancipation of adolescents. Freud thought that males past twenty suffered greatly from abstinence (1908), but he saw teenage abstinence as a vital prerequisite to the development of aim-inhibited and sublimated social bonds that would presumably constrain and channel our inborn aggression into socially useful pursuits (Freud, 1933, chap. 5). Reich disagreed. Reich saw sociability as something inborn, instinctive, and destructiveness as an artifact of patriarchal civilization. In the preface to the third edition of his classic work, *The Mass Psychology of Fascism,* Reich declared:

> Extensive and painstaking therapeutic work on the human character has led me to the conclusion that, as a rule, we are dealing with three layers of the biopsychic structure . . . these layers of . . . character . . . are deposits of social development, which function autonomously. On the surface layer of his personality the average man is reserved, polite, compassionate, responsible and conscientious. There would be no social tragedy . . . if this layer of his personality were in contact with the deep natural core. This, unfortunately, is not the case. The surface layer is not in contact with the deep, biologic core of one's selfhood; it is born by a second, intermediate layer, which consists exclusively of cruel, sadistic, lascivious and envious impulses. It represents the Freudian "unconscious" or "what is repressed" . . .
>
> [My work] made it possible to comprehend the Freudian unconscious, that which is anti-social in man, as a secondary result of the repression of primary biologic urges. If one penetrates through this second layer . . . one always discovers the third, deepest layer, which we [that is, Reichians] call the biologic core. In this core, under favorable conditions, man is essentially honest, industrious, cooperative, loving and, if motivated, a rationally hating animal.   (1970, pp. xii–xv)

Reich's clinical credo is clear. Man is a naturally sociable animal. Our second nature is not civilized, as Freud imagined, but sadistic and perverse, while the surface—like Jung's *persona*—has all the hallmarks of social adaptation. Apart from specific formulations on the relationship between drive and defense, Freud's error, Reich intimated, lay in taking the second, intermediate layer for the biologic core, and not penetrating to the deeper strata of human personality. After *Character Analysis* (1932), Reich saw pathology increasingly as something expressed in differing intensities and modalities of alienation from the real self or biologic core, and sought to rectify these disturbances by dissolving the "character armor" (or resistance) embedded in the musculature, with the hope of strengthening and reviving the remainder of healthy (but inhibited) personality. Reich saw no better way of gaining access to the biologic core of personality than through orgasm; accordingly, he spent less and less time in the analysis of resistances, which had been his forte, and focused exclusively on the facilitation of "orgastic potency." Once this had been established, presumably, a more healthy and satisfactory mode of relatedness to the world would follow automatically; a hope seldom borne out by clinical experience.

Nowhere were the differences between Freud and Reich more apparent than in their theories of character formation. Freud thought that character is formed as a result of processes of organic repression, sublimation, and reaction-formation against primitive pregenital drives. One dynamic striving could have a variety of manifest expressions, depending on its degree of secondary transformation. For example, at its most primitive, anality is expressed in *anal eroticism*, which, apart from the overtly sexual connotation, expresses itself in a slovenly and indifferent attitude toward personal appearance and cleanliness. At the anal stage, dirt or excrement is not yet experienced as something dangerous or disgusting, either in appearance or in smell. In time, however, through processes of sublimation, reaction-formation, and so on, which are facilitated by toilet training and socialization, anality manifests itself in exacting standards of cleanliness and punctuality and in tendencies toward hard, methodical, perfectionistic work habits, collecting rocks, insects, specimens, and making lists, to any number of obsessional or compulsive behaviors that may or may not be adaptive, depending on the degree to which the person is attuned to reality (Ferenczi, 1914). Similarly, according to Freud's collaborator Karl Abraham, oral, cannibalistic tendencies may be expressed in greed and impatience or, in more regressed individuals, in paranoid fears of being persecuted, engulfed by the other, in which their own unconscious contents are projected onto the external world.[2]

In Reich's thinking, by contrast, character structure may also derive from anal or oral strivings and from more or less ingenious methods of negating or sublimating them at the level of manifest behavior. However, in Reich's opinion, character serves the additional function of armoring and insulating the individual from the natural and healthy biological pulsations that would tend to establish a healthy and mature intrapsychic and interpersonal equilibrium, by restricting the range and intensity of affective experience. The resulting neurotic equilibrium, like its Freudian counterpart, is a creature of conflict and compromise, the difference being that *what* is repressed includes many healthy and prosocial tendencies. Character as a *constricting* variable, in Reich's view, is not merely a "civilizing" influence for the secondary transformation of instincts, but a *deforming structure* whose internalization alienates people from their authentic human possibilities (Reich, 1932b).

Fromm, Reich, and Object Relations Theory

Unlike Freud and Reich, Fromm never devoted much effort or attention—in print—to deciphering the various meanings and historical layerings of neurotic symptomatology. Like Reich, however, Fromm denied that malignant destructiveness—as opposed to rational or reactive hatred—is instinctive to man, and looked to other cultures and to prehistory for corroboration of his beliefs. Clinically, Fromm (and Horney) resembled Reich in emphasizing the rediscovery and strengthening of the authentic self buried beneath faulty or excessive socialization, rather than the analysis of symptoms per se. Like Reich, Fromm (and Horney) was concerned to establish and maintain contact with the alive and healthy core of patients, and to strengthen and consolidate it before confronting pathology (Thompson, 1950, p. 210). However, Reich regarded the patient's core and the alienation from selfhood as fundamentally rooted in a somatic process of drive and defense, even after he ceased using verbal interpretations altogether. Though not denying the significance of biological rigidity or of alienation from bodily functions, Fromm soon jettisoned the drive-reduction theory of motivation and characterological development, according the need for relatedness primacy over the satisfaction of tissue needs.

The development of Fromm's clinical orientation evinces a certain inner logic that can best be reconstructed in light of the debates in Freudo-Marxist circles in the 1930s. However, the character of Freudo-Marxist literature from this period permits no clear demarcation between clinical theory and social psychology. They were as intimately intertwined in this literature as they were, in fact, for Freud himself in the 1920s and 1930s.

Reich stressed the role played by the repression of genitality in deforming character, and singled out the authoritarian, patriarchal family as the chief agency of socialization entrusted with this task in the interests of maintaining class rule. A corollary assumption, therefore, was that the widespread proliferation of unconstrained genital sexuality (and a corresponding atrophy of its sadomasochistic distortions and derivatives) would buttress revolutionary and democratic sentiments in the population at large, ensuring the future of socialism. Although Fromm concurred with Reich's assessment of the family, he differed with Reich in emphasizing the primacy of the self-preservative or ego-instincts over the sexual drives. Fromm never meant to imply that the ego-instincts play a greater role in character formation than sexual ones. But in the event of conflict between the two groups of instincts, self-preservation takes precedence, since sexual appetites and aims can be deferred, sublimated, or repressed almost indefinitely or gratified through fantasy without any threat to actual survival. By contrast, the ego-instincts require real and immediate gratification to support life; they are not nearly so malleable as their sexual counterparts (Fromm, 1932a).

Fromm shared Reich's views on the deleterious effects of sexual repression and cautioned that prolonged nonsatisfaction of "normal" genitality led to intensification of sadistic trends and was therefore undesirable from a sociological standpoint (Fromm, 1932a), but he took no steps toward reorienting clinical theory around orgasm or around Freud's theory of the actual neuroses. On the contrary, Fromm's first deviation from classical Freudianism, and from the drive/defense orientation Reich shared with the analytic mainstream, involved some prescient reflections on object-relationships. In 1932, for example, Fromm observed that

> Freud established a close connection between the sexual drives and the "erogenous zones," and assumed that the sex drives are called forth by

stimulation of these erogenous zones. In the first stages of life, the oral zone and its associated functions . . . is the center of sexuality . . . then, from three to five, the genital zone gains in importance. Freud designates this first blush of genital sexuality as the "phallic phase," because he assumes that for both sexes it is only the phallus (or the phallically experienced clitoris) that plays a role, along with tendencies toward forceful invasion and destruction.

However, Fromm continued,

It is important to make a distinction between . . . erogenous lust and a person's object relationships. The latter are the person's (loving or hating) attitudes towards himself and other people . . .

These object relationships are seen as having a very close connection with the erogenous zones. The connection is understandable when you consider the fact that specific object relationships first develop in connection with specific erogenous zones and that these connections are not fortuitous. At this point I really do not want to raise the whole question of whether the connection is really as close as much of the psychoanalytic literature would have it; nor do I want to consider whether and to what extent an object relationship, typical of a particular erogenous zone, can also develop independently of that particular zone.   ([1932b] 1970a, pp. 166–167)

Yet in a footnote to his paper on Bachofen, published two years later, Fromm did just that. Here he remarked that

there is a basic difference between the typology based on pregenital character structures and the matricentric and patricentric typology. The former signifies a fixation to the oral or anal level, and is basically opposed to the mature, "genital character." The latter conceived in terms of the dominant object-relationship does not stand in opposition to the genital character. The matricentric type *can* be an oral character; in that case the person is more or less passive, dependent and in need of others' help. But the matricentric type can also be a genital character, i.e., psychically mature, active, not neurotic or arrested.

Here we cannot enter into a full discussion of the psychoanalytic categories . . . I do believe, however, that a typology based on object-relationships, rather than on erogenous zones or clinical symptomatology, offers fruitful possibilities for social research . . .   ([1934] 1970a, p. 131)

Despite this bold beginning, Fromm never developed this genial intuition. It stands as an isolated assertion, resonating with promise and thoughtfulness but essentially unfulfilled. Still, these thoughtful but inconclusive musings on the putative nexus between object-relationships and erogenous zones anticipated the central theoretical preoccupation of Fromm's Scottish contemporary W. R. D. Fairbairn. In a remarkable paper on schizoid phenomena, Fairbairn suggested in 1941 that object-relationships do indeed undergo a measure of autonomous development independently of their original somatic anchorings. Fairbairn claimed that the need for relatedness as such takes precedence over the vicissitudes of drives in the etiology of neurosis; a view pithily expressed in his famous contention that the libido is object-seeking, not pleasure-seeking. Like Fromm, Fairbairn saw the pursuit of raw drive satisfaction as symptomatic of a severe deterioration of interpersonal relationships (Fairbairn, 1941; Fromm, 1941). Like Fromm, Fairbairn saw psychopathology as an inability to maintain open, trusting, and giving relationships with others because of a preponderance of unresolved issues regarding the receiving, taking, incorporating, and holding of "good objects" or psychic nutriment, and because of hysterical and exhibitionistic preoccupations about *seeming* to give of oneself, to feel deeply, and so on, which merely mimic authentic relatedness, masking a deeper alienation within. Summarized, Fairbairn's final theoretical position was that the dynamics of phobias, obsessions, exhibitionism, and the Oedipal drama itself all represent different compromise formations between the regressive lure of symbiotic fusion and the progressive solution of individuated fellowship (Fairbairn, 1951); a position that, in substance, if not in the specific nuances of formulation, is identical with Fromm's clinical psychopathology after 1938.

The parallels between Fromm and Fairbairn seem obvious in retrospect, but they were not apparent to Harry Guntrip. Although Guntrip commended Fromm and Horney for dropping the drive theory as untenable, he reproached them for having contributed nothing to the knowledge of endopsychic structure, and for their manifest lack of interest in developments in Great Britain (Guntrip, 1961, chap. 8). Like Fairbairn, Guntrip labored to disentangle Freud and Klein's object-relations theory from the drive theory, arguing that the latter is clinically superfluous (1961). But Guntrip also spoke of restoring the capacity for ego relatedness in language that is strikingly reminiscent of what Fromm termed "core to core relatedness" (1968).[3]

Guntrip's critique of Fromm and Horney might have been balanced if Fairbairn, his own teacher, had interested himself in American psychoanalysis. As it happens, though, both Fromm and Fairbairn worked in relative isolation, and Fromm expressed only the barest acknowledgment of what were actually profound affinities between him and the British middle school in an interview for German radio in 1975 (1986, p. 82). Apart from the possibility of rivalry, parochialism, or sheer indifference—which can never be ruled out in the history of psychoanalysis—there were profound intellectual and stylistic differences between the two men, which might account for the fact that no one except David Schechter (1973) has ever commented on the astonishing parallels in their clinical orientations.

One obvious difference between them was that Fairbairn, following Melanie Klein, explored the conflicts characteristic of obsessional, hysterical, schizoid, and phobic symptomatology from the standpoint of unconscious fantasy and the way it shapes our feelings, fears, and expectations and our (conscious and unconscious) experience of people and events. Although the notion of unconscious fantasy was already implicit in Freud's concept of transference, it was a peripheral issue when ego psychology took center stage in the United States. The British gave this domain of analytic inquiry a new lease on life, but in ways that Fromm found difficult to assimilate. Bernard Landis relates that during a conversation about unconscious fantasy Fromm vigorously objected to the notion of split off, of internalized objects as being at odds with the "clinical phenomenology" of patients' utterances (personal communication, November 1988). (Fromm never worked with psychotic patients.) Douglas Carmichael, in a slightly different vein, emphasizes the profound differences between Fromm and Fairbairn on questions of technique, Fairbairn's being classical (Guntrip, 1975), and Fromm's being very active and empathic (personal communication, May 1983).

For reasons that need no elaboration, then, I would hesitate to characterize Fromm's post-Freudian endeavors as embodiments of object-relations theory. But despite intervening changes in emphasis and terminology, there is a striking continuity in spirit between Fromm's early, object-relations orientation and his later clinical formulations. In *The Heart of Man* (1964), for example, Fromm merely revived an earlier train of thought when he noted that, for Freud and his followers, the degree or severity of pathology is determined by the temporal (or sequential) proximity of the trait or process in question to the genital phase. On this line of reasoning, Fromm noted, phallic exhibitionism and intrusiveness would be less pathological than a preambivalent oral fixation. However, Fromm insisted, the earlier, preambivalent oral orientation is characterized by more openness and trust in the world and a lesser admixture of sadism. Consequently, Fromm suggested,

> the problem cannot be solved by the evolutionary assumption that the earlier orientations are the roots of the more pathological orientations. As I see it, each orientation in itself has various levels of regression, reaching from the normal to the most archaic . . . I propose therefore to determine pathology not according to the distinction between levels of libido development, but according to the degree of regression *within* each orientation . . .   (1964, pp. 112–113)

In other words, in 1964 Fromm still seemed to concede that the ontogenetic sequence described by Freud is essentially sound, and that appropriate modifications within this framework might yet yield a workable system for diagnostic purposes. Yet in 1966, in conversation with Richard Evans, Fromm doubted whether there *is* any ontogenetic sequence (Evans, 1966). It is impossible to determine whether Fromm was even conscious of this ambiguity and, if so, what importance he attached to it. What cannot be disputed, however, is that the great burden of emphasis in Fromm's work suggests that the various libido positions described by Freud are not universal ontogenetic sequelae, but merely different ways or strategies of meeting our (physical and emotional) needs, with characteristic modes of relatedness to the world (Fromm, 1947, chap. 3; Fromm and Maccoby, 1970, pp. 11–16). And this, in essence, is what Fairbairn believed as well.

Finally, Fromm's idea of character structure and Fairbairn's notion of unconscious fantasy are highly convergent, though differing in pedigree. Fromm's idea of character structure, though shaped by his early meditations on object-relationships, was influenced chiefly by Freud and Reich and was modified in the spirit of existential humanism. Fairbairn and his associates, working in proximity to Klein, were more impressed by the notion of primitive introjects in the defective or punitive superego and by the role of "splitting." However, the fact remains that both character structure and unconscious fantasy ostensibly result in distinctive modes of assimilation and socialization, and in distinctive hopes, fears, and expectations that shape manifest behavior whose roots are deeply unconscious.

Fairbairn, then, like Fromm, came to regard the various syndromes and processes he described as solutions to the problem of relatedness rather than concomitants of an epigenetically preprogrammed maturational itinerary that gets "stuck" at a certain point of unfoldment (compare Fairbairn, 1946; Fromm and Maccoby, 1970, chap. 4). Like Fromm, he saw character as a more open system than did Freud—as something liable to change in response to better or worsening conditions well into the teens, or indeed, throughout life. And like Fromm, he vigorously objected to attempts to reduce ethical or philosophic problems to the epiphenomena of repressed infantile sexuality or a repressed nucleus of pathogenic conflicts (Fairbairn, 1956).

But differences remain. Although Fairbairn took issue with Freudian forays into philosophy and ethics, he seldom made reference to religious, philosophical, or historical ideas. And unlike Fromm, Fairbairn wrote for clinicians alone. In style as well as in substance, his revisions to classical theory represent an immanent critique whose successive phases and underlying rationale were chronicled with great care, and with the express intention of maintaining the link between psychoanalysis and the natural sciences that Freud had forged and Reich tried to deepen in another direction, albeit mostly in vain. Fromm, by contrast, felt no affinity for the natural sciences and ranged freely through philosophy and the social sciences in all his published work, although, like Reich and Fairbairn before him, he saw himself as following in Freud's footsteps as well.

Any dialogue between Fromm and Fairbairn would have foundered on their irreconcilable attitudes toward Marx. By his own admission, Fairbairn accorded scant significance to the role of economic conditions in shaping social psychology. From a Marxist standpoint, he cherished a naive and reified conception of the family as a transhistorical constant, and not as an entity shaped by class divisions and changing material conditions (Fairbairn, 1935). His was a deeply conservative but nevertheless ahistorical conception of the family.

By contrast, long after he abandoned the libido theories Fromm saw the family as an agency of socialization that is exquisitely responsive to changing requirements of prevailing economic circumstances. In this important respect, his later work is entirely consistent with his earlier ideas. However, as Fromm abandoned the libido theories he accorded less and less significance to sexual repression as an instrument of social control in contemporary life. In *Greatness and Limita-*

tions of Freud's Thought, for example, there is a passing reference to Reich,

> who thought that inhibition of sex creates antirevolutionary characters and that sexual freedom would create revolutionary characters . . . Of course, Reich was quite wrong, as later developments showed. This sexual liberation was largely part of the ever increasing consumerism . . . It is after all the most simple and the cheapest of all consumption. Reich was misled because at his time the conservatives had a strict sexual morality and he concluded from this that sexual liberation would lead to an anticonservative, revolutionary attitude. Historical development has shown that sexual liberation served the development of consumerism and if anything weakened political radicalism. Unfortunately Reich knew and understood little of Marx and could be called a "sexual anarchist." (1980, p. 135)

This is Fromm at his most thoughtless and polemical. The intent of this passage was clearly twofold: to obscure the fact that he had once shared Reich's hopefulness on this score (with qualifications), and to have the proverbial last word in what had quickly become a contentious relationship bereft of comradeship or genuine collaboration. Worse still, the assertion that sexual liberation—inasmuch as it promotes consumerism—weakens political radicalism is eerily reminiscent of the rhetoric the hard-core Leninists in the Communist party used to discredit Reich when they ousted him from their midst. Moreover, Fromm implied that Reich would have endorsed the so-called sexual revolution of the 1960s and 1970s wholeheartedly, that sexual liberation is inherently consumeristic and antirevolutionary—an absurd concoction of fabrications, half-truths, and misattributions.

Still, Fromm's charge that Reich did not understand Marx is more intelligible in relation to Reich's late excursions into biological mysticism, a far cry from his Freudo-Marxist endeavors. In Fromm's work, the continuity of Marx's influence is more pronounced. Fromm's early concept of a shared libidinal structure—the precursor to what he would later call social character—was predicated on the primacy of the self-preservative drives, whose overriding demands for satisfaction hinged on the realm of work and its vicissitudes and, by implication, on what Marx had termed the prevailing "mode of production," with its attendant social relationships (Fromm, 1932a). Fromm's invocation of the instincts was not destined to last, but he continued to see the family as the mediator for more impersonal imperatives of social adaptation.

With regard to character and instinct, Fromm's thinking changed in the 1940s. Fromm noted that as a general rule the cortical development of an animal species is in inverse proportion to the degree of instinctive adaptation to its surroundings; that humans possess a large cortex, and presumably, as a result, little instinctual hardware. This does not mean that innate predispositions do not affect individual development. Indeed, Fromm supposed we are all born with an innate *temperament,* which makes a tangible contribution to our overall personality and is more or less fixed. Character, by contrast, is a product of experience and environment rather than genetic endowment. Personality represents the synthesis of temperament and character (Fromm, 1947, chap. 3).

Although Fromm recognized various theories of temperament as being useful (for example, those of Hippocrates, Jung, Ernst Kretschmer, and William Sheldon), his clinical interest focused on character, which is open to change. According to Fromm, character can be understood along two dimensions, namely, modes of assimilation and modes of relatedness or socialization. The former refer to the characteristic way in which we attend to physical needs; the latter to the way we relate to others. Although Fromm had a tendency to treat modes of assimilation and socialization as discrete entities, a moment's reflection indicates that they are not. The way in which biological need satisfaction is mediated by interpersonal relationships from earliest infancy to adult life in increasingly interdependent systems of production, distribution, and exchange suggests that the boundary between assimilation and socialization, though useful theoretically, is fluid in practice, as with the analogous processes of assimilation and accommodation in Piaget's cognitive theory (Gruber and Voneche, 1977, preface).

In the absence of a preset instinctual orientation to the environment, Fromm theorized, character enables us to respond to environmental contingencies and interpersonal situations without having to reflect, and to mediate our activity through complicated processes of deliberation, evaluation, and so on. If only for this reason alone, the real roots of character are deeply unconscious and very difficult to change. Although Fromm did not discuss modes of socialization until 1964, he spelled out the modes of assimilation as early as 1947, enumerating various positive and negative manifestations of what he termed the receptive, exploitative, hoarding, and marketing orientations. The first three correspond to the oral-receptive, oral-aggressive, and anal phases in Freud's psychosexual schema. The marketing character, by contrast, has no analogue in Freudian thinking, and no erogenous zone to anchor it in our somatic makeup. It deserves more attention than it has received hitherto, and comes in for critical scrutiny in Chapter 5.

Fromm's Concepts of Destructiveness and Symbiosis

In addition to its analysis of characterological orientations or modes of assimilation, *Man for Himself* (Fromm, 1947) contained a thoughtful analysis of the pathogenesis of aggression and destructiveness that harked back to a paper in 1939 in which Fromm's break with Freud had become quite apparent. In "Selfishness and Self-Love," Fromm already distinguished between a reactive or rational hatred, which is a biologically conditioned response to (real or imaginary) threats to one's well-being, and a characterologically conditioned hatred, which is an abiding quality, rather than a transient response to a noxious stimulus. Operating on instinctivistic assumptions, Fromm charged, Freud had assumed that destructiveness represents a (more or less) fixed quantity of instinctual energy that is constantly operative in the organism and, like the libido, directed either inward or outward. Fromm maintained, to the contrary, that the virulence and intensity of pathological hatred varies from individual to individual, between different cultures—and thus is not fixed—and that self-hatred and hatred of others, instead of being alternatives, invariably go hand in hand (ibid., chap. 4, sec. 5). Moreover, he claimed that destructiveness proper, as opposed to "rational hatred," represents a secondary potentiality of the human psyche that surfaces only after the primary potentiality for growth and development has been blighted by adverse environmental conditions. In his own words,

> the degree of destructiveness is proportionate to the degree to which the unfolding of the person's capacities is blocked. I am not referring here to occasional frustrations of this or that desire, but to the blockage of spontaneous expression of man's sensory, emotional, physical and intellectual capacities . . . If life's tendency to grow, to be lived, is thwarted,

the energy thus blocked undergoes a process of change and is transformed into life-destructive energy. *Destructiveness is the outcome of unlived life.* Those individual and social conditions which make for the
blocking of life-furthering energy produce destructiveness, which in
turn is the source from which the various manifestations of evil spring.
(Ibid., p. 218)

In 1955 Fromm adopted a slightly different approach to destructiveness, one that heralded the emergence of his philosophical anthropology. He now tended to characterize destructiveness as the
response of a crippled, distorted person to the existential problem of
"thrownness" (*Geworfenheit*) and to the accidental, contingent character of human existence. Man, said Fromm,

is thrown into this world without his knowledge, consent or will, and
he is removed from it again without his consent or will. In this respect
he is not different from the animals, from the plants, or from inorganic
matter. But being endowed with reason and imagination, he cannot be
content with the passive role of the creature, with the role of dice cast
from a cup. He is driven by the urge to transcend the role of the creature,
the accidentalness and passivity of his existence, by becoming a "creator."

Man can create life. This is a miraculous quality which he indeed
shares with all living beings, but with the difference that he alone is
aware of being created and being a creator . . . In the act of creation man
transcends himself as a creature, raises himself beyond the passivity and
accidentalness of his existence into the realm of purposefulness and
freedom.

To create presupposes activity and care. It presupposes love for that
which one creates. How then does man solve the problem of transcending himself, if he is not capable of creating, if he cannot love? *There is
another answer to this need for transcendence; if I cannot create life, I can
destroy it. To destroy life makes me also transcend it.* Indeed, that man can
destroy life is just as miraculous a feat as that he can create it, for life
itself is the miracle, *the* inexplicable. In the act of destruction, man sets
himself above life; he transcends himself as creature. Thus, the ultimate
choice for man, inasmuch as he is driven to transcend himself, is to
create or destroy, to love or to hate . . . Creation and destruction, love
and hate, are not two instincts which exist independently. They are both
answers to the same need for transcendence, and the will to destroy
must rise when the will to create cannot be satisfied. However, the
satisfaction of the need to create leads to happiness; destructiveness to
suffering, most of all, for the destroyer himself.   (1955b, pp. 41–42)

Here, then, is another interpretation of destructiveness; one that complements, rather than contradicts, the first. What is uniquely "Frommian" about this view is not the ideas themselves, which have ample precedent elsewhere, but the fact that they appear in what purports to be a *psychoanalytic* treatment. Evil as negative transcendence, as a compensation for the impotence and isolation occasioned by the inability to love, care, create, or merely to assert one's existence, to be heard and appreciated, is a leitmotif of drama and literature, used to explain and "humanize" villains and outcasts in works such as Shakespeare's *Richard III,* Milton's *Paradise Lost,* Mary Shelley's *Frankenstein,* and Goethe's *Faust.* Indeed, all the antinomies of psychoanalytic thought—such as the conflict between the evolution versus the regression of the libido, the conflict between life and death drives, the gradual emergence of consciousness from the sphere of unconscious instinctual life, and the quest for the recovery of the "real self" buried or distorted by irrational authority and convention—reverberate with the nineteenth century's literary and philosophical preoccupations about consciousness, individuality, and the fate of the individual (Burston, 1989). This is probably why Freud and Jung found so many vivid instantiations of their clinical conjectures in literary texts, and why they made such deft use of literary artifice in the presentation of their own theories. Their ideas, couched in the language of instinct and archetype, were reinvested by Fromm with a more openly literary and philosophical quality—to the obvious annoyance of Abram Kardiner (Kardiner, 1961).

In any event, pathological destructiveness was only one area in which Fromm put forward hypotheses that conflicted with Freud's. *The Sane Society* (Fromm, 1955b), for example, was also noteworthy for its discussion of pre-Oedipal dynamics in clinical psychopathology and their links to historical and social psychological phenomena. The opening chapters, with their attempts to derive collective psychopathology (for example, tribalism, nationalism, "idolatrous fixation") from incestuous symbiosis or a presexual fixation on the mother, may owe more to Jung and Rank than to Freud (for example, Jung, 1913, 1935, 1943), although Bachofen alone is given credit here. After all, Fromm was conversant with them before *Escape from Freedom* was published (for example, Fromm, 1935b). But although Fromm strove to disguise or minimize his resemblance to Jung—whether consciously or otherwise—I suspect that his more orthodox counterparts smelled heresy and dismissed him accordingly. And the more Fromm's clinical formulations were appended to (or embedded in) discussions of social, political, and philosophical issues, the more his reputation as a dilettante grew.

Fromm and Jung

Apart from some reflections on individual and group narcissism (1964, chap. 3), the twin foci of Fromm's attention as clinical theorist from this point onward continued to be destructiveness and incestuous (or symbiotic) fixation. *The Heart of Man* (1964) deepened and extended Fromm's reflections on these subjects. Already in *The Sane Society* (1955b), and with equal emphasis in *The Art of Loving* (1956a), Fromm had affirmed that human existence constitutes a problem, and that the varieties of psychopathology represent more or less abortive responses to that problem. Owing to our lack of an instinctive adaptation to our surroundings, Fromm contended, we seek communion with others to alleviate a potentially devastating sense of isolation and helplessness, whose net outcome, if not addressed, is madness; a theme Fromm returned to again and again (for example, 1960d; 1962, chap. 12; 1968, p. 95).

However, if aloneness is the problem, how we overcome it becomes the critical question. In Fromm's estimation, the various solutions contrived by individuals really resolve themselves into two basic alternatives, which Fromm sketched in outline in *The Sane Society* and discussed at greater length in *The Heart of Man*. These are the regressive and progressive solutions. In the regressive solution, the individual enmeshed in idolatrous fixation is incapable of developing her or his specifically human powers of love and reason, and therefore, by implication, the core to core relatedness to another that constitutes the most durable refuge from loneliness. The progressive solution, by contrast, is based on a continuing search for communion with humanity and nature mediated by the development of one's powers of love and reason, and overcoming the narcissistic and symbiotic strivings that characterize our attachment to "idols" and prevent our development as human beings.

Fromm was not the first to draw attention to the contrast between the regressive, symbiotic, and "progressive-spiritual" orientations to reality. As early as 1913, in *Symbols of Transformation,* Jung, apparently leaning on Bachofen's Dionysian/Apollonian dichotomy, distinguished between the regressive and progressive deployment of the libido—albeit a desexualized, monistic libido, such as Fromm himself endorsed (1964, p. 100n). Several features differentiate Fromm from Jung on this score, however. Whereas Jung emphasized the specific *mode* of relatedness to external reality in his theory of psychological types (1935), the role that communion and the interpersonal dimension played in his thought are unclear. For example, in "Seven Sermons to the Dead," a fragment appended to his memoirs, Jung, adopting the authorial voice of the Gnostic Basilides, construed all forms of communion or community as flights from authentic individuality; as a necessary evil, at best (1963, pp. 386–388). In contrast to Jung, Fromm saw individuation as a *prerequisite* to genuine relatedness, as did Martin Buber, Fromm's former associate from the Freie Jüdische Lehrhaus (Buber, 1965, chap. 2).[4]

Finally, for Jung the regressive orientation of the libido—or introversion—is not necessarily a pathological phenomenon. By cathecting ever-deeper levels of unconscious fantasy, according to Jung, introversion reaches beneath the ego to the "collective sphere" and taps a phylogenetic inheritance of universal symbols, the "collective unconscious," issuing either in madness or in a psychic rebirth (Jung, 1943). Though not disputing the existence of universal symbols, Fromm placed more emphasis on present-day social and cultural determinants in shaping character and the unconscious, evidenced in his theory of social character and the "social unconscious" (1962, chap. 9). This gave his thinking a greater degree of historical specificity, so that, whatever its shortcomings, it did not lapse into Jung's mystical obscurantism (ibid., p. 114n).

However, important resemblances remain. Like Jung, Fromm regarded the aim of therapy as more than mere symptom alleviation. Analytic therapy had initially been conceived of as the alleviation of target symptoms (for example, phobias, obsessions, conversion symptoms, and psychogenic impotence) and the dissolution of parental fixations. But Fromm felt its ultimate goal lay in the recovery and gradual derepression of modalities of experience that are normally proscribed by society for purposes of social control (1960d). These modalities include both archaic and more complexly differentiated dimensions of cognitive and affective functioning than are normally accessible to consciousness. Accessing these new experiential levels involves more than dismantling a purely individual or intrapsychic censorship that operates on sexual and aggressive impulses; it also involves deconstructing "social filters" that selectively screen out both the "higher" and "lower" dimensions of psychic activity. Only when we penetrate beneath the socialized self, with its conventional blinkers on reality, will we experience our universal or common humanity, which encompasses the entire gamut of human experience, from the most archaic and depraved passions to the most exalted and sublime. In learning to recognize the sinner and the saint, the madman and the child, the murderer and his victim within oneself, one acquires a deeper sense of solidarity with the whole human species, which issues in a kind of spiritual or existential rebirth (Fromm, 1960d). The tendency to regard the unconscious as more than the sum of repressed pathogenic material distorted by an individual censorship, to ascribe a transcendent function to analysis as a bridge to universal humanity, was very like Jung, though couched in the context of an existential or radical humanism, which stresses the imperative of relatedness.

Fromm's Theory of Necrophilia

Sometime after 1961 Fromm reformulated what he termed the progressive and regressive solutions to human existence in terms of "syndromes of growth and decay" and introduced the concepts of biophilia and necrophilia into his clinical vocabulary (1964). Although Fromm accorded these concepts considerable importance, they seem to represent less a true conceptual innovation than a change in terminology or emphasis that served an important subjective function for him. More important, Fromm represented this ostensible deepening and clarification of ideas as a kind of "return to Freud." For despite Fromm's resolutely anti-instinctivist posture, his thinking in his later years, polarized as it was between life- and death-promoting forces, came to resemble Freud's in many respects.

However, in introducing the concept of necrophilia, Fromm was obliged to qualify and rethink some of his earlier insights on the origins of destructiveness. The results are interesting from several points of view. On the one hand, they urge us to discriminate between different forms and sources of pathological aggression, introducing new ideas that are rich, suggestive, and intuitively compelling. On the other hand, they are exceedingly problematic from a logical and methodological standpoint.

In *Man for Himself* (1947) Fromm had distinguished between rational aggression, which is in the service of life and biologically conditioned, and destructiveness proper, which is a result of "unlived life," of the warping and suppression of the primary strivings toward growth and development. In a similar vein, in *The Sane Society* (1955b) Fromm treated destructiveness as a mode of negative transcendence, linked to the need to overcome our "creatureliness" and the contingent, accidental character of human existence, which differs from animal existence in that we are acutely conscious of that fact.

However, *The Heart of Man* (1964) involved a subtle reordering of Fromm's conceptual categories. Instead of merely opposing rational (or adaptive) aggression to destructiveness proper, Fromm now speculated that there are several sources of aggression, all of which, to varying degrees, are in the service of life, including reactive/defensive aggression; aggression prompted by frustration, envy, or jealousy; revengeful violence; compensatory violence; and archaic bloodlust, rooted in an overpowering urge to return to a state of symbiotic, preindividuated union with nature. Thus, instead of being construed as the preeminent source of destructiveness, the need to transcend one's creatureliness, and the twisted passions that derive from its frustration, were now subsumed under *compensatory* violence and contrasted with a new category, called necrophilia. No explanation was given for this obvious (and potentially far-reaching) shift in emphasis.

According to Fromm, various forms of "benign aggression," and particularly sadism and bloodlust, shade imperceptibly into the necrophilic domain. But what characterize the truly necrophilous person are a deep-seated indifference or hostility to life and a passionate interest in all that is dead and mechanical. This striving may manifest itself in an overt sexual perversion (which is rare) or in more common and socially conventional ways, as in the bureaucratic tendency to reify people—a tendency that characterizes the "progress" of Western industrial society and reached a grisly apotheosis in the Nazi concentration camps. Furthermore, Fromm now contended, the necrophilous orientation is generally allied to strong narcissistic and symbiotic-regressive (incestuous) tendencies, which collectively form what he termed a "syndrome of decay."

Had Fromm left it at that, perhaps, we would assume that the notion of negative transcendence as the chief source of malignant aggression, which he had entertained a decade previously, had now been replaced with a more discerning schematization. After all, Fromm's new description of the syndrome of decay—the confluence of a deep underlying narcissistic-pathology fascination with death, decay, and new technology—is thoroughly consistent with what we know about the history and psychology of fascism. Modris Eksteins' recent book *The Rites of Spring* (1989), which probes the psychology of fascism from the standpoint of the cultural historian, provides ample confirmation of Fromm's fundamental intuitions. But in 1973 Fromm presented yet another set of categories and explanatory hypotheses, with a perfunctory apology and no explanation of the deliberations that had given rise to these latest changes. "Malignant aggression," previously equated with necrophilia, now encompassed forms of aggression that had previously been termed "benign" (such as vengeful aggression, sadism); and the frustrated need for creativity, (that is, evil as negative transcendence) slipped into a kind of conceptual limbo.

There is still more. In *The Heart of Man* (1964), *The Anatomy of Human Destructiveness* (1973), and *Greatness and Limitations of Freud's Thought* (1980), Fromm added a new dimension to his theory of necrophilia that was flagrantly inconsistent with the premise that malignant aggression—as opposed to adaptive or benign aggression—is a uniquely human, that is, noninstinctive, phenomenon. Here Fromm speculated that anal dynamics (which in intensified form result in necrophilia) are grounded in a regressive reactivation of a prehominid, four-legged orientation to reality, described as an "anal-olfactory-hateful" mentality, which contrasts markedly with the "genital-visual-loving" orientation characteristic of evolving humanity. In entertaining the possibility of a regression to an earlier phyletic stage, Fromm seemed to be conjuring with Freud's notion of organic repression by invoking the apparent links between anality, sadism, and coprophilic instincts. Freud had remarked in a letter to Fleiss in November 1897: "I have often had a suspicion that something organic plays a part in repression . . . (the notion was linked to the changed role played by the sensations of smell: upright walking, nose raised from the ground, and at the same time a number of formerly interesting sensations attached to the earth becoming repulsive—by a process still unknown to me)" (Masson, 1985, p. 279). Similarly, Fromm observed:

> If one wants to entertain a biological speculation one might relate anality to the fact that orientation by smell is characteristic of all four-legged mammals, and that the erect posture implies the change from orientation by smell to orientation by sight. The change in function of the old olfactory brain would correspond to the same transformation of orientation. In view of this, one might consider that the anal character constitutes a regressive phase of biological development for which there might even be a constitutional-genetic basis. The anality of the infant could be considered as representing an evolutionary repetition of a biologically earlier phase in the process of transition to fully developed human functioning.   (1980, p. 124)

But even if there is a clinical correlation between sadism, coprophilia, and anal traits in humans, the link between sadism and the sense of smell on evolutionary grounds seems a gratuitous slur on many species of primates and four-legged mammals that rely extensively on smell for survival but whose typical species behavior puts the relative sociability of our species to shame. Besides, it is fundamentally incompatible with the idea Fromm adduces elsewhere, to the effect that repression is chiefly social in origin and traceable to the fear of isolation (Fromm, 1935, 1962; Fromm and Maccoby, 1970).

Because of its lack of internal consistency, Fromm's notion of necrophilia, though intuitively and descriptively quite compelling at times, fails to meet the most elementary requirements of a genuine scientific theory. This does not mean that Fromm's critique of Freud—which stands or falls on its own merits—is necessarily unsound. Nor does it mean that people afflicted by a fear of and aversion to life and by a corresponding attraction to what is decaying, dead, or mechanical do not exist, or that their perverse attitude to life is not tied to strong narcissistic and symbiotic pathologies or is not prevalent enough to warrant a special diagnostic label—in which case, "necrophilia" is as good a term as any other. What it does mean, however, is that Fromm's alleged alternative to Freud's theory of innate biological destructiveness is deeply contradictory and therefore not really an alternative.[5] Realistically speaking, there is no theory here, and it remains for us to account for the phenomena Fromm described in a more cogent fashion, and without relapsing into an instinctivist construal of malignant destructiveness (which Fromm wanted to avoid).

Inward Identity and the Loyal Opposition

Given the theoretical problems with Fromm's concept of necrophilia, the question arises why someone who had devoted so much of his career to refuting the idea of the "death instinct"—and who had done so, on the whole, quite effectively—suddenly undermined the very premise on which his argument was based. In the absence of detailed knowledge about Fromm's thoughts and feelings, we can only speculate. Fromm's late excursion into psychobiology is extremely suggestive, and possibly quite revealing of the man.

Like many writers of the 1950s and 1960s who addressed social and psychological issues, Fromm rejected the stance of the psychologist *qua* natural scientist in favor of that of the social scientist or existentialist philosopher. This approach enabled Fromm to introduce into his work two themes that he shared with Jung and Rank, namely, the role of current (as opposed to infantile) conflicts and their ethical implications, greater emphasis on the therapist's personality and the countertransference, and the synthetic, self-actualizing dimensions of the psyche, as expressed, for example, in religious symbolism.

During this same period, however, Fromm also advised trainees dealing with troublesome symptoms to drop the prevailing emphasis on character analysis and to implement the "classical technique" of Freudian therapy, dating to around 1915–1917 (Wolstein, 1981). By the "classical technique," Fromm probably meant the approach embodied in Freud's case histories, in which the meaning and roots of various individual symptoms are interpreted through dreams and free-association, but with scant attention to characterological resistances or healthy defense mechanisms. Ironically, this approach to technique evolved within a theoretical framework of instinctivistic and genetic assumptions that was radically at odds with the ideas Fromm incorporated from his religious, philosophical, and sociological background. Fromm seems to have been unconsciously trying to reconcile some deeply contradictory ideas and commitments. It was

at this point—just after 1960—that he presented the theory of necrophilia.

In view of the obvious similarities between Fromm, Jung, and
Rank, which threatened Fromm's identity as Freud's "pupil and
translator," the idea of a "return to Freud" must have appealed to this
aging Freudo-Marxist. It enabled him to reaffirm his core identity and
to honor his commitment to celebrate Freud's genius in a critical,
methodical, but sympathetic fashion. The ferocious polemics between Fromm and Herbert Marcuse (Marcuse, 1955, 1956; Fromm,
1956, 1970a) probably prompted Fromm to reconsider the "death
instinct" more closely. Now, instead of rejecting it outright, he concluded that the idea, though flawed, represented a dramatic step
beyond the mechanistic materialism in which Freud had couched his
earlier discoveries. His derivation of anality-necrophilia in specula-
tive-evolutionary terms may also attest to a nagging sense that Freud
was on to something after all.

In any case, Fromm's belated biologizing and his protestations of
fidelity to Freud indicate that he wanted to be remembered (and to
see himself) as a faithful member of the psychoanalytic brethren, if
only in its loyal opposition. David Riesman, a friend and colleague of
Fromm's, expressed some skepticism regarding this interpretation
(personal communication, July 9, 1985). Noting a variety of circumstances, including the fact that Fromm had criticized Erikson sharply
for lingering with the Freudian ontogenetic schema in order to be
accepted into the mainstream, Riesman inferred that Fromm was too
proud to desire the kind of corporate identity afforded by membership
in analytic circles. As proof, Riesman cited Fromm's abiding admiration for Trotsky "as revolutionary thinker, as general, as exile."

In addition to plausibly explaining Fromm's conscious attitudes,
Riesman's observations on Fromm's feelings for Trotsky illumine
aspects of his sense of inward identity that have never been critically
analyzed. Trotsky regarded himself—and was seen by many others—
as a representative of authentic Marxism, who played a historic role
in exile by disseminating the truth in the midst of the Stalinist night-
mare of the 1920s and 1930s. Given the likelihood that Fromm did
indeed admire and identify with Trotsky, it seems plausible that, like
Trotsky, he actually embraced his dissident status, having an elevated
conception of his broad historical function. And indeed, there is
evidence for this. Fromm often wrote as if his admittedly revisionist

brand of psychoanalytic theory retained the essence of Freud's system, but purged of the contingent and historically conditioned features that encumbered the unfettered growth of the new science, such as Freud's sexism and mechanistic materialism (Fromm, 1970a).

Fromm's attitude is quite consistent with what we know about other Freudo-Marxists. Much as they differed from Freud—on our inborn sociability, the nature and origins of pathological destructiveness, the role of social and economic conditions, and so on—a central part of their personal identity was invested in repeatedly authenticating their fidelity to Freud, and thereby expressing their loyalty and gratitude to him. Wilhelm Reich, for example, was crushed when Freud had him expelled from the International Psychoanalytic Association in 1934. But this did not deter him from developing what he took to be the core of Freud's discoveries to their ultimate logical conclusions.

To judge from past performance, then, Freudo-Marxists do not crave acceptance in the psychoanalytic mainstream. They see themselves as members of the loyal opposition. But they also consider uncritical acceptance of Freud to be disloyalty on a par with virtual defection. They are true to what they take to be Freud's essence, and this sense of loyalty provides consolation and a sense of moral rectitude and inner strength in the face of an unsympathetic audience or a jeering crowd. If they cannot gain acceptance and widespread recognition, then theirs is the bittersweet solace of resolute isolation or, as in Reich's case, martyrdom.

However, Freudo-Marxists show little sense of solidarity. Each arrogates to himself the status of true defender of the faith and seeks to excommunicate those whose visions differ from his own. Their disciples and expositors mount the same platforms and make similar denunciations, vigorously perpetuating old schisms. In this sad, comic, and slightly revolting spectacle, Fromm was attacked more than any other member of this fractious enclave. With the exception of his polemic with Marcuse, remarkable for its length and bitterness, and the posthumous rejoinder to Wilhelm Reich, which was as mean-spirited and obfuscating as Reich's initial salvo, Fromm seldom responded on a personal level to the many insults hurled his way. On balance, I believe, Fromm showed more charity, forbearance, and good judgment toward his fraternal adversaries than many other Freudo-Marxists. And unlike many of them, who tended to ape the orthodox, Fromm never alluded to the names and ideas of Adler, Jung, and Rank in a derogatory way, much as he distanced himself from them; he kept Freud in an altogether different and more elevated category at all times.

In view of his Freudo-Marxist beginnings and his midlife abandonment of Freud's instinct theories, Fromm's late flirtation with biological explanations for malignant destructiveness may reflect a feeling that his own approach was inadequate and had to be supplemented biologically. His brief speculative excursion and his musings on the death instinct may have represented both a kind of homage to Freud and an attempt to authenticate his own claim to be working in Freud's spirit, although his own approach to malignant aggression had been radically different for many years previously.

Ultimately, any sympathy we feel for Fromm's putative inward identity must rest on whether his actual role in the psychoanalytic movement corresponds to his self-chosen vocation; whether it was rooted and redeemed in reality. And there are several ways in which Fromm can be said not to have been a true Freudian.

First, as discussed earlier, Freud's antinomies between evolution and regression, between life and death, and the emergence of consciousness from the preindividuated matrix of unconscious mental life were all typically nineteenth-century ideas. Freud's originality lay in restating these ideas in instinctivistic language and in situating all clinical psychopathology along a hypothetical developmental trajectory culminating in "genital primacy." The biological underpinnings of Freud's model, ingenious at the time, are now hopelessly out of date (Sulloway, 1979). But even if it was justifiable to reject the mechanistic materialism in which Freud mummified the Romantics' philosophical anthropology, as Fromm did (see Chapter 8), it was not justifiable to relinquish the whole developmental dimension that Freud introduced into the study of mental illness. Fromm was demonstrably inconsistent in his commitment to this approach: some of his utterances suggest that he took it seriously, others that he merely paid it lip service.

Moreover, despite his occasional espousal of "classical technique," most of the data suggest that Fromm's approach to treatment was at variance with classical Freudianism. Fromm's divergences and their effects—whether his changes in technique yielded a demonstrable gain in therapeutic efficacy—are the final considerations in this chapter.

Fromm's Therapeutic Posture

Three themes persist in Fromm's writings on therapy: the dangers of excessive cerebration, the need for a core to core relationship between therapist and patient, and the importance of present-day conflicts and of socioeconomic factors and aspirations that shape or impinge on the patient's life, including their role in unconscious motivation. Fromm regarded the concept of analytic neutrality as impracticable or unproductive (1935a; 1962, pp. 151–152). But he did insist on the therapist's attentiveness, respect, and disinterested dedication to the welfare of the patient (Thompson, 1950, p. 210). Fromm inveighed against abstract, rationalistic interpretations based on a priori theoretical expectations (1980, pp. 16–21), arguing that in order to address an unconscious issue in a patient and to "interpret" it effectively, that is, to bring it to consciousness, the therapist must first feel its resonance within his or her own psychic interior (Landis, 1981).

Given the frequency with which Fromm urged his students to read and reread classics in philosophy, religion, drama, and literature, few would venture to describe him as anti-intellectual. Yet Fromm repeatedly warned against the dangers of abstract intellection as a substitute for direct experience; he insisted people must experience their inner conflicts, their repressed needs and feelings, bodily, on a "gut level." In a seminar with analysts in training in Locarno, Switzerland, in 1974, Fromm illustrated the difference between thinking and awareness with an example from the practice of meditation:

> To feel your breathing does not mean to think about your breathing. Once you think about your breathing, you don't feel it. I say that in order to emphasize the difference between thinking and awareness . . . Your body is aware of your breathing. It is not a thought . . . And that holds true for practically all experiences. Once you think about them, you stop experiencing them . . . Awareness is not only a matter of the intellect, as it is the fashion to believe today. Awareness is a matter of one's whole body sensing something clearly which does not itself appear as a thought.

Similarly, in the analyst's case, it is important to remember that the chief curative factor "is not an interpretation, which describes the patient as an object with various defects, and explains their genesis, but it is an intuitive grasp. It takes place first in the analyst and then, if the analysis is to be successful, in the patient. This grasp is sudden; it is an intuitive act which can be prepared for by many cerebral insights but can never be replaced by them" (Fromm, 1959a, p. 200).

Today many of these ideas would be subsumed under the notion of empathy. Fromm's emphasis on active engagement and on direct intuitive perception into the core of the person's subjective dilemma echoes the earlier recommendations of Georg Groddeck, Frieda Fromm-Reichmann, and Harry Stack Sullivan and is echoed in turn in those of Heinz Kohut. Still, there is a danger in appeals to empathy and to direct, intuitive insight into the patient's situation. It is the appeal to therapeutic "virtuosity." Despite the varying abuses to which it has been subject, the concept of neutrality was originally intended to ensure the optimal degree of self-discovery and self-disclosure, and a minimal reliance on the analyst as a source of solutions or of "wisdom" concerning one's own predicament or perplexity. Despite the conformist uses to which it was put (Fromm, 1935a), analytic neutrality was intended, in part, in a democratic spirit: to encourage a collaborative search for truth and, ultimately to foster self-reliance (Maccoby, 1983). Modifications to technique— which vary from one therapist to another, one school to another— ought to be made in this spirit as well.

According to Herbert Spiegel and Michael Maccoby, Fromm's greatest shortcoming as a therapist was that he was attentive to aspects of patient's utterances that tended to confirm his own theories and preconceived ideas, but inattentive, impatient, or actually dismissive of those facets of their experience and self-representations (or "self-reports") that did not coincide with his "intuitive" sense of their problems and situation (Maccoby, personal communication, May 14, 1985; Spiegel, personal communication, Nov. 24, 1987). Having formulated a patient's "core" problem to his own satisfaction, he would often adopt a didactic, prescriptive stance and interpret conflicting testimony, no matter how compelling, as "resistance." In this respect, Maccoby suggests, Fromm departed from Freud's model of the analytic process as a collaborative enterprise aimed at patiently uncovering the truth, toward a master-disciple model of therapeutic interaction, in which the therapist becomes an idealized role model, like a Zen master or medieval mystic. Unfortunately, as Maccoby points out,

> For a patient with repressed infantile impulses and grandiose ideals, such a therapy can both increase transference resistances and a sense of

guilt about one's unworthiness, one's unproductiveness, and dependency. Instead of remembering or experiencing childlike drives, humiliations, rages, and fears as a means to mastering them, the patient attempts to resolve his conflicts by becoming an ideal person, like the master. In so doing, he may again submit to authority and repress sexual or angry impulses directed against the parent. As a result, some Frommian patients identify with the master and self-righteously direct their irrational feelings at others.   (1983, p. 79)

Accordingly, although many patients experienced Fromm as a deeply empathic individual and benefited immensely from his therapeutic interventions, others were poorly served. The irony is that Fromm's scattered formulations on technique were intended to redress the conformist and sadistic abuses of neutrality, which Fromm pinpointed with devastating accuracy (1935a). But they may have the opposite effect. In practice, if not in theory, "Frommian" analysts can be as authoritarian as their Freudian counterparts if they fall into the abortive trap of false idealization and pseudo-authenticity.

In short, Fromm's sense of inward identity as Freud's loyal opposition, or of himself as the Trotsky of the psychoanalytic movement, was not justified in the clinical domain. Rather than strengthening the positive dimensions of Freud's approach to technique, in his writing Fromm entirely lost sight of the democratic element in Freud's notions of neutrality and "working through." The net result, though dramatically different in emphasis, was probably no better or worse than the orthodox approach. For in addition to accounting for the many dramatic breakthroughs and transformations that Fromm purportedly helped engender in patients (and that they engendered in him), it exempted him from having to think about therapeutic failures as the expression of his own overly knowing and prescriptive approach.

4 *Fromm's Existentialism*

Reason, Induction, and the Human Situation

One of Fromm's chief contributions to psychology was his concept of "existential needs." Here Fromm's approach resembled that of an Aristotle or a Spinoza, in that he *began* with a concept of human nature (1962, p. 174). Like the neo-Freudians, Fromm was keenly aware of the influence of social conditions and gender roles on the development of character (1943) and on the prevalence of traits such as cooperation or competitiveness in any given society (1973). But he also believed that there is a universal human nature or "essence" that can be distinguished from the various "accidents" that constitute an individual's existence in all its particularity. To judge from his remarks in a variety of contexts, these "accidents" presumably include inborn temperament, constitution, and intelligence, ethnic and religious affiliations, and the other socially and historically conditioned contradictions that shape our character and personal fortunes (for example, Fromm, 1949a, p. 112; 1968a). Fromm was fond of quoting Terence (also Marx's favorite maxim): "I am a man: nothing human is alien to me." That is, there is something we share with other people, apart from uniformities of organismic structure, that enables us to sense something central to their existence. This does not mean that the other is ever totally transparent to us. But despite the manifold obstacles to interpersonal understanding, Fromm thought that inasmuch as we are human, reason discloses what that "something" that unites us is. Fromm's "reason" was not the complex and elegant ratiocination of logical demonstration and proof; he often failed to supply the kind of evidence a professional philosopher would require. On the other hand, his method was not purely "intuitive" either. Fromm's concept of reason evinces certain properties of what logicians call "inductive inference," which, in light of manifold particulars, deduces the existence of an underlying uniformity that can account for phenomena; a uniformity that may be variously described as an essence, a law, or, more modestly perhaps, as an empirical generalization.

Clearly, Fromm's approach to ascertaining the essence of human nature was different from that of most psychologists. When using inductive inference, positivist psychologists gather data that are pertinent only to their specialized field of inquiry, such as perception, cognition, or clinical psychopathology, and restrict the scope and domain of their theoretical conclusions accordingly. By contrast, in attempting to explicate human nature Fromm harked back to the tradition of philosophical humanism, which takes humanity *as such* as its object (Fromm and Xirau, 1968). The average clinician or experimental psychologist, whose approach to her or his subject matter is ahistorical, may balk at the seeming indiscipline of Fromm's methodology. But there are sound scientific reasons for not ascribing transhistorical validity to traits and features of human behavior that are a product of contemporary conditions, and for using information from history and all the human sciences as material for observation, speculation, and theory building. As Fromm noted in the 1930s, any theory of human nature that universalizes on the basis of contemporary social character and its corresponding neuroses is inadequate both humanly and scientifically. This criticism is particularly compelling with regard to orthodox Freudian social psychology, which constructs the psychology of "normal" people in bygone eras or different cultures by analogy with neurotics in its own milieu (Fromm, 1932a).

Contrary to what we might expect, however, Fromm did not seek to identify traits or attributes for the human species that are invariant, that transcend the vagaries of cultural and historical circumstance and are common to all humanity. He contended that isolating or enumerating transhistorical traits or processes—for example, Homo sapiens as a social animal (Aristotle's *zōon politikon*), a toolmaking animal (*homo faber*), or a symbol-creating animal (Cassirer)—though useful, fails to penetrate to the problems at the core of human existence (Fromm and Xirau, 1968, pp. 3–7). To borrow a term from Heidegger, the human essence consists in our sense of "thrownness" (*Geworfenheit*)—the precarious, contingent character of our existence in the world, which is rendered all the more problematic by the fact of human self-consciousness. As Fromm put it, "man's essence lies in the very contradiction between his being in nature, thrown into the world without his will, and taken away against his will, at an accidental place and time, and at the same time transcending nature by his lack of instinctual equipment and by the fact of his awareness—of himself, of others, of the past and the present" (quoted in Funk, 1982, p. 57).

As a result of our "thrownness" and our distinctively human self-consciousness, Fromm suggested, we have certain psychological needs that, though the result of unparalleled cortical complexity and a long evolutionary development, are not reducible to bodily needs or the exigencies of erogenous satisfaction. Because we are self-aware, conscious of our separateness, and capable of imagining our death or nonbeing, our existence (and potential nonexistence) acquires a problematic cast. We are driven to make some kind of sense of existence and to transcend our sense of finitude, isolation, and helplessness. These needs emerge as a result of self-consciousness, even if they are not always conscious as such. The problem then becomes *how* we go about making sense of life, how we achieve transcendence, say, through the development of our powers of reason and love, of individuated fellowship and communion, or through conformist or regressive solutions, in which self-consciousness is blunted or abolished through an attempted return to childish, intrauterine, or animal existence (Fromm, 1956a, chap. 2; 1964).

Linked closely to the ascertainability of the human essence in Fromm's work are universal norms of right and wrong, or adequate and inadequate answers to the problem of human existence (1947, chap. 2). For although there are various avenues to the experience of oneness and to the transcendence of isolation, not all are equally conducive to our well-being. Any striving or norm of conduct that impairs the individual's capacity for autonomous judgment, for love, and for reason is *objectively* wrong, regardless of the degree of consensual validation that attaches to it. Consequently, the equation of mental health with "adjustment," which varies from one culture to another, relativizes the concept of health, robbing it of any substantive content, making it subject to circumstance and impervious to rational evaluation (Fromm, 1955b, chap. 4).

Fromm's discussion of "the pathology of normalcy," of socially patterned defects, and of the other topics examined in the following chapters logically presupposes a norm of human development and conduct that diverges from the cultural prototype. Without an ostensibly universal norm for human development, critical thought loses its bearing, its point of reference. It is impossible to speak of a deformation of subjectivity without some notion, however implicit, of what an undistorted subjectivity is like.

Notwithstanding the objections of Herbert Marcuse (1955), Martin Birnbach (1961), and others, the weakness in Fromm's universalism and its application to psychology was not his search for norms of human conduct and well-being that have—or ought to have—cross-cultural validity. It was the naive and dogmatic spirit in which he approached this task. For any norm of human development held in contrast to the prevailing cultural pattern is itself a cultural and historical product and is often modeled on the idealization of previous epochs or other cultures (for example, Maccoby, 1983). This fact need not invalidate the objective or transhistorical validity of such ideal constructs completely, since some cultures may pattern behavior in ways that are actually more conducive to the development of a rational sociability. But it does require considerable caution. In principle, one would have to establish and reconcile the historical specificity of a given set of ideals with their allegedly universal applicability.

Moreover, to cite religious preceptors or "Masters of Living" as issuing convergent testimony in one's favor, as Fromm did, lends an argument superficial plausibility at best. It amounts simply to another appeal to authority or consensus. Even admirers of Isaiah, Heraclitus, Socrates, Buddha, Meister Eckhart, and Spinoza will recognize the weakness in this approach. Recourse to authority and consensus are still commonplace in scientific discourse, but philosophers since Bacon and Descartes—in principle, at any rate—have sought to ascertain truth by appeals to empirical evidence or logical ratiocination alone. Fromm's appeals to venerable old masters are oddly scholastic or talmudic gestures, and not calculated to enhance his credibility here.

Existential Needs

Notwithstanding these limitations, Fromm's concept of existential needs remains an important contribution. Fromm enumerated various needs that flow directly from the human situation, starting with the need for a framework of orientation and devotion (1950) and eventually including needs for relatedness, transcendence, rootedness, a sense of identity, a framework of orientation and devotion, drama and ritual, a sense of effectiveness, unity, and excitation and stimulation (1955b, chaps. 3–5; 1973, chap. 10). On reflection, three of Fromm's existential needs are basic: (1) a framework of orientation and devotion, (2) a sense of rootedness, and (3) a sense of transcendence. They resemble the related strivings for cosmological coherence, ontological grounding, and transcendence that are rooted in our sense of thrownness, or lack of instinctive oneness with our surroundings. This reclassification, however, does not involve a straightforward reduction; several of Fromm's needs could fit under two (or all) of the new headings simultaneously. For example, the need for a framework of orientation and devotion could be classed under the need for cosmological coherence (orientation) *and* ontological grounding (devotion). What is important here is not whether these terms are exactly equivalent, but the concept of existential needs as an integral dimension of existential and depth psychology.

To begin with, the need for a sense of *cosmological coherence* subsumes the needs for a framework of orientation and devotion, a sense of rootedness, a sense of identity, and drama and ritual. It entails specifically human needs for intelligibility, meaning, and purpose to existence in the face of suffering, aloneness, and death. Freud himself acknowledged the need for intelligibility as the preeminent force behind animistic thought, whereby the mysteries of nature are rendered intelligible through the creation of imaginary entities whose propitiation helps overcome feelings of helplessness and victimization. In *The Future of an Illusion*, Freud observed:

> Impersonal forces and destinies cannot be approached; they remain eternally remote. But if the elements have passions that rage as they do in our own souls, if death itself is not something spontaneous but the violent act of an evil will, if everywhere in nature there are Beings around us of a kind we know in our own society, then we can breathe freely, can feel at home in the uncanny and can deal by psychical means with our senseless anxiety. We are still defenseless, perhaps, but we are no longer paralysed; we can at least react. Perhaps, indeed, we are not even defenseless. We can apply the same methods against these violent supermen outside that we employ in our own society; we can try to adjure them with the same methods that we employ in our own society,

to appease them, to bribe them, and, by so influencing them, we may rob them of a part of their power. (1927, pp. 16–17)

But intelligibility or coherence, though essential, is not enough. People also need a sense of purpose, of experiencing their place or role within the wider scheme of things, to lend existence some semblance of meaning in an otherwise absurd and haphazard universe. No one saw this more clearly than Max Weber. Noting the wild profusion of divergent belief systems in the history of religion, Weber observed:

> One could wish to be saved from political and social servitude and lifted into a Messianic realm in the future of this world; or one could wish to be saved from being defiled by ritual impurity and hope for the pure beauty of psychic and bodily existence. One could wish to escape being incarcerated in an impure body and hope for a purely spiritual existence. One could wish to be saved from the eternal and senseless play of human passions and hope for quietude of the pure beholding of the divine . . . One could wish to be saved from peonage under the astrologically conceived stellar constellations and long for the dignity of freedom and partaking of the substance of the hidden deity . . . One could wish to be saved from the cycle of rebirths with their inexorable compensations for the deeds of times past and hope for eternal rest . . . Many more varieties of belief have, of course, existed. Behind them always lies a stand toward something in the actual world which is experienced as specifically "senseless." Thus the demand has been implied; that the world order in its totality is, could and should somehow be a meaningful "cosmos." (1923, pp. 280–281)

From Weber's remarks and similar reflections in Fromm's work we can infer that magical, religious, and metaphysical systems address similar or related needs without necessarily supplying a uniform answer. In other words, the *need* is universal, but the solutions vary. But as Fromm often observed, intellectual constructs of reality, however penetrating, have a tentative, provisional character and are destined to be superseded in the course of time (1980, chap. 1). A viable solution, existentially speaking, is less a question of what we believe than of how we relate ourselves practically to the world.

Related to the need for cosmological coherence is the need for *ontological grounding*. Fromm's notions of the needs for rootedness, relatedness, and a sense of identity are all implicated here. However, whereas the quest for cosmological coherence characteristically manifests itself in the development of or adherence to certain belief systems, as an intellectual—though not merely intellectual—response, the need for ontological grounding can elude conscious ratiocination, expressing itself in a need for a *prereflective sense of connectedness,* of rootedness in reality. Indeed, the need for ontological grounding in the prereflective sense is more fundamental than the need for cosmological coherence, since many people function admirably without ever posing religious, metaphysical, or existential questions on the meaning of life as long as their relatedness to the world is not impaired by suffering or death. In these instances, the need for ontological grounding bypasses the sphere of reflective intellection and expresses itself directly in biological reproduction and child rearing, the day-by-day reproduction of society in work, or the exercise of our creative faculties.

Linked closely to ontological grounding is the need for *transcendence,* a term Fromm uses in three distinct senses. Above all, perhaps, the need for transcendence implies a need to rise above our sense of thrownness or creatureliness by becoming *creators* in our own right; by furthering or engendering life (Fromm, 1955b, p. 41). Transcendence in this sense is closely linked to what psychoanalysts call transforming passive into active, or the need for mastery. But it is important to distinguish healthy from pathological manifestations of this need. Life, as Fromm reminds us, is *"the* miracle, the inexplicable"* (1955b, p. 42), and the uninhibited destroyer enjoys a sense of power and exultation similar in intensity, if not in kind, to that of the creative person. This avenue of transcendence is a warped and distorted expression of what presumably might have been healthy human faculties—a product of inner misery, not of joy.

In other contexts, Fromm's notion of transcendence signifies an ability to transcend the boundaries and limitations of our own ego. This transcendence of the ego in Fromm's vocabulary parallels what Jean Piaget termed *decentration,* or what Ernst Schachtel called *allocentric perception,* except that more than cognitive and perceptual qualities are involved. For Fromm, increased objectivity in cognitive, perceptual, or interpersonal functioning presupposes the diminution of greed, fear, and repression (1976). Interpersonally, transcendence of the ego involves the active penetration of the other's world through love, which yields a knowledge of the other that cannot be acquired or experienced in any other way. Knowing the other in this sense is not commensurate with having any amount of merely factual "information" about that person (Fromm, 1956a).

Fromm's third, closely related use of transcendence is as a specifically human striving to step outside the sphere of routine, of mundane concerns, and to experience our life as having a quality and meaning above and beyond this restricted sphere. Apart from affirming cosmological coherence, religious ritual—when it is not merely routine—has the function of consecrating the individual for a spiritual goal beyond mere getting and spending. In Judaism, the Sabbath ritual is an outstanding example of this need and its symbolic fulfillment (Fromm, 1951, chap. 7, sec. 4; Heschel, 1951).

Relatedness and Self-Affirmation in Fromm, Buber, and Marx

By Fromm's reckoning the many solutions to the problem of human existence in different social and historical circumstances basically resolve themselves into two types: those that foster the progressive growth and unfolding of the individual's powers of love and reason, and those that inhibit them. What Fromm termed the "syndrome of growth" (1964), based on reason and love, is rooted in a sense of solidarity with the entire species, which transcends national or ethnocentric ties and perspectives. However, development in this direction can be exceedingly problematic if our deepest human self-interest is at odds with the constraints of adaptation, which demand that certain inborn powers and potentialities be blunted, or allowed to atrophy in the struggle for survival. Meanwhile, if true self-actualization is hindered, compensatory and substitutive mechanisms to redress the problem of our thrownness, such as the sense of cosmological coherence, ontological grounding and transcendence afforded by corporate identity, or by symbiotic or conformist solutions, will soon emerge. But no matter how genuine or satisfying these seem at first, they lapse ultimately into inauthenticity, into forms of relatedness and experience that are destructive of our humanity, because they are not rooted in our selves—the self-active development of our latent sociability.

Closely related to this perspective is another element in Fromm—his belief that self-love and love of others are complementary, and not antithetical, as Freud thought (Fromm, 1939a; 1947, chap. 4, sec. 5; 1956a, chap. 3, sec. d). Classical Freudianism and the existentialism of Heidegger and Sartre converge in the belief that self-affirmation and the affirmation (or love) of others (that is, authenticity and relatedness) tend to cancel each other out. According to Freud, the individual lends his energies to the species "against, or at any rate without any volition of his own," while the emergence of object-libido depletes our reserves of narcissistic energy (1914, p. 14). According to Sartre, "hell is other people," and the exercise of one's own freedom invariably involves the encroachment on or diminution of others' (Marcuse, 1948).

Fromm, in contrast, resembles Martin Buber in thinking that relationships based on reciprocal validation and individuated fellowship are not only possible but in fact a prerequisite to the emergence of authentic selfhood. Buber's views are rooted in a faith in a personal creator God who is keenly interested in our spiritual welfare, who addresses man through the Covenant and His actions in human history (Buber, 1965). Fromm's thinking, though influenced by religious values, is secular, steeped in the humanism of the German Enlightenment and the Hegelian left. Marx, who in Fromm's estimation stood at the apex of this tradition, expressed his faith in the possibility of reciprocally affirming relationships in his concept of nonalienated labor. In a passage in *The Economic and Philosophic Manuscripts of 1844* Marx declared:

> Supposing that we had produced in a human manner; each of us would in his production have doubly affirmed himself and his fellow men. I would have: (1) objectified in my production my individuality and . . . thus . . . enjoyed realizing that my personality is objective . . . (2) In your enjoyment . . . I would have had the direct enjoyment of realizing that I had satisfied a human need . . . (3) I would have been for you the mediator between you and species and thus acknowledged . . . by you as a necessary part of yourself . . . (4) In my expression of my life I would have . . . realized my own essence, my human, communal essence.   (Quoted in McLellan, 1977, p. 25)

In short, for Marx, the reciprocal validation of individuals, whether in labor or in "sensuous enjoyment," is predicated on both individuals' discovering in themselves, through relating to the other, their unique individual powers, and recognizing in each other their essential *species character*. For Marx, as for Buber, there is no genuine and lasting self-discovery outside of relatedness to others. But for Marx—or at least the young Marx—work, considered as conscious, free activity, has an almost sacramental character. Marx did not come by this emphasis on work as our primary mode of self-actualization because he was bent on working-class emancipation. After all, if one did not conceive of work as being integral to human happiness in this way, emancipation would simply involve a more equitable distribution of wealth and leisure. This was only one of Marx's objectives, and not his primary one at that (Fromm, 1961b). Under the prevailing system of alienated labor, Marx insisted in 1844, an enforced increase in wages "would be nothing more than a better remuneration of slaves, and would not restore, either to the worker or to the work, their human significance and worth" (quoted in ibid., p. 107).

In the interests of understanding Fromm, let us ponder the dramatic contrast between Freud and Marx on the psychology of work. In Freud's estimation, we have an inborn aversion to work that civilization strives to overcome (1927, chap. 1). Only brute necessity and a prodigious capacity for sublimation render work possible. But among the motives that prompt us to work, Marx reckons drives toward mutual recognition and self-objectification, which today would be called self needs, needs for object-relatedness or self-actualization. For Marx, antipathy to work or to society at large is a product of alienating social conditions, not of biological endowment. There is a parallel line of conceptualization in Heinz Kohut's "self psychology" (1984), in which the unbridled pursuit of "instinctual gratification" is a "breakdown product" occasioned by the impossibility of actualizing the "nuclear program of the self." For Kohut, however, the pursuit of raw instinctual pleasure is a breakdown product occasioned by damage to the self as a result of failures in "empathic mirroring" or early interpersonal relationships (1971, 1984). For Marx, the one-sided satisfaction of "animal functions," that is, the pursuit of "drive gratification" in the Freudian sense, is occasioned *not* by untamed instincts, but by an asocial division of labor and its rewards, or alienation in the labor process. Fromm mediates between Kohut and Marx, inasmuch as he insists that patterns of early childhood socialization tend to be preparatory for functioning in the adult world and pressed into the service of prevailing economic conditions. After all, if "self-disorders" were not indicative (or exaggerated versions) of an underlying pathology of normalcy characteristic of our time, it would be difficult to account for their apparent proliferation in our narcissistic age.

Fromm's philosophical anthropology was closely tied to his inter-pretation of the Old Testament. Like many German thinkers before him, Fromm emphasized that alienation, the birth of self-conscious-ness, and the search for union or unity with nature, oneself, and one's fellows are all the result of the loss of an instinctive, prereflective oneness with the cosmos (Abrams, 1971, pp. 181–182). In "The Prophetic Concept of Peace," Fromm declared:

> Man has to experience himself as a stranger in the world, estranged from himself and from nature, in order to be able to become one again with himself, with his fellow man, and with nature. He has to experi-ence the split between himself as subject and the world as object as the condition for overcoming this very split. His first sin, disobedience, is the first act of freedom; it is the beginning of human history. It is in history that man develops, evolves, emerges. He develops his reason and his capacity to love. He creates himself in the historical process which began with his first act of disobedience, which was the freedom to disobey, to say "No." ([1960c] 1963a, p. 205)

By the "freedom to disobey," Fromm was referring to Eve and Adam's choice to eat of the tree of knowledge against God's express com-mand, which Fromm took to be emblematic of the step toward growth and emancipation. His essentially *positive* reading of the Fall (1966, chap. 4) has no analogue in rabbinic literature, which inter-prets disobedience to God negatively, as sin (Schechter, 1961, chap. 14; Block, 1968). But it resonates with sentiments expressed by Schiller, Boehme, Milton, and, indeed Saint Ambrose, whose doc-trine of the *felix culpa* suggested that the Fall affords humanity the hope of even greater felicity than existed before the Fall, and is therefore part of a grand providential design (Abrams, 1971, p. 208).[1] Accordingly, like Hegel, but unlike Marx, Fromm saw alienation as more than merely a sociohistorical phenomenon, or a product of social conditions, which is destined to be definitively overcome or abolished. For Fromm, some measure of alienation is rooted in hu-man existence and prerequisite to our full personal development:

> Only when I can distinguish between the world outside and myself, that is, only if the world becomes an *object*, can I grasp it and make it my world, become one with it again. The infant, for whom the world is not yet conceived as an "object," can also not grasp it with his reason and reunite himself with it. Man has to become alienated in order to over-come this split in the activity of his reason. (1962, p. 57)

Similarly, Herder, Lessing, Goethe, Kant, Fichte, and Schelling had interpreted the biblical drama of the Fall and redemption as metaphors for the historical progression of humanity from undifferentiated unity and unconsciousness through an evolutionary sequence culminating in a higher kind of communion premised on differentiation and the full development of our faculties (Fromm, 1966, p. 15; Abrams, 1971, chap. 4).

To summarize, then, the differences between Marx and Fromm's models of human nature are as follows. Marx saw alienation as arising from the disparity between our essence and the actual conditions of our existence; a disparity engendered by class domination and exploitation. When our essence becomes a *means* to our existence, rather than being something embodied and expressed therein, we feel dominated by alien forces and are chronically estranged from ourselves, from nature, and from the species. Like Marx, Fromm anticipated a time when we will be able to transform social relations so that we can finally bring our latent sociability and productive powers to full and unimpeded expression. But unlike Marx, Fromm insisted that our essence is given in the conditions of our existence, as a state of thrownness or homelessness occasioned by the emergence of consciousness from the adualistic, unconscious union of the animal with its natural surroundings. The implication is clear; even in the absence of oppression or privation, we would still struggle for a newfound unity with ourselves and the cosmos in a life filled with effort and suffering. Here Fromm sounded a sad and sober note that is entirely absent in the younger Marx's unbridled utopianism.

But if alienation and suffering are rooted in the human condition and will persist despite changes in our social, political, and economic arrangements, why accord such importance to economic conditions specifically? And if suffering will endure, why bother to change society? How could it be different from or better than the present scheme of things?

Fromm's answer to these questions was twofold. First of all, a social order based on exploitation cannot exist without lies and illusions. To the extent that we embrace or accommodate the prevailing ideology within an oppressive or unjust society, we collude in maintaining its ethical blindness and self-deceptions and are unable to think critically and compassionately about the reality around us (1962). Another feature of class society that deforms the human spirit is the conditioning we continuously receive to estrange us from what Fromm called the *being* mode, and to make us consumed with acquisitiveness or the *having* mode, which, as Fromm explained, in capitalist society colors every dimension of human experience (1961a, 1976). Those who scoff at Fromm's attempt to link Marx's critique of political economy to the Old Testament idea of idolatry (1961a, 1962) and to values espoused in the New Testament (1976) forget that the term *historical materialism* refers to a method of analysis, not to a system of values per se. Despite his atheism, the values underlying Marx's critique of political economy were anything but materialistic. For example, in his early manuscripts Marx described the methodical accumulation of capital as an alienated objectification of the human essence, a congealed and static expression of human life that is used in a privative and dominating way. In a passage Fromm was fond of quoting from *The Economic and Philosophic Manuscripts of 1844,* Marx declared:

> Political economy, the science of wealth, is therefore, at the same time, the science of renunciation, of privation and of saving . . . This science of a marvellous industry is at the same time the science of asceticism. Its true ideal is the ascetic but usurious miser and the ascetic but productive slave . . . the less you eat, drink, buy books, go to theater or to balls, or to the public house, and the less you think, love, theorize, fence, etc., the more you will be able to save and the greater will be your treasure which neither moth nor rust will corrupt—your *capital.* The less you *are,* the less you express your life, the more you *have,* the greater is your alienated life and the greater is the saving of your alienated being.   (Quoted in Fromm, 1961b, p. 144)

In light of the following chapter, it is interesting to note that Marx's "ascetic but usurious miser" combines the hoarding and exploitative traits that Fromm contended were dominant in nineteenth-century social character. The satirical reference to "treasure which neither moth nor rust will corrupt"—and Jesus' call to relinquish worldly goods in order to attain the kingdom of God—suggests that under capitalist auspices, acquisitiveness has displaced the message of the Gospels as the real religion of society, despite the pronouncements of clerical officials. In describing the "having" mode more than a century later, Fromm merely generalized Marx's thinking on greed for material possessions to all acquisitive passions that operate to the detriment of our need for solidarity with other human beings, such as an alienated pursuit of power, prestige, knowledge, or intimacy

(1976). Indeed, the idea that the way a particular society constrains people to satisfy their *material* needs colors all spheres of human interaction, and is generally at variance with their human or *existential* needs, is a constant theme in Fromm's writings, and central to his idea of social character.

5 *Studies in Social Character*

Theoretical and Historical Perspectives

Fromm's studies of social and political psychology span almost five decades, beginning with "The Dogma of Christ" (1930a) and ending with *To Have or to Be?* (1976). Most of his writing was theoretical and historical in orientation and was based, by his own account, on the thinking of Max Weber, Werner Sombart, Ferdinand Tonnies, W. H. Tawney, and, of course, Marx and Freud (Fromm, 1941, pp. 68–70; 1962; 1973, p. 236). In "The Dogma of Christ," Fromm discussed the development of social character in the Mediterranean in the first four centuries of the Christian era. *Escape from Freedom* (1941) was concerned with the psychology of Nazism. In other works Fromm advanced a general theory of social character (1962) or focused on social character in postwar industrial society (for example, 1955b, 1968b, 1973, 1976).

There is an impressive continuity between Fromm's later research on social character and his early inquiries into the prevailing "libidinal structure" of society, which antedated American psychoanalytic publications on culture and personality by several years. This fact is seldom acknowledged in the literature because the stimulating dialogue between anthropology and psychoanalysis that gave rise to the American theories was already under way when Fromm arrived in the United States. Although Fromm contributed to this movement in no small measure, his own ideas originated in an entirely different context.

Fromm's psychoanalytic social psychology began with the assertion that a consistent application of the method of individual psychoanalytic inquiry would dispense with analogies between social and intrapsychic processes, would enjoin a thorough study of the history and life conditions of the group in question, and would derive psychic structure from social structure, rather than vice versa (1932a). Moreover, Fromm insisted that normal individuals in any given society are characterized by a (more or less) adequate adaptation of their psychic apparatus to the exigencies of survival within it; so that analogies between the psychic processes of modern neurotics and of normal people living under vastly different circumstances are doubly misleading. Fromm did not dispute the universality of the incest taboo but declined to give it chief importance; he argued that the ambivalence toward the father that Freud universalized was a social artifact, not a biological given, and that in clinical research the domain of character was much more important for social psychology (1932b).

Fromm shared much of his general outlook with two other psychoanalytic investigators, Abram Kardiner and Erik Erikson, who developed in a similar direction more or less contemporaneously. In *My Analysis with Freud*, Kardiner relates how his thinking changed under the influence of anthropologists Ralph Linton and Cora du Bois:

> It was . . . in 1938 that I really . . . realized the necessity for certain innovations in psychoanalytic theory. The libido theory assumes that most human development was propelled by certain inborn energies and occurred under a certain preordained order proved to be unwieldy and unable to yield the new information in the study of social processes. What was needed was a method for the empirical study of ontogenesis, particularly under greatly varying conditions . . . The seminars with Linton's material gave me the opportunity to observe the impact of social institutions on the human mind and on character formation. I felt I was on the right track, because character defines the nature of human interaction within a society. If the interaction is in the main cooperative, then the society holds together. However, if the social institutions change too rapidly or create too much tension within individuals, cooperative feelings, which are the glue that holds any society together, may dissolve and the society falls apart. (1977, p. 113)

Fromm likewise expressed indebtedness to Ralph Linton, with whom he taught at Yale in 1948–49 (1973, p. 193n). However, whatever insights Fromm gleaned from collaboration with Linton came well after his own formulation of these issues. He came by his distinctive brand of social psychology *before* he dropped the libido theories and their corresponding nomenclature in the early 1930s.

As indicated earlier, Fromm's first papers expressly rejected the notion of a "collective subject." Indeed, as early as 1929 Fromm declared that

> the psychoanalyst must emphasize that the subject matter of sociology, society, is actually constituted of discrete individuals, and that it is these people, and not an abstract "society" as such, whose behavior, thought, and feelings are the domain of sociological research. These people do not have an individual psyche that functions when the person acts as an individual . . . and an adjacent but separate collective psyche endowed with vague attributes such as community feeling, solidarity, or mass instincts, which spring into action when the individual acts as part of the collective . . . There are not two souls in the human breast, but one, in which the same mechanisms and laws obtain.   (Quoted in Funk, 1984, pp. 73–74; my translation)

Though apparently couched as an oblique rebuttal to Emile Durkheim's brand of sociology, Fromm's rejection of the idea of a collective mind bears a clear resemblance to the ideas of philosophers Moritz Lazarus and Heymann Steinthal and sociologists Georg Simmel and Alfred Weber. Simmel, for example, emphasized that only individuals are irreducibly, ontologically real, but that inasmuch as they enter into relations with others for the satisfaction of their needs in culturally predetermined situations, the constraints and possibilities of culture—itself the product of concerted individual wills—in turn become a determining influence (1908a, 1908b). Likewise, although he rejected the idea of a group mind per se, Fromm would argue that social attitudes, cognitive templates, and aesthetic sensibilities that have a widespread social distribution are "objective," and hence legitimate subjects of scientific inquiry, even though they exist only in and through the psychic activity of individual subjects (1962, chaps. 8, 9). Lazarus and Steinthal and later Wilhelm Dilthey did much the same thing in their discussions of social psychology (Makkreel, 1975, chap. 8; Danziger, 1983).

In view of the German-Jewish background to Fromm's work and the influence on Freud of Gabriel Tarde and Gustave Le Bon, one can scarcely exaggerate the difference between the German-based *Geisteswissenschaften* and French "crowd psychology" at the turn of the century. Although they dismissed the collective psyche per se, Lazarus and Steinthal, Dilthey, Simmel, and Alfred Weber stressed the inescapable rootedness of the individual in collective life, as well as the idea that forms of collective behavior and belief that are today considered irrational and anachronistic may have been exquisitely adapted to the exigencies of life in an earlier period, and therefore "rational" in their original context. From their point of view, Tarde and Le Bon's reflections on the role of suggestion in political life and social turbulence (such as the general strike and political demonstrations) narrowed the scope of inquiry unnecessarily by excluding religious and juridical norms and linguistic, aesthetic, and musical forms, and seriously denigrated collective life. They vigorously opposed the crowd psychologists characterization of social groups as loose aggregations of emotionally labile individuals bound together by their irrational desire to submit to charismatic authority; an idea Freud wholeheartedly embraced.

But liberal and left-leaning proponents of the *Geisteswissenschaften* also advocated a position that differed from the reactionary and irrationalist conception of *Volkgeist*, which in the early nineteenth century was already alloyed with anti-Semitic ideas, in seeming anticipation of Nazi ideology. Lazarus and Steinthal, Dilthey, Simmel, and Alfred Weber saw the individual, no matter how differentiated, as rooted in cultural life. But they also viewed culture itself as a product of concerted individual agency in historical time, not as some mystical, ontic essence existing prior to the individual, and in which individuals must deliberately submerge themselves to discover their authentic vocation in life.

Nevertheless, in the political domain, the French theories of the irrational crowd, and the irrationalist emphasis on the primacy of instinct and the group that was gathering force in Germany possessed an odd complementarity. Crowd psychology was aristocratic, elitist, and nominally rationalist: collective behavior was "inferior" because it was irrational (Moscovici, 1985). The Romantics, by contrast, tended to exalt irrationality and collective sentiment at the expense of discursive rationality, which they deemed bloodless and antilife. These reactionary populists saw a source of strength in what the French construed as a contemptible sign of weakness. Nevertheless, both elitist rationalism and reactionary populism were essentially antidemocratic, and it is no accident that Hitler, who championed the mystical conception of *das Volk*, also studied Le Bon's characterizations of the collective mind in order to be a more effective leader and propagandist and courted the favor of reactionary aristocrats to finance his militarist and antidemocratic schemes (Fromm, 1941, chap. 7; Moscovici, 1985, pp. 63–64).

By and large, Lazarus and Steinthal, Dilthey, Simmel, and Alfred Weber opposed both programs. Their premises about the relationship between individuals and their cultural setting harked back to J. G. Herder and Giambattista Vico. At present, not enough data on Fromm's university studies, rough manuscripts, and lecture notes are available to allow us to do more than speculate how or when these theorists influenced him. But it is likely that as a student of sociology at Heidelberg Fromm read Lazarus, Steinthal, and Simmel because they, like him, were Jewish and opposed the racist collectivism of "Aryan" ideology (Kalmar, 1987). Or he may have encountered them still earlier, in his teens, at the Freie Jüdische Lehrhaus, where their work was doubtless discussed.

Fromm's theory of social character, then, was inspired not only by Bachofen, Marx, and Freud but also by proponents of nineteenth-century *Geisteswissenschaften* and the *Verstehende* approach to sociology. This fact and its manifold implications for theory were lost on his American audience, so that the secondary literature abounds in misconceptions. Fromm's first published study of "the shared libidinous, and largely unconscious attitudes" that characterize a society, "The Dogma of Christ" (1930a), was not translated into English till 1963, and his empirical research from the late 1920s and early 1930s was published only posthumously. As a result, most of Fromm's professional audience in America knew him only by *Escape from Freedom* (1941) and credited these basic ideas to theorists such as Kardiner or Erikson (for example, Hall and Lindzey, 1954). And because Kardiner and Erikson continued to cultivate their ties to the Freudian establishment, many of Fromm's critics found it fashionable to make invidious comparisons, insinuating that Fromm (and Horney) had diluted the real core of Freudian teaching in order to pander to the American public. In fact Fromm and Horney did enjoy widespread popularity "because their views are more in accord [than Freud's] with the dominant stream of social psychological thought in [the United States]" (Hall and Lindzey, 1954, p. 174). But to imply, as many have, that Fromm was opportunistic or not original, that he packaged his work to suit American tastes, is to deny the overriding continuity between Fromm's earliest and later efforts.

Thus, despite the popularity of his work, fundamental aspects of

Fromm's theories, which originated in a European context, failed to register with his American interlocutors and critics. For example, psychologist William Sahakian stated: "In addition to his individual character, Fromm posited that a person possesses a social character, the traits of which are those shared by the majority of his group" (1974, p. 174).

This assessment is erroneous in two respects. First, character—even social character—is not something one "possesses" that is distinct and apart from oneself. It is something one *is*. Second, Fromm repudiated as early as 1929 the notion that social character is something one "possesses" over and above (or in addition to) his or her individual traits and characteristics. The idea that Fromm's "social character" is something that exists independently of or alongside individual character is not uncommon, if only because, for heuristic purposes, we discuss them as if they were two separate entities.

But this raises the inevitable question: What, then, *is* social character? If it does not reside in individuals next to their individual peculiarities, where can it be found, and how can it be studied? Following the later Fromm, we might define social character as the dominant patterns of assimilation and socialization in a given society, owing to prevailing economic conditions and cultural-historical factors (for example, Fromm, 1941, appendix; 1955b). However, to infer from this that social character exists independently of or alongside the constituent individuals composing a society is to succumb to reification, or the fallacy of misplaced concreteness. In reality, social character is an abstraction. It does not have the same ontological status as a rock, a tree, or a human individual. It is not a concrete existent with extension and duration in space and time. Unlike the actual individuals composing a society or class, social character is not a found object existing in the external, phenomenological world of the observer, any more than irrational numbers and logarithms or the legal and national entities we create by law, convention, or collective agreement. On the contrary, like Max Weber's "ideal type," social character is an idea that enables us to grasp an underlying uniformity among manifold particulars of social behavior, which is not in itself directly observable.

However, although it is, properly speaking, an abstraction, social character is not a *statistical* abstraction. A mainstream statistical approach to "social personality" would attempt to discover the sum total and distribution of "traits" and their various correlations in a given population, in ways that Fromm considered to be radically misleading. Social character as Fromm understood it, though presumably susceptible to empirical inquiry, elucidates the *function* of widespread characterological traits and their *history* in the course of social development (1941, 1955b). Functional and historical conceptualization explains prevailing attitudes and behavior in terms of the requirements of the system in which they are embedded, and only secondarily as objects of statistical inquiry.

This brings us to a problem that bears on the methodological foundations of *all* psychoanalytic social psychology, namely, the search for structural invariants that define the human situation. For Freud, the one invariant feature of any consequence shared by all societies was the incest taboo, which he traced to a "core complex" persisting, with minor variations, from remote prehistory to the present. Freud's superordinate emphasis on one structural factor and his reckless willingness to generalize from the present to the past made his theory breathtakingly coherent but also pervasively indifferent to material and historical factors. In Fromm, by contrast, the context of shifting constraints and possibilities pertinent to elucidating social behavior is what Marx termed "the mode of production," or the prevailing methods of production, distribution, and exchange of essential goods and services, and of the corollary juridical, political, and artistic ideas that arise as a consequence (Fromm, 1961b, chap. 8; Fromm and Maccoby, 1970, chap. 1; Maccoby, 1983). The only invariant property of these systems is that they make some provision for human needs—physical, emotional, and intellectual. The function of social character is to render the adaptation to prevailing social conditions as smooth as possible, "to shape the energies of the members of society in such a way that their behavior is not a matter of conscious decision as to whether or not to follow the social pattern, but one of *wanting to act as they have to act* and at the same time finding gratification in acting according to the requirements of the culture" (Fromm, 1955b, p. 77).

Presumably, in this endeavor the various agencies of socialization, such as home, school, and the mass media, march in lockstep. The recognition that socialization is a process of continuous adaptation to one's surroundings, and not something settled in early childhood, differentiates Fromm somewhat from Kardiner, who emphasized child rearing as the chief instrument of socialization. Moreover, Fromm's suggestion that social character minimizes inner friction so that people *enjoy* doing what they actually *have* to do introduces an element that, if not actually foreign, is very different in tone and in emphasis from those prevailing in Erikson and ego-psychology (Fromm and Maccoby, 1970). Clearly, Fromm assigns to socialization, rather than to ontogenetic development, the function of creating a (more or less) "conflict free sphere of ego operations" adapted to surrounding conditions. From his standpoint, then, the idea of a conflict-free sphere of ego operations, or of an identity harmonious with one's social role, is no longer necessarily indicative of health. For, as Michael Maccoby notes, "the social character itself may be alienating, since needs for survival and sanity conflict with needs stemming from the nature of man with its inherent need for human solidarity and the development of reason and creative talents" (1983, p. 75).[1]

Under such circumstances, presumably, a "conflict free sphere of ego operations" may be indicative of a "socially patterned defect," not of genuine health, while neurosis may be indicative of a struggle against a dehumanizing environment (Fromm, 1941, pp. 159–161).

The Authoritarian Character and Empirical Social Research

In 1929 and 1930, with the support of the Frankfurt Institute for Social Research, Fromm directed a study of the character and attitudes of German blue-collar workers that had serious repercussions for the history of psychology. This project anticipated many features of *The Authoritarian Personality* (Adorno et al., 1950). According to Marie Jahoda, the questionnaire Fromm developed for his study

> is remarkable both for its similarities and differences with that developed in the California studies [i.e., Adorno et al.] As far as content is concerned it contains more than thirty questions which come close to what we have now learned to call the PEC scale (political and economic conservatism); and some forty questions about Weltanschauung which correspond to the F scale (fascism) items. In addition, it contains many questions on actual family relations designed to elicit patterns of domination and submission, i.e., the authority structure of the family, and a much more detailed account of the respondent's actual life situation than the data in *The Authoritarian Personality* reveal. (Christie and Jahoda, 1954, pp. 13–14)

Apart from its intended size and scope, the subject matter, rationale, and methodology of Fromm's study gave it a landmark status in the history of social psychology. It was a pioneering attempt to determine the prevalence of "authoritarian" or profascist tendencies among any group, anywhere. The concept of the authoritarian character, now so familiar, was quite new at that time. As Russell Jacoby has pointed out, the concept of the patriarchal authoritarian character dates back to Paul Federn's 1919 paper "On the Psychology of Revolution: The Fatherless Society." Federn contrasted the father-centered mentality of obedience to authority in a hierarchical social order with that of the "band of brothers" that supposedly characterized a primitive (matriarchal?) democracy, arguing that the former is inimical to socialism but probably destined to prevail by dint of custom, education, and its transmission through the patriarchal family (Jacoby, 1975, pp. 84–85).

Federn did not develop this line of thought, but Fromm and Wilhelm Reich became deeply interested in the idea. They argued that widespread tendencies to compliance, to idealization of and identification with authority, to obsessive guilt, and to sadomasochism— which Freud had ascribed to an "archaic inheritance" of inherited guilt feeling—are rooted in dynamics that are peculiar to the patriarchal family, and are therefore social artifacts rather than genetically determined.

But although psychoanalysis provided the subject matter for Fromm's inquiry, it had little to offer by way of empirical research methodology. Here Fromm relied on his sociological training and on the active involvement of his collaborators Hilde Weiss, Adolph Levenstein, and Ernst Schachtel, who contributed to its design. (Paul Lazarsfeld was statistical consultant; Anna Hartoch and Herta Herzog helped distribute and gather the questionnaires.) Weiss and Levenstein were familiar with a research methodology in empirical social psychology, pioneered more than a decade previously by Max Weber, that had evolved to assist in the development of social policy. As Wolfgang Bonss points out, nineteenth-century studies of the living conditions, attitudes, and aspirations of German workers had been biased because of the prevalent practice of soliciting information about subjects from third parties, such as employers, teachers, clerics, and physicians. In 1908 Max Weber designed a survey that finally discontinued this paternalistic practice, substituting a twenty-seven-item questionnaire to be jointly filled out by the worker and the surveyor in a face-to-face interview. Weiss and Levenstein, though apparently unacquainted with psychoanalysis, had extensive experience with Weber's protocols (Bonss, 1984, pp. 11–12).

But the *rationale* underlying Fromm's study differed somewhat from Weber's. In Weberian sociology, the sole objective of empirical research is to inform, correct, and enrich theoretical conceptualization—not to obliterate theory in a mass of empirical data. This goal was quite congruent with Fromm's objectives. However, the purpose of Weber's study had been to determine (1) the effects of large-scale industry on the personal character and nonoccupational life style of the worker and, more important, (2) how large-scale industry is restricted in its development by beliefs and dispositions that are prevalent among workers as a result of tradition and poor living conditions. The focus was on streamlining production and making it more profitable. By contrast, Fromm's research was undertaken with no regard for its usefulness to big business. His objective was to elucidate the prospects and preconditions for general emancipation, rather than to maintain or augment the hegemony of corporate interests.

Fromm used a strikingly new methodology, combining features of Weber's protocols with ideas adapted from psychoanalytic theory in an "interpretive questionnaire." Instead of conducting face-to-face interviews guided by a preordained series of questions, as Weber did, or full-scale analytic interviews, which allow for no reliable quantification and standardization, Fromm and his collaborators had their respondents respond in writing to open-ended questions on a 271-item questionnaire. According to Fromm and Schachtel, spontaneous responses to certain questions regarding women's issues, abortion, corporal punishment, political leadership, friendship, money, entertainment, and matters of taste and dress had a "physiognomic" character, indicating what weight should be attached to other responses on purely political topics, such as voter preferences, attitudes toward the right, the judiciary, and state power, which were liable to elicit stereotyped responses or "the party line" among their predominantly left-leaning sample (Fromm, 1930b, chap. 1). Accordingly, subtle discrepancies were sought between a subject's conscious ideas, or nominal preferences, and his or her real, underlying attitudes, which were gauged on the basis of the "physiognomic" responses and peculiarities of literary style, including vague or elliptical replies or the avoidance of certain items, whose specific import could be determined only in light of the entire questionnaire (Fromm and Maccoby, 1970, pp. 24–29; Bonss, 1984).[2]

Fromm and Schachtel's attempts to design a psychoanalytic instrument for social research were linked to a profound disenchantment with extant methods for assessing personality. In 1937 Schachtel argued that the whole field of personality research was one-dimensional, having been colonized by industrial psychology, the interests of management, and the requirements of smooth bureaucratic administration. Earlier still, in a section outlining the aims of their Weimar study, Fromm discussed the limitations of questions that restrict responses to "yes/no" or "graded" alternatives:

> Attitude measures and personality tests, which lead to a set of scales for adding up answers which have been given fixed numerical values, require homogeneous responses as a precondition . . . This restriction on the range of answers enables one to give each answer a standard value, with the possibility of achieving further refinements by subtracting contradictory responses or developing the quota. The result of measurements arrived at by adding up the value of each answer signifies a far-reaching devaluation of individual responses. The same overall score for two respondents can be derived from totally diverse answers, which lose their original significance when torn from their original context and turned into numbers. What is being measured remains ultimately unclear and indefinite; the individual structure of the attitude or personality is lost. Another disadvantage of . . . the restriction of answers to a few fixed alternatives [is that] a prescribed list will hardly allow for all possible answers. It puts words into the respondent's mouth which he only gives because he has to decide in favor of one of the alternatives and which he might never have arrived at himself.   (1930b, pp. 46–47)

Methods of statistical inference and research have developed apace since 1930. But according to some (for example, Lamiell, 1981, 1986), the approach remains fundamentally unchanged, suggesting that Fromm's misgivings remain relevant. Numerical values for "traits" such as depression, aggression, and introversion/extroversion are often misleading in ways that cannot be corrected by even the most elaborate statistical checks and balances. False, misleading, or superficial data, contaminated at the source by loss of the subjective and contextual determinants of a given response, cannot provide an accurate picture of the subject's state.[3]

In addition to the issues Fromm raised with respect to the answering and scoring of questions in mainstream personality research, there are palpable problems with the questions themselves. In most paper-and-pencil inventories and measures, questions are trite, ambiguous, and based on blinkered or biased assumptions regarding what constitutes a "normal" response, irrespective of how culture, ethnicity, and the vicissitudes of personal development shape one's emotional makeup. The circumstances of an individual's upbringing or current life-world may *warrant* attitudes summed up in such statements as "People are only out for themselves," "My father (mother) was weak, dishonest; didn't care for me," or "The primary function of the police is to harass the poor and minorities and to protect the wealthy and privileged," or even "Sometimes life is so painful it doesn't seem worth living." People who ordinarily show strength and sensitivity to others may occasionally utter or endorse such statements on clinical or personality tests, and the presumption that such a response is indicative of pathology or of abstract personality "traits," rather than of environmental factors, candor, or even health, is just that, a presumption, unless or until it is informed or qualified by a detailed knowledge of the individual's life history. Considered in the abstract, the kinds of questions to which these statements might constitute a response often reveal as much about the people who design such tests as about their subjects.[4]

Whatever its shortcomings by contemporary standards, the modified psychoanalytic approach that Fromm and Schachtel adopted was useful in shattering some widespread misconceptions. Many Freudo-Marxists believed that the social situation of workers would engender a higher proportion of revolutionary or "genital" characters among them than among the middle or upper class. It was on them, presumably, that the future of socialism depended. In fact, however, Fromm and his colleagues discovered a very high proportion of workers who voted for the left merely out of habit or convention, and whose tepid sympathies could thus be easily undercut by conformism and parochialism in an emergency, precluding a real will to fight fascism. Worse still, about 10 percent of left-wing respondents evinced strong sadomasochistic tendencies and might therefore be expected actively to abet a repressive, sadistic regime. Contemporaneous studies, based solely on voters' *conscious* preferences and opinions, minimized the threat of fascism because of the left's historic popularity with the electorate, which showed no immediate signs of abating. Fromm, by contrast, reluctantly predicted Hitler's rise to power, on the grounds of inadequate opposition (1986, pp. 117–133).

It seems likely that the nature of Fromm's conclusions regarding the character of the workers was a hindrance rather than a help to their publication. Commenting on Max Horkheimer's unwillingness to publish the study, Herbert Marcuse recalled misgivings among the institute staff that Fromm's analysis would be twisted for ideological purposes to argue that workers became Nazis *because* they were socialists (Bonss, 1984, p. 29). In an interview for German radio in 1974, Fromm was deliberately evasive about the whole matter (Fromm, 1986, pp. 125–132) but agreed that his study, had it been published promptly, might have helped mobilize resistance to Hitler.

But irrespective of its political repercussions or lack thereof, the fact that Fromm's study was not published until after his death had notable scientific consequences. For notwithstanding the horrors of Stalinism, the "F-scale" designed by Nevitt Sanford and Daniel Levenson to measure profascist tendencies seemed to involve a tacit equation between right-leaning sympathies and authoritarianism, on the one hand, and left-leaning views and "democratic" trends on the other, ignoring the "authoritarianism of the left" (Shils, 1954; Kirscht and Dillehy, 1967). Although it is possible to understand both the motives that obstructed the initial publication of Fromm's study and Americans' ignorance of it, the apparent inability or refusal of Horkheimer and Adorno to take cognizance of Fromm's findings about the authoritarianism of the left, and to alert their colleagues to design their study and instruments accordingly, is both odd and reprehensible.[5]

Apparently other issues were also involved in the Frankfurt Institute's decision not to publish or publicize Fromm's study. Rainer Funk relates that Horkheimer and associates doubted the reliability of the interpretive questionnaire, although they had no experience as analytic practitioners on which to base such an evaluation (1984, p. 95). The presumption here seems to be that *had* they had the appropriate clinical experience, they would have credited Fromm's methods. But this seems unlikely. After all, working with several seasoned clinicians, Adorno and associates made extensive use of in-depth interview data in *The Authoritarian Personality* (1950). More likely, Horkheimer and his colleagues expressed such grave doubts about the validity and reliability of Fromm's data because Fromm relied on neither clinical interviews nor psychological tests to buttress his inferences about his respondents' character or intrapsychic processes. By contrast, in their California studies of anti-Semitism in the late 1940s, Horkheimer, Ernst Simmel, and their collaborators took the wise (and historic) precaution of administering Thematic Apperception Tests and Rorschachs to all their subjects (Simmel, 1946, chap. 6). Likewise, *The Authoritarian Personality* rested its conclusions on extensive test data, in-depth interviews, and questionnaires—a strength Fromm's early study clearly could not boast. Perhaps as early as 1938, Horkheimer declined to publish Fromm's work in the belief that the institute could do better, hoping to buttress psychodynamic interpretations with test data. It is also possible that Horkheimer and his colleagues were not entirely frank in their criticism because they had future plans that did not include Fromm. This might account for their obvious reticence on the subject, and for the angry and occasionally obtuse tone of Fromm's rejoinders.

In any case, Fromm learned a valuable lesson from *The Authoritarian Personality* (Adorno et al., 1950). His next foray into empirical social research, a massive multidimensional study of a Mexican village conducted from 1957 through 1963, included a modified version of his 1930 questionnaire, plus in-depth history-taking face-to-face interviews *and* psychological test data for the majority of villagers (Fromm and Maccoby, 1970). Fromm even tried to outdo Horkheimer and Adorno in the rigor and thoroughness of his research; in addition to these controls, Fromm gathered detailed demographic, historical, and anthropological data on the 162 households in question and involved numerous researchers as participant-observers in the daily lives of the peasants, while minimizing any disruption of the rhythms of daily life in the village. According to Dr. Dario Urdapilleta, Fromm even conducted two one-year postgraduate seminars with Dr. Lorette Cenourne and several Mexican analysts in the anthropology of pre-Columbian cultures before embarking on this massive undertaking, to familiarize himself with the indigenous culture.

In addition to psychologists and psychiatrists from the United States and Mexico, Fromm's coworkers in the field included teachers, public health officials, and anthropologists. Their prolonged involvement with the village of Chiconcuac afforded them opportunities for long-term observation that render this one of the most intriguing experiments in the history of social psychology, albeit one seldom cited in the literature (Fromm and Maccoby, 1970).[6]

Despite what he learned from it, however, *The Authoritarian Personality* did not seem to impress Fromm. He once remarked to Michael Maccoby that its research methodology was shallow and "positivistic," that it failed to distinguish between a traditionalist and an authoritarian or sadomasochistic orientation, and indicated how little Horkheimer and Adorno understood his own approach to social psychology (personal communication, May 14, 1985). Adorno did, of course, distinguish between the "conservative" and "pseudo-conservative" types, and on the face of it there may be some correlation between these typological distinctions. Was there any justice in this harsh assessment?

Let us start by recalling that Adorno and his associates emphasized the American conservative's firm attachment to capitalist values of competition and the necessity of economic insecurity as engines of social progress, making the absence of ethnocentrism and racial hostility the criterion for differentiating the conservative from the pseudo-conservative (1950, pp. 181–182). This rationale followed organically from their initial interest in anti-Semitism (Simmel, 1946; Jay, 1973). By contrast, Fromm's typology reflects the agrarian setting in which he worked. In this context, the traditionalist, or what Fromm and Maccoby called the "traditionalist authoritarian," organizes his or her life around traditional attitudes and activities. In the precapitalist milieu, work is viewed either as a necessary evil that guarantees subsistence and, by implication, the spiritual or leisure pursuits that lend dignity and meaning to life; or as a means to self-expression and self-development; or as a means to perfect one's product. Fromm also pointed out that in the traditional milieu, production and exchange are chiefly for use and enjoyment, not for profit per se (1941, chap. 2). The idea of producing as much as possible, by any means possible, to increase one's stock of material wealth over and above one's traditional or hereditary status by "beating the competition" is deemed foolish or mercenary. Even when work is customarily considered no more than a necessary evil, the mechanized and impersonal methods of capitalist production seem demeaning or irrational to the traditionalist mind.[7]

Fromm's description of work in the precapitalist milieu derives, by his own admission, from Marx, Max Weber, and W. H. Tawney. However, it also accords well with Ferdinand Tonnies' critical distinction between *Gemeinschaft* and *Gesellschaft,* or communal and contract-based societies, and the findings of substantivist economists such as

Karl Polanyi (1944, 1968). In this sense, Fromm was quite correct in charging Adorno and associates with ignoring the traditionalist in their portrait of conservatives; for in a study of American society, there is practically no room for the traditionalist in Fromm's sense, whose character is rooted in the peasant, aristocratic, or guild-centered values of a precapitalist mode of production. The nearest equivalent to the agrarian or craft-based traditionalist conservative in America is what Michael Maccoby calls "the craftsman"—a small cadre of designers and technicians who exist in an uneasy symbiosis with monopoly capitalism and are characteristically concerned less with profit and the company's interests (as management sees them) than with quality of workmanship and maintaining their own creative autonomy, and accordingly demand great respect and managerial skill from their employers to remain productive (Maccoby, 1976, chap. 2).

Moreover, one could argue that Adorno's emphasis on ethnocentrism, though illuminating, gives a one-sided portrait of even the capitalist conservative. Conservatism in any milieu involves complexly interwoven systems of beliefs and values, and ethnocentrism—or its absence—is just one part of the picture. For example, in rural Mexico both the traditionalist and the authoritarian stress the value or necessity of hierarchy in social relations. Unlike the authoritarian, however, the traditionalist does not idealize (or identify with) authority or believe that the ability to exercise power confers moral authority. Though reluctant to change, the traditionalist can adapt to new circumstances if they do not threaten her or his life and livelihood. Unlike the authoritarian, who is emotionally isolated and hostile to spontaneous and expressive behavior, the traditionalist emphasizes values of personal dignity and the enjoyment of life in indigenous folk art and ritual, and a strong family life—a life-affirming response to the encroaching commercialism and anomie of industrial society (Fromm and Maccoby, 1970, pp. 80–82).

Experience suggests that the traditionalist and conservative can be distinguished from the sadomasochistic, authoritarian character on a variety of dimensions, including a disposition to truth and attitudes toward social hierarchy, conflict resolution and the use of violence, family and faith, and strangers and the disadvantaged. Eventually social psychology must distinguish between the agrarian, guild, or *Gemeinschaft* traditionalist and his or her capitalist counterpart, and the varieties of authoritarianism characteristic of precapitalist and capitalist societies. In the meantime, the following description of the traditionalist versus authoritarian orientations furnishes a useful point of departure.

Whether in an agrarian or capitalist context, life-affirming conservatives characteristically insist on deference to one's elders as the principle for conflict resolution between generations. But respect for authority, though deeply rooted, will not prompt them to repress feelings of anger or resentment for being ill used. Moreover, they do not believe that the mere capacity to use force confers moral authority. This revulsion toward force is coupled with a capacity for compassion toward the disadvantaged, and a cautious openness toward strangers that can blossom into respect and trust. They value honesty and a truth-loving disposition and in certain situations are capable of rising above banal or stereotyped perceptions of people and events. Their child-rearing practices promote deference to elders and respect for religious and family values but do not damage the growing child's sense of self, integrity, or inner worth.

By contrast, authoritarians defer to elders *because* they are more powerful. Without power, elders lose authoritarians' respect, admiration, and envy. Conflict resolution through violence attracts them. Strangers are hated, feared, and admired if they are more powerful, and objects of contempt if they are not. Solidarity with strangers, outgroups, or the disadvantaged—the ethnocentrism of Adorno et al.—is considered crazy or suspect. They have no love of truth, so that their criteria of truth, beyond mere expediency, are influenced by loyalty to authority figures. Authoritarian child rearing inculcates compulsive obedience, defiance of authority, or both, but family solidarity and closeness are emphatically delegitimized if they interfere with loyalties to the state, party, or religious order.

It is easy to see why social and political psychologists have been bewildered by the boundaries between traditionalism and authoritarianism. In the precapitalist world, organized religion reinforced ethnocentrism and unquestioning obedience and sought expedient alliances with despotic powers. In other words, it tended to foster authoritarianism together with a traditionalist outlook, rendering it difficult, from a purely experiential standpoint, to disentangle the traditionalist outlook from the authoritarian, and both from the new-style capitalist conservative. More discriminating distinctions among these various types and their social and historical admixtures are rendered possible by the fascist phenomenon and by the ambiguous role of organized religion in movements for political emancipation since the Second World War.

Let us examine recent trends. In both right- and left-wing dictatorships, the authoritarian in the capitalist or state capitalist context makes religious and family piety expendable or illegitimate if it constrains the exercise of power by his or her interest group. By adhering to traditional norms of political conduct, organized religion may pose a challenge to state authority and actually promote movements toward liberty and the preservation of human dignity. In the postwar context, this applies both to "liberation theology," which challenges prevailing structures of domination in Marxist (that is, economic) terms, and to the still-dominant alloy of traditionalist authoritarianism characteristic of Roman Catholicism. Pope John Paul IV combines the church's historic emphasis on obedience to authority and male dominance in the clerical hierarchy with a strong streak of life-loving traditionalism, with its concern for human welfare and dignity. This enables him to be critical of unbridled capitalism, to relinquish some of the church's historic collusion with oppressive right-wing regimes, and to foster growing political alliances with progressive forces in eastern Europe. From almost any point of view, of course, the church is a conservative and hierarchical institution. In its internal workings, it is feudal and antidemocratic to the core. Nonetheless, the alliance of "conservatives" and "progressives" in Communist society who are rapidly dismantling the frightful legacy of Stalin demonstrates how the traditionalist mentality can oppose unbridled authoritarianism and oppression.

Unfortunately, research on the authoritarian character tends to ride roughshod over these distinctions, which are vital to an understanding of twentieth-century politics. Anyone attempting to update *The Authoritarian Personality* for today would have to provide a more credibly nuanced and discerning discussion of the historic relationship between family (or antifamily) and religious (or antireligious) values and political ideology, and to take explicit cognizance of the difference between conservatism in capitalist and agrarian contexts.

Traditionalists in a peasant or aristocratic context are suspicious of capitalism, with its disruption of traditional rhythms of life. They put great store in personal loyalty and honor and expect their position in society to be respected, often preferring gradual impoverishment to wholesale adaptation to new methods of production and norms of life, such as mechanization, impersonal administration, and a high degree of personal mobility. Moreover, they tend to be religious. The conservative in the capitalist context, by contrast, believes in "progress" and sees adaptation to technological innovation as an imperative, has no respect for hereditary rank, and, though capable of loyalty and honor, redefines their content and limits in accordance with capitalist norms, which are out of step with a *Gemeinschaft* society. The conservative capitalist evinces a great faith in the capacity of "the system" to effect the greatest possible human happiness, even in the absence of overt religious beliefs.

Thus, although life-loving traditionalists in both the capitalist and agrarian contexts tend to be relatively free from ethnocentrism, on other levels their outlooks vary widely. Indeed, capitalist conservatives invest all their piety and trust in a system that wreaks havoc on the structures and sensibilities that previous eras deemed traditional. As capitalist conservatism takes root, displacing the older, agrarian-based values, sensibilities that were once characteristic of a traditionalist outlook may be alloyed to liberal attempts to humanize capitalism, or to radical critiques of the capitalist system, including those encompassed in the environmentalist movement that has recently sprung up.

Fromm never analyzed the difference between the *Gemeinschaft* and *Gesellschaft* conservative explicitly, which is why his remark about Adorno seems so harsh. Yet apart from the psychology of politics and social attitudes, the idea of the *Gemeinschaft*-traditionalist as opposed to the capitalist conservative is useful in understanding Fromm the man and his profound antipathy toward American culture. Despite his deep reverence for Marx, his radical critique of Freud, and so on, Fromm was, in many respects, a traditionalist of the older, precapitalist stripe, who felt more at home in the villages of rural Mexico than in the cities of the United States (Funk, 1984, pp. 119–122). Indeed, Rainer Funk makes it plain that Fromm felt his own antipathy to our consumer society was rooted in the precapitalist values of his religious preceptors and forebears (1984, chap. 1).

From Fascism to the Marketing Character

Fromm's *Escape from Freedom* (1941), a study of the transition from feudalism to modernity was informed by a wealth of theological and sociological erudition. Though connected to his empirical work on authoritarianism ten years previously, it was a chiefly historical and theoretical inquiry. In a very important sense, however, *Escape from Freedom* also set the stage for the next phase of Fromm's work, embodied in *The Sane Society* (1955b), in which he became increasingly concerned with the postwar manifestations of what he had previously termed "automaton conformity" (1941, chap. 5, sec. 3). By 1947 Fromm replaced this term with the "marketing character," which in one way or another insinuates itself into practically everything Fromm wrote after this point, particularly with respect to the "chronic, low grade schizophrenia" that he felt characterizes the pathology of normalcy in the present age (for example, 1968b, pp. 33–43; 1976, pp. 133–139).

In *The Sane Society* Fromm dwelt at length on the differences between nineteenth- and twentieth-century social character. But he also noted that capitalism in the nineteenth and mid to late twentieth centuries share certain basic structural features. They were—and indeed, still are:

1. the existence of legally and politically free men
2. the fact that free men (workers and employees) sell their labor to the owner of capital on the labor market
3. the existence of the commodity market as the mechanism by which prices are determined and exchange is regulated
4. the principle that each individual acts with the aim of seeking profit for himself, and yet that, by the competitive action of many, the greatest advantage is supposed to accrue for all (1955b, p. 80)

Another uniform feature of capitalism Fromm noted is that production, in the first instance, is for sale, exchange, and profit, not for *use*. Working people no longer produce for others in a direct, human fashion. They produce for their employer, who distributes goods through a whole series of intermediaries, whose interest in the quality of the goods, though tempered by the requirements of the marketplace, is diminished for lack of a personal investment in them, and whose treatment of the customer is often as routinized and impersonal as the process of production, requiring few skills or foresight and little more than the passive execution of a small repertoire of mechanical tasks (Fromm, 1941, chap. 4; 1955b, chap. 5).

According to Fromm, the consumer society, the relative affluence and widespread conformity in the West during the 1950s, was presaged by developments before the Second World War (1941, chap. 4; 1955b, chap. 5). Chief among them were the advent of monopoly capitalism and the increasing sense of powerlessness and alienation it engendered in the population at large (Fromm, 1937). For unlike peasants or artisans, or indeed, early capitalists, most people under monopoly capitalism do not own their own means of production, and consequently are obliged to sell their labor. No matter how well they are rewarded, their utter dependence on wage incomes for economic support renders them more helpless to deal with market forces. This (generally unconscious) sense of helplessness deepens as capital is concentrated in fewer hands, and the remaining small to medium-size concerns have to contend with the market machinations and ungovernable crises of mammoth corporations (Fromm, 1937; 1941, chap. 4).

Moreover, Fromm suggested, the impersonality and unpredictability of market forces put an adaptive premium on the success of individuals' "personality," or their willingness to fit a (more or less) interchangeable position in the chain of production or distribution, many of which require no great skill but do require an appropriate "attitude." And to the extent that all of life is shaped by market forces, people increasingly experience *themselves* as commodities for sale, and accordingly, their sense of self-worth fluctuates in response to external symbols of acceptance, competence, and recognition (1941, p. 141; 1947, pp. 75–89). On the face of it, misery of this sort seems a far cry from fascism. Many psychologists would insist that we are dealing with disparate phenomena—and indeed we are. But there is a real connection between them.

In Fromm's estimation, the social character of nineteenth-century industrial society was predominantly a blend of hoarding (that is, anal) and exploitative (oral-aggressive) orientations, which were rooted in the exigencies of competition and material scarcity (1955b, chap. 5). The virtues rewarded in reality were industry, thrift, sobriety, and a kind of grim honesty in one's business dealings that does not preclude a callous disregard for the needs and interests of others, whose misfortunes were construed as the will of God, a law of nature, or the just desserts of moral and intellectual inferiority. This concatenation of dynamic strivings and beliefs derived credence and respectability from social Darwinism, which served as a kind of secular theodicy or cosmology and legitimated individualistic, self-aggrandizing, and distinctly predatory attitudes toward others, including the ravages of colonialism (Harris, 1968, chap. 5; Kumar, 1978), although, curiously, the last scarcely entered into Fromm's analysis.[8]

Like Wilhelm Reich during the early 1930s, Fromm saw the chief support for the fascist menace as emanating from the lower middle class. In retrospect, this evaluation still makes sense. Apart from captains of industry and the petite bourgeoisie, the lower middle class benefited most from the first great surge of capitalist production and colonial expansion. Accustomed to thrift and industry, having access to education, being individualistic and eager to improve their social standing, the lower middle class tended to find social Darwinism a congenial philosophy. They were also the first to suffer in a crisis, but they clung fiercely to the outlook that had presided over their brief and precarious enjoyment of the spoils of unbridled imperialist expansion. Their profound disappointment, as global capitalism faltered, provided a fertile breeding ground for fascist demagogues preaching racist and nationalist variants of social Darwinism, which promised to extinguish the pain and humiliation of economic decline in an orgy of nationalist frenzy and sadistic scapegoating. Fueled by the paralysis and blindness of its opponents, by depression, unemployment, inflation, and ready cash from reactionary elements of the aristocracy and bourgeoisie, fascism rapidly became a global threat of terrifying proportions (Kitchen, 1975).[9]

But though Fromm never said so in so many words, the full development of productive forces unleashed by the new economic order demanded a different kind of conformity from that practiced under fascist auspices. An economy on a wartime footing poses certain advantages for industry but cannot be maintained indefinitely, if only because one side must eventually lose. Despite the Second World War and the crises that led up to it, the automated manufacture of the nineteenth and early twentieth centuries, and the incredible innovations in transportation and communication, accelerated by the First and Second World Wars, issued inexorably in a consumer society in which the vicissitudes of manufacture (costs of labor, raw materials, new capital investments) were eclipsed by the necessity to find (or create) new markets for consumer goods, to forestall the crises of overproduction that could create new and potentially threatening revolutionary situations, whose ultimate outcome, it was feared, would be socialism.

Consequently, contrary to Marx's prediction of the accelerating impoverishment of the working class—but also, in part, *because* of it—extensive pay raises gave a hitherto propertyless proletariat a stake in the new system and came to the aid of the middle class as well. In the consumer society that followed, the vicissitudes of manufacture were eclipsed by those of salesmanship. For as machines replaced industrial armies, the problems of finding (or creating) new markets assumed unprecedented proportions, while the growth of conglomerates, trusts, and multinationals shifted control of production from small and medium-sized concerns controlled by individual capitalists to proliferating managerial cliques (Fromm, 1941; 1955b).

This shift, in turn, called for the development of "team players" rather than the rugged individualists of a bygone era (Maccoby, 1976). Unlike their grandfathers, great-grandfathers or remote feudal forebears, whose economic role identities were rigidly circumscribed, team players cannot rely on tradition, skill, or hard work alone. They require the flexibility to assume any persona that might facilitate their advancement or spare them the trials of going it alone; an option that poses fewer and fewer advantages as capital becomes concentrated in the hands of multinational corporations. This new kind of economic symbiosis occurs within the highly mobile, competitive, and impersonal world of monopoly capitalism, not on the village green or under the benevolent eye of the parish priest or local squire. In other words, it is a symbiosis without the deep or enduring emotional bonds that were likely to develop under feudalism.

According to Fromm, the motto of the marketing person, who experiences herself or himself as a commodity for sale, is: "I am as you want me to be." This statement expresses extremes of autoplastic adaptation, dependence on others' acceptance and approval, and the lack of a core of convictions, values, and personal attributes that imparts a sense of integrity and continuity through the temporal transformations that characterize human life. By a curious paradox, the marketing type is both the seller and the commodity being sold, so that to the extent that employment, acceptance, and success in a fickle and changing market constitute the preeminent objectives of the individual, his or her locus of self-esteem and framework of orientation and devotion lie chiefly outside; whatever traits or convictions the marketing person seems to possess are more a function of a persona demanded by a particular social role than something rooted deeply within (Fromm, 1947). And although Fromm did not say so explicitly, it seems reasonable to speculate that the premium on moving up (or moving on) that corporate life imposes on its employees makes the maintenance of relatively superficial relationships a pragmatic necessity. The result is an erosion of basic trust, which in turn requires a veneer of superficial sociability to allay anxiety and maintain the conduct of social relations without too much friction or open antagonism.

Despite important resemblances and the fact that both are rooted in capitalist societies, however, the heteronomous orientation of the marketing type differs from the sadomasochism of the authoritarian character—Fromm's chief target in *Escape from Freedom* (1941). The authoritarian is closer to the obsessive-compulsive or anal character and evinces a harsh and relentless superego that promotes obedience, irrational doubt and anxiety, feelings of worthlessness, impotence, or identification with the aggressor, and strivings to dominate, hurt, or control others. This sort of heteronomy is more characteristic of early industrial capitalism than of the more recent phenomenon.

By contrast, the marketing type flourishes in economic conditions that are inimical to old-fashioned patriarchal authority but witness a dramatic rise in consumerism and the administration of society by manipulated, rather than coerced, consent. Although marketing trends can be alloyed with authoritarian, sadistic ones or with oral aggression, in the more typical case the marketing orientation is blended with receptive dynamics, suggesting that the person lacks the punitive superego and the desire to exploit, control, and humiliate others. Anxiety stems from his or her own passivity and aloneness, which are continually reinforced through an autoplastic orientation and lack of genuine contact or interest in others.

Fear of Death, Necrophilia, and Schizoid Trends

Long before Ernest Becker's best-seller, *The Denial of Death* (1973), Fromm argued that repression of the fear and awareness of death is one of the most salient features of our culture (1941, pp. 270–272). For those who are philosophically minded, there is an interesting parallel between Fromm's marketing syndrome and Heidegger's "they self," adopted by those whose "fall" into inauthenticity renders them incapable of self-mediated reflection and a "resoluteness toward death," which is one of the "ownmost" possibilities of being (Fromm and Xirau, 1968, pp. 296–300). Unlike Heidegger, however, Fromm stressed the potential of this existential realization for enhancing deep personal bonds between people, which are characteristically absent in contemporary life. For Heidegger, by contrast, genuine community predicated on the preservation and enhancement of one's autonomy is not a real option. Either one falls in with the centerless, indiscriminate sociability of "the they," or one pursues one's own solitary path. Either way, one is never really "at home" in the world, although one is aware of that fact only in the solitary mode of authenticity (Heidegger, 1927).

No doubt Fromm would have agreed with two psychologists at Rutgers University, George Atwood and Robert Stolorow, who argue that Heidegger ontologized one mode of human estrangement, making it constitutive of the human condition as such (1984, pp. 15–23). Accordingly, as they suggest, Heidegger's *Being and Time* represents "a *symbol* of an anguished struggle for individuality and grounded authenticity in a world where one is in perpetual danger of absorption in the pressures and influences of the social milieu" (ibid., p. 23)

There are also parallels between Fromm's view of modernity and that of psychiatrist Viktor Frankl. Though trained as a Freudian, Frankl concluded, like Fromm, that the exigencies of drive or tension reduction and the pursuit of erogenous satisfaction do not provide an adequate model for many of the conditions and disturbances he encountered clinically. Like Fromm, Frankl emphasized that loneliness, suffering, and radical uncertainty are ineradicable dimensions of experience for the deeply alive and sane individual living in an imperfect world (compare Fromm, 1955b, pp. 173–174, and Frankl, 1959, pt. 2). In the present climate, Frankl claimed, the "cure of souls" may depend as much on restoring the authentic capacity to suffer as on the capacity to enjoy. In a similar vein, Fromm noted:

> A person who is alive and sensitive cannot fail to feel sadness or sorrow many times in his life. This is so, not only because of the amount of unnecessary suffering produced by the imperfection of our social arrangements, but because of the nature of human existence. Since we are living beings, we must be sadly aware of the necessary gap between our aspirations and what can be achieved in our short and troubled life.

Since death confronts us with the inevitable fact that either we die before our loved ones or they before us—since we see suffering, avoidable and unavoidable, around us every day, how can we avoid the experience of pain and sorrow? The effort to avoid it is only possible if we reduce our sensitivity, responsiveness and love, if we harden our hearts and withdraw our attention and our feeling from others, as well as from ourselves.   (1955b, p. 178)

Frankl, then, criticized Freudian theory for emphasizing the pleasure principle to the detriment of meaning. Fromm, in a similar vein, criticized contemporary "mental health" practice for attempting to flatten and trivialize dimensions of human experience that fall outside a narrow and parochial conception of maturity in the interests of social control:

In our society emotions in general are discouraged. While . . . any creative thinking . . . is inseparably linked with emotion, it has become an ideal . . . to live without emotions. To be "emotional" has become synonymous with being unsound or unbalanced. By accepting this standard the individual has become greatly weakened; his thinking is impoverished and flattened . . .

In the process of tabooing emotions modern psychiatry plays an ambiguous role. On the one hand its greatest representative, Freud, has broken through the fiction of the rational purposeful character of the human mind and opened a path which allows a view into the abyss of human passions. On the other hand, psychiatry, enriched by these very achievements of Freud, has made itself an instrument of the general trends in the manipulation of personality. Many psychiatrists, including psychoanalysts, have painted the picture of a "normal" personality which is never too sad, too angry or too excited. They use words like "infantile" or "neurotic" to denounce traits or types of personalities that do not conform with the conventional pattern of the "normal" individual. This kind of influence is in a way more dangerous than the older and franker forms of name-calling. Then the individual knew at least that there was some person or some doctrine which criticized him and he could fight back. But who can fight back at "science"?   (1941, pp. 270–272)[10]

Among the things often repressed by psychiatry were "the sense of tragedy" and "the awareness of death":

There is one tabooed emotion that I want to mention in particular, because its suppression touches deeply on the roots of personality; the sense of tragedy . . . the awareness of death and of the tragic aspect of

life, whether dim or clear, is one of the basic characteristics of man. Each
culture has its own way of coping with death . . . Our own era simply
denies death and with it one of the fundamental aspects of life. Instead
of allowing the awareness of death and suffering to become one of the
strongest incentives for life, the basis for human solidarity, and an
experience without which joy and enthusiasm lack intensity and depth,
the individual is forced to repress it . . . Thus the fear of death lives an
illegitimate existence among us. It remains alive in spite of the attempt
to deny it, but being repressed it remains sterile. It is one source of the
flatness of other experiences, of the restlessness pervading life, and it
explains, I would venture to say, the exorbitant amount of money this
nation pays for its funerals.   (Ibid., p. 271)

But although people today may be deeply afraid of death, and
indeed, more so than if they harnessed their fear in the service of life,
there is another sense in which Fromm believed they are *attracted* to
it, and afraid of or repelled by all that is alive. According to Fromm,
the necrophilous strain in contemporary culture is expressed in the
arms race and in our inability to plan for the future and to manage our
environment sanely (1968b, chap. 3). It is also expressed in widespread tendencies toward schizoid detachment, boredom and passivity, and our perverse cultural romance with machinery and gadgets.
Fromm also detected tendencies in this direction among the nominal
opponents of conformist banality, epitomized in the fascist ravings of
an avant-garde artist such as F. T. Marinetti (1973, pp. 31–32, 382–
384).

Fromm's notion of necrophilia and its underlying rationale are
quite muddled. It could hardly be called a "theory." Still, from a
purely descriptive standpoint, it touches on some profoundly disturbing truths. One need only reflect on escalating crime rates, the prevalence of violence and murder in the media and popular culture, and
the unconscious death wishes of televangelists preaching Armag-
gedon in the name of salvation to appreciate how prevalent necrophilia is. However, an important distinction must be made. The
violence, bitterness, and contempt for life characteristic of the nec-
rophile are all too visible among criminals, drug addicts, and marginal
people whose hope seems irrevocably shattered. They dramatize and
express their inner reality with relative lack of restraint, having nothing more to lose. The more dangerous (because less visible) varieties
of necrophilous passion attach themselves to the apparently more

sane and "normal" individuals most likely to denounce or scapegoat the more deviant variety; to reproach the hopeless and destitute for their selfishness and lack of restraint and to call for more punitive measures against them; those whose cynicism and lack of compassion are rationalized or masked by what passes for good sense.

Whether or not necrophiles are criminal in a technical sense—and they often are—is essentially beside the point. The structure of social relations allows for all sorts of ways to damage, cheat, and humiliate others in a perfectly "legitimate" manner, and not just individually, but en masse. Ironically, self-righteous death worshipers who habitually blame the victim are often unconscious of their own victimization, which is correspondingly less visible than among the underprivileged, and just as much part of the system they idealize and hope to buttress or restore as the endemic tragedies they blame on feminism, permissiveness, minorities, atheism, and so on.

Apart from the marketing and necrophilous trends, but as part and parcel of the modern psyche, Fromm mentioned a taboo on strong emotions that psychiatry helps to maintain (1941, chap. 7). Linked to this perhaps is what he termed the merely "reproductive" realism of the schizoid person, who registers events in external reality realistically but is deeply estranged from his or her own subjective feelings and processes (1947, pp. 108–113). In his view, this alienation, though statistically quite prevalent, is just as insane, humanly speaking, as the opposite extreme found in psychosis, in which *only* the person's subjective feelings and processes are experienced as real (Landis and Tauber, 1971, p. 414). Along similar lines, in *The Revolution of Hope* (1968b) Fromm noted that the schizoid person, like the paranoid, can be perfectly logical without being rational, and that genuine rationality presupposes a balance and synthesis of thought and feeling that are rare today. Indeed, to the vast majority, those who have *not* lost the vital connectedness between head and heart often seem "crazy" as a consequence (ibid., pp. 42–43).[11]

Age, Youth, and Gender Equality

Fromm's characterization of contemporary social character does not take into account several trends that play an enormous role in modern life. One example is the growing revolt, since the Second World

War, against domesticity and traditional sex roles. The little that
Fromm said on this subject suggests that he was extremely uncom-
fortable with it (1956a, pp. 12–13), despite his relentless critique of
Freud's patriarchal bias. For example, Fromm reproached Freud for
misunderstanding erotic love by supposing that libido is essentially
masculine in both men and women (ibid., chap. 2, sec. 3c). By
contrast, Fromm insisted, genuine love or communion between people is predicated on the reality, the appreciation, and the enhancement of their differences. In an essay titled "Sex and Character"
Fromm argued that ever since the Enlightenment, people have
tended to confuse or conflate equality with sameness, through an
unconscious capitulation to a tendentious feature of reactionary rhetoric.

> The implicit assumption underlying much reactionary thinking is that
> equality presupposes the absence of differences between persons or
> social groups. Since such differences obviously exist with regard to
> practically everything that matters in life, their conclusion is that there
> can be no equality. When, conversely, liberals are moved to deny the fact
> that there are any great differences in mental and physical gifts and
> favorable or unfavorable accidental personality conditions, they only
> help their adversaries to appear right in the eyes of the common man.
> The concept of equality, as it developed in the Judaeo-Christian and in
> the modern progressive tradition, means that all men are equal in such
> basic human capacities as those making for the enjoyment of freedom
> and happiness. It means furthermore, that as a political consequence of
> this basic equality, no man shall be made a means to the ends of another
> man, no group a means to the end of another group . . . Thus equality is
> the basis for the full development of differences, and it results in the
> development of individuality.   ([1943] 1963a, p. 112)

These remarks indicate that, in Fromm's view, inasmuch as we are
all unique we are all entitled to equal rights and opportunities to
develop and express our distinctive gifts. But although we should,
without exception, be treated equally in this respect, the fact that
women have—or ought to have—the option of entering the work
force on equal terms with men does not necessarily imply that they
ought to exercise these rights in a concerted flight from domesticity
and childbearing. The suggestion that *they have to* in order to be equal
with men—which, though now passé, was quite prevalent among
feminists while Fromm was alive—Fromm found repugnant and

absurd. In his estimation, this would only foster an increasing masculinization of women and a *depolarization* in the relations between the sexes (1956a, pp. 12–13).

Fromm saw a differently motivated tendency to efface sexual differences in what he perceived as the matriarchal ethos of the counterculture of the 1960s and 1970s. His remarks are illuminating both as a critique of the counterculture and as an expression of a peculiar ambiguity in his outlook, in which a radical, antipatriarchal ethos was blended with a strong traditionalist streak. In connection with the rejection of prevailing patriarchal norms, Fromm noted:

> Certain matriarchal tendencies can . . . be observed in some sectors of the—more or less—radical youth. Not only because they are strictly anti-authoritarian; but also because of their embracing of the . . . values of the matriarchal world as described by Bachofen and Morgan. The idea of group sex (whether in its middle-class, suburban forms or in radical communes with shared sex) has a close connection with Bachofen's description of the early matriarchal stage of mankind. The question can also be raised as to whether the tendency to diminish sexual differences in appearance, dress, etc., is not also related to the tendency to abolish the traditional status of the male, and to make the two sexes less polarized, leading to a regression (emotionally) to the pregenital stage of the infant. ([1970b], 1970a, p. 105)

The way in which Fromm posed the problem suggests either an imperfect command of the English language or a tacit assumption that genital primacy, which he equates with maturity and differentiation, is contingent on the preservation of "the traditional status of the male." Fromm never elaborated on this point, so it is impossible to determine precisely what he meant. For most people, however, "the traditional status of the male" means nothing less than being dominant economically, often in the household as well as outside it, and having this dominance sanctioned by religious tradition. Perhaps Fromm did not mean to imply this. Nevertheless, his choice of words suggests that behind his critique of patriarchy lay powerful sentiments of a far more conservative character. (Note his wayward invocation of Freud's psychosexual schema, which he ostensibly rejected, to sanction his thoughts on maturity; further evidence of his ambivalence in this regard.)

Fromm also had little to say about contemporary society's general orientation toward youth. Freud contributed to this trend by demonstrating the roots of adult personality in childhood experience. But on a more pervasive level, this phenomenon stems from society's interest in training the workers, technicians, and consumers of the future, and in its ceaseless revolutionizing of its technological infrastructure. In order to sustain economic growth, capitalism depends on an ever-increasing level of technical expertise to propel the engines of competition. As a result, the skills, knowledge, and attitudes of older people, not to mention their social and aesthetic sensibilities, are deemed obsolescent with each revolution in technology. This attitude fosters a decline of the extended family, and what Erikson termed "trans-generational identification." To his lasting credit, Erikson drew attention to the need of the aging for a sphere of "generativity" that links them to the lives of the new generation, and the complementary needs of the young for a positive experience of old age and all it holds in store. The "missed mutuality" occasioned by the widespread perception that the elderly have nothing worthwhile to transmit does incalculable damage to young and old alike (Erikson, 1960). As a consequence, the *fear* of aging, the premium put on youth, and so on contribute to what can only be termed the infantilization of popular culture. At a time when their concerns should embrace the young and the old equally, many people in their twenties, thirties, and forties flee responsibility, remaining trapped in the peer-group perspectives of late adolescence. To them, old age seems a curse rather than a blessing, as it often did in precapitalist settings, where the pace of technological change was slow and modulated by traditional values. An inevitable corollary of all this is that, in all age brackets, the demand for psychotherapy has risen enormously since the late nineteenth century.

Other Views of Contemporary Social Character

Given the acerbity of Fromm's view of the modern psyche, it is not surprising that some of Fromm's students found his formulations exaggerated, and prone to overlook the positive potentialities inherent in the transformations wrought by the technological revolution. David Riesman and Michael Maccoby, both analysands and colleagues of Fromm's, contrasted Fromm's assessment of prevailing trends with their own views regarding the productive and potentially liberating potentialities of an increasingly technological and market-oriented society (Riesman, 1950; Maccoby, 1976, 1983). Maccoby, a student of Riesman's, has criticized Fromm for contrasting prevailing social character with a normative ideal of productive self-realization modeled on the qualities of artists or mystics who developed in a feudal context, which are discrepant with current conditions, in which Fromm's ideal is scarcely attainable by anybody, and even its desirability is somewhat moot (Maccoby, 1983). According to Maccoby, in Fromm's writings on social character the essentially historical and empirical methodology that informed his best work is confounded with a prescriptive, moralizing stance that implies the possibility of a "pure" productive type of development. In fact Fromm believed that there is no such thing as a "purely" productive character; rather, all of us possess admixtures of the various characterological orientations in varying strengths and combinations (1947). But he was not always clear on this in his writings. Maccoby's misgivings along these lines, which arose in the late 1960s, prompted Fromm and him to drop the "productive character" as an independent construct from their Mexican study, and to refer instead to varying intensities and admixtures of "productivity" with receptive, exploitative, hoarding, or marketing trends (Fromm and Maccoby, 1970b).

Fromm and Maccoby's study of the Mexican village was published when interest in social character was on the wane, and it elicited far less interest than it deserved. However, Riesman's highly acclaimed *The Lonely Crowd* (1950) was explicitly indebted to Fromm's *Escape from Freedom* (1941) and *Man for Himself* (1947). In keeping with Fromm's typological distinctions between character, temperament, and the whole personality, Riesman began his reflections on American social character

> by defining character structure as the more or less permanent, socially and historically conditioned organization of an individual's drives and satisfactions. The term as thus defined is less inclusive than "personality," the word which in current usage denotes the total self, with its inherited temperaments and talents, its biological as well as psychological components . . . My reason for selecting from this complex the abstraction called "character" is that . . . I propose to deal with those components of personality that also play the principal role in the maintenance of social forms—those that are *learned* in the lifelong process of socialization.   (1950, p. 4)

Another facet of Riesman's approach that was indebted to Fromm was his distinction between "adjustment" and "autonomy." By autonomy, Riesman meant more or less what Fromm meant by the "productive character," that is, the capacity for relating to the world through one's powers of love and independent judgment. Adjustment, for Riesman, connotes conformity. Riesman was acutely aware that there may be wide discrepancies between individual character and social character, and that adoption of the values embodied in the prevailing institutions and mores of a society may exact a severe toll on the individual: "Mere adjustment is a hardship, and a temptation, for people who can recognize autonomy within themselves; to become and remain autonomous is never easy" (1950, p. 356).

Nevertheless, Riesman deliberately did not use Fromm's concept of the marketing character to describe the contemporary scene. Instead Riesman suggested that the overall trend of Western society was from a "tradition directed" (feudal) to an "inner directed" (early modern) to an "other directed" (late capitalist) orientation of character. And whereas Fromm's marketing orientation is, by definition, heteronomous, Riesman saw greater possibilities for autonomy within the "other directed" framework than Fromm did (Riesman, 1950, pp. 300–306). Riesman's optimism was premised on the assumption that modernity involves a growing degree of self-awareness as a concomitant to trends toward consumerism and an increasingly market-oriented outlook; that the average "outer directed" individual is more self-aware than his or her feudal or early capitalist counterparts. In time, Riesman hoped, there would emerge a "saving remnant" whose powers of reflexive awareness would enable them to sensitize their contemporaries to the possibilities for self-estrangement inherent in the other-directed outlook, effecting wide-ranging social transformations. Though more hopeful than Fromm about the possibilities for transformation *within* the prevailing system, Riesman neglected to buttress the ostensible correlation between "other directedness" and increasing self-consciousness with convincing proofs, or to explain how the "saving remnant" of the future would extricate themselves from slavish allegiance to peer-group perspectives and market trends, and coalesce as an effective social catalyst.

Nevertheless, one merit of Riesman's study was that he discerned how "other directed," cliquish, and covertly conformist many bohemian enclaves in society actually are, and how the relaxation of traditional sexual constraints may further the incursion of the market mentality into interpersonal relationships—a prescient observation, given the times in which it was written. More important, Riesman devoted far more explicit reflection and analysis to education and the mass media as agents of socialization than Fromm did. For although Fromm never said so, the proliferation of mass education and the electronic media in the postwar era has effected a relative decline in the importance of the family as an agent of socialization. Emphasis on the family as the chief transmitter of prevailing economic imperatives and values may already be anachronistic, however central the family was in the feudal and early capitalist milieus.

But if Fromm neglected these (and other) facets of the contemporary scene, he did acknowledge the more diffuse ideology that sanctions and sustains them. It is the belief that the production of more and more things, through more and more efficient means, is "Progress"; that if something *can* be done, it *ought to* be done (Fromm, 1968b). Ironically, twentieth-century capitalism takes the ethos of "Progress" as its birthright but empties the idea of most of its original content—a shift no less real for being widely ignored. The goals of reason, of autonomy, and of a profound and spontaneous sociability that animated progressive thinkers since the French Revolution have been displaced in twentieth-century capitalism by a preoccupation with material prosperity and by the overarching designs of technological society.

Progress, we are told, is a good thing. And once upon a time, it was. But the widespread attenuation of the ideals that animated our predecessors to cast off the shackles of feudalism makes the twentieth-century god of "Progress" so naive, mechanical, and stupid that it scarcely warrants comparison with its early modern forebear. Granted, Fromm's descriptions of contemporary life sound shrill and alarmist to many people. But for many popular thinkers today, including Marcuse, Lacan, Foucault, Baudrillard, and their followers, Fromm's denunciation of modernity was not nearly shrill enough. Yet attempts to "unmask" or deconstruct normative ideals such as "individual autonomy" or "sociability" as being ideological in their very essence leaves no goal for emancipatory social praxis other than the purely negative one of critique. Even here, it will be wanting. For any emancipatory project—whether individual or social—must hold to some implicit standard of human liberty and well-being in order to be intelligible, let alone persuasive. Structuralist and "postmodern" thought tends to end in nihilism or bombast because it makes a conscious and deliberate strategy of what was already a prevalent (if unconscious) trend in late capitalist society—to empty of their meaning the normative ideals that guided the inception of capitalism. Fromm, by contrast, attacked what he called "the illusion of individuality" in contemporary life (1947, chap. 7) but retained some conception of autonomous choice and personal development as nonideological normative criteria and as goals for democratic socialism.

6 Consensus, Conformity, and False Consciousness: "The Pathology of Normalcy"

Normative Humanism versus Consensual Validation

The phrase "the pathology of normalcy" appears but once in Fromm, in the second chapter of *The Sane Society* (1955b). The book as a whole is concerned with the pervasive alienation of postwar industrial society. But "the pathology of normalcy" does not merely refer to so recent or specific a phenomenon. Like the very idea of a sane society, it derives from a broader anthropological and historical outlook that Fromm termed "normative humanism." Its controversial premise is that a society as a whole can be sick or "insane," inasmuch as it fails to address existential needs that are vital to the growth and development of the human individual (Fromm, 1955b, 1973). Among Fromm's targets in *The Sane Society* were mental health ideologues who saw adaptation or conformity to the emerging technocratic order as a necessary or sufficient condition of sanity and well-being:

> It is naively assumed that the fact that the majority of people share certain ideas or feelings proves the validity of these ideas or feelings. Nothing is further from the truth. Consensual validation as such has no bearing whatsoever on mental health . . . The fact that millions of people share the same vices does not make these vices virtues, and the fact that they share so many errors does not make the errors to be truths. (1955b, p. 23)

Fromm hastened to add, however, that consensually validated errors and vices do involve certain rewards; for example, people subject to a socially patterned defect experience less inner conflict and neurotic misery or are merely less conscious of their conflicts and cognitive distortions than their overtly neurotic counterparts. For whereas the neurotic's rationalizations reflect personal conflicts and desires and may be transparent to an outsider, an indifference or hostility to truth characteristic of conformist psychology has lower social visibility, because it is socially shared and reinforced (Fromm, 1973, p. 396). Here resistance to insight and to change on the individual level is less the product of individual censorship and repression than of shared perspectives anchored securely in one's sense of corporate identity and in consensual models and definitions of reality. This situation is effectively summed up in Fromm's oft-repeated aphorism that, for the majority of people in society, "most of what is real is not conscious, and most of what we are conscious of is not real" (1975, p. 403).

Clearly, Fromm's thinking here is at variance with conventional wisdom and with the prevailing theory and practice of the mental health professions. When it comes to questions of fundamental sanity, laypeople and clinicians alike are accustomed to gauging the sanity of thought processes in terms of the degree of consensual validation that attaches to their content, and in terms of the adequacy or intelligibility of their underlying process (so far as we can apprehend it). Many of the diagnostic instruments and protocols used by mental health professionals are merely refined and systematic extensions of these commonsense assumptions. Accordingly, the idea that for the average person, what is real is not conscious, and what is conscious, unreal, will strike the majority of people in any society, including its more thoughtful and reflective members, as extravagant. For if the majority of people thought that their counterparts were defective or impaired in some vital capacity, all trust in consensual systems of belief and rituals of daily interaction would tend to break down. That being the case, what prompted Fromm to espouse this disturbing viewpoint?

Before answering this question, it may be useful to note that the *idea* of the pathology of normalcy—unlike the specific locution—is actually not original to Fromm. Indeed, it is as old as philosophy itself. Its best-known philosophic articulation is the celebrated Myth of the Cave in Plato's *Republic*. But both before and after Plato, Hindu and Buddhist sages and Greek philosophers such as Thales, Anaxagoras, Heraclitus, Pythagoras, Parmenides, Empodocles, and Epicurus entertained similar ideas regarding the widespread prevalence of mass delusion, which only a rigorous apprenticeship of the mind or spirit can undo. For these men, the apprehension of truth is simply beyond the grasp of the average individual, who, by virtue of past lives, constitutional inferiority, a matter-enmeshed mode of livelihood, or all three, simply cannot grasp the timeless, unchanging reality clothed in the temporal appearance of change, growth, and decay by liberating themselves from the sensual appetites that bind them to illusion. For them, the pathology of normalcy is principally a defect of cognition and is delineated by way of contrast with an essentially disincarnate intellect and a hypothetical state of grace attainable only by an elite of ascetic saints and intellectual virtuosi who are truly and metaphysically in the know.

Two other traditions linking false consciousness to normality that are more germane to Fromm are rabbinical learning and the elements of the Sophist and Stoic philosophies of ancient Greece and Rome that were incorporated and transfigured in the concept of natural law (Bloch, 1961; Fromm, 1961b). In contrast to the ascetic and elitist philosophies of pagan antiquity, these traditions did not disparage the body or the senses much, and stressed the potential participation of *all* people in the divine. And on the whole their emphasis was ethical, not metaphysical and was incipiently democratic rather than elitist. For example, the Hebrew concept of idolatry was premised on the assumption that all men are created in the image of God (Fromm, 1966, chaps. 1–3). Although the Jews were consecrated as a holy or "chosen people," God's covenant with all humanity, embodied in the Noachite Commandments, implies that all of us are related to God through Adam and through the avoidance of idolatry, violence, and deception; that no one has a monopoly on truth or righteousness (ibid., pp. 41–43; Loewe et al., 1966).[1] Despite the residual tribalism invested in the "chosen people" ideology, the prophetic critique of false consciousness was universalistic in outlook, and became increasingly so as Israel's claims to territorial sovereignty became no more than a faint historical recollection (Fromm, 1960d, pp. 65–66, 108–110).

The idea that all men are equal in the sight of God, and are capable of wisdom and righteousness regardless of class or ethnic origins, had parallels in ancient Greece. Following certain Sophist and Cynic teachers, the Stoics argued that all men are essentially equal and are infused with a "divine spark" or *logos spermatikos* emanating from God, who was conceived of monotheistically or pantheistically (Bloch, 1961; Baldry, 1965). This belief expressed itself in Stoic doctrine in its emphasis on the dignity of labor and its corresponding repudiation of the aristocratic-elitist theory that individuals engaged in manual labor are either constitutionally or vocationally unfit for wisdom, virtue, and political life (Edelstein, 1966, p. 76).

Since the emphasis in Stoic and rabbinic messianic thought was chiefly ethical, we are apt to ignore its cognitive or epistemic component, which expressed itself in a variety of ways. Fundamentally, for example, the Hebrew concept of idolatry implies the misrecognition and reification of our own divinely begotten essence, which, like the burning bush, is in a process of continuous and inextinguishable *becoming,* and is not something finite, static, or dead, like a graven image (Fromm, 1966, chap. 2). Indeed, from a philosophical perspective, it is precisely this failure of cognition, not mere disobedience to a higher authority, that produces the profanation of man and God; a point emphasized by Maimonides in *The Guide to the Perplexed* (Funk, 1982, pp. 183–188). Similarly, in the Stoic tradition, philosophers and men of letters expressed profound joy in the realization and celebration of being "world citizens," or *cosmopolites,* and called on humanity at large to renounce the illusions of ethnic and religious particularity (Baldry, 1965).[2]

Despite diametrically opposed perspectives regarding the suitedness of common humanity for apprehending truth, there is one respect in which the pagan/ascetic and Stoic/Hebraic theories of false consciousness agree, however. Both of them suggest that the failure of cognition that estranges us from truth represents more than a mere lack of information. Fundamentally, it represents the lack of a *disposition to truth,* which only a profound awakening and conscious choice can alter. Thanks to the Christian synthesis of pagan asceticism and otherworldliness with Stoic and Hebraic ideas in the late Roman and medieval periods, Jewish, Christian, and Islamic thinkers came to associate sin, or ethical dereliction, with a willful estrangement from the underlying bedrock of truth that supposedly sustains our fleeting existences. However, in the hands of the orthodox, who claimed privileged access to the ultimate ground of being, what were tools for critical consciousness in preceding epochs became powerful instruments of domination and persecution, and the enforcement of unthinking conformity to a punitive social order. In short, in the course of their historical development, these ideas, once alloyed with dogma, became more of a hindrance than an incentive to independent and rational inquiry into truth.

The advent of scientific rationalism, with its challenges to revealed truth and popular superstition, gave a whole new complexion to the idea that the broad mass of humanity is sunk in ignorance and superstition. One of the first to do this—though he is seldom recalled in this connection—was Francis Bacon. Like Freud much later, Bacon was a gifted debunker. His deep and sincere antipathy to organized religion, his vaulting personal ambition, and the historical and polemical context in which he wrote, all prompted Bacon to distance himself from his remote religious and philosophical forebears. David Rapaport's brief history of associationism sheds interesting light on Bacon's theory of false consciousness, or the consensual validation of imaginary belief systems through the idols of the tribe, of the marketplace, and of the theater (Rapaport, 1938, pp. 7–20). As Bacon no doubt realized, the use of philosophical argument to restate the ancient idea of false consciousness or mass delusion in associationist terms in the interests of promoting natural science was something of a coup. For it sundered the medieval marriage of philosophy and religion—in which science was subordinate—and turned the charge of false consciousness on the defenders of revealed truth, as well as on popular superstition.

As science rounded on religion to secure its emancipation from dogma—subverting philosophy wherever possible—it became increasingly difficult for modern theorists of false consciousness (and their audiences) to recognize the affinity between their ideas and the critical theories of pre-Christian antiquity, although Bacon's use of the term *idols* with reference to popular delusion obviously invites such comparisons. Accordingly, if you tell a modern psychoanalyst or social scientist that temperamentally, if not culturally, Freud was a Platonist, with strong affinities for the ascetic/elitist tradition of pagan Greece, whereas Fromm was a prophetic and Stoic thinker, and that this fact is of considerable consequence for the history of psychoanalysis, you are more likely to be greeted with derisive laughter or stony incomprehension than with a nod of sympathetic understanding.

The idea that the average individual is enveloped in a welter of delusions that are buttressed or reinforced by convention, consensus, or the prevailing social order—radical and extreme though it may sound—is vividly inscribed in the prophetic and Platonic consciousness. Indeed, the diligent historian of ideas is confronted with a strange situation that most clinicians seem loath to contemplate. It is this: that in most societies, the majority of those deemed normal, who share in consensually validated belief systems and are free of manifest mental illness (according to prevailing standards), think of themselves and their fellows as being eminently sane. By contrast, a sizable number of their thinkers, philosophers, and prophets—in a proportion that varies somewhat from one society and period to another—regard the majority of their contemporaries as deluded and as radically, often willfully, estranged from the truth.

Freudian Social Psychology: Normality, Development, and the Social Order

Aside from his sensational sexual theories, Freud's claim to preeminence among twentieth-century thinkers rests in large part with his ability, like Ludwig Feuerbach, Karl Marx, Arthur Schopenhauer, Friedrich Nietzsche, Henrik Ibsen, and others, to puncture our most cherished illusions. In his clinical practice Freud demonstrated what they intuited in their philosophical, literary, and scientific endeavors, namely, that naive self-consciousness is mostly false consciousness, and that the constructions we put on our own thought and behavior are often superficial or misleading; a product, one might say, of motivated ignorance (Fromm, 1962, chap. 2).

Among Freud's boldest contributions along these lines was his insistence that normality is not simply a self-evident given, but a phenomenon whose characteristics warrant analysis like any other. In *Three Essays on the Theory of Sexuality* (1905), Freud stated that normality (defined as heterosexual object choice accompanied by a modicum of aim-inhibited affection and sublimation) is a far from self-evident affair and, like all the vagaries of desire, presumably subject to a lawful course of development, which he purported to supply in psychosexual terms. For Freud, the concepts of health and normality remained pretty much coextensive, just as they do in everyday usage. But Freud also stepped resolutely beyond commonsense conceptions. For he regarded normality as (1) something to be explained in causal terms commensurate with our knowledge of anomalous experience and behavior, and, more important for our present purposes, as (2) a product of external constraints and inner vicissitudes whose origin and direction are inextricably intertwined with the whole direction of cultural development (Freud, 1908).

In response to Jung's desexualized theory of libido—which Fromm endorsed (1964, p. 100)—Freud speculated that in the course of individual development we undergo a basic differentiation between our "narcissistic libido," a primordial reservoir of energy invested in our own egos, and "object libido," which forms the basis for erotic and emotional attachments and anchors us in external reality (1914). Civilization, Freud maintained, is built up through the progressive deployment of raw instinctual energy—that is, object libido—whose creative inhibition and secondary transformation foster the rational mastery of nature, and aim-inhibited love, which creates solid social bonds necessary to implement these intellectual achievements, and to tame the aggressive and narcissistic impulses that would otherwise interfere with their collective planning and execution (1933). But despite real gains in material prosperity and social order, society's ever-escalating demands on available erotic energy render us "enemies of civilization" in our deepest instinctual core. Indeed, Freud noted, "A good part of the struggles of mankind center around the . . . task of finding an expedient accommodation between this claim of the group and that of the individual; and one of the problems that touches the fate of humanity is whether such an accommodation can be reached, or whether this problem is irreconcilable" (1933, p. 96).

By stating the problem this way, Freud left open the possibility that this problem can be resolved. But an "accommodation," especially an "expedient accommodation," suggests something more in the way of an armed truce than a historic rapprochement. Clearly, Freud was deeply pessimistic on this score, though arguably in splendid company. For pessimism was part of his cultural milieu. Schopenhauer and von Hartmann had long since linked their psychologies of the unconscious with profoundly pessimistic philosophies of history (Mann, 1933). In the same vein, in "On Narcissism," Freud asserted:

> The individual does actually carry on a double existence; one designed to serve his own purposes and another as a link in a chain, in which he serves against, or at any rate without, any volition of his own. The

individual himself regards sexuality as one of his own ends; while from another point of view he is merely the appendage of his germ-plasm, to which he lends his energies, taking in return a toll of pleasure—the mortal vehicle of a (possibly) immortal substance—like the inheritor of an entailed estate which survives him. The differentiation of the sexual instincts from the ego-instincts would merely reflect this double function of the individual.   (1914, p. 14)

This statement, tendered in connection with clinical concerns, draws us closer to the heart of Freud's social psychology and philosophy of history. Freud supposed that we are born narcissistic, meaning that our energy is invested in our own bodily well-being. Subsequently, our reliance on others—to begin with, our mothers—dictates that psychic energy be channeled along anaclitic lines, in libidinal cathexes with those who tend to our bodily needs. Eventually the sexual instinct abandons its moorings in the oral zone, becoming anal, then genital in focus. But though suited, perhaps, to the purely biological imperative of reproduction, raw sexual energy is incapable of bonding more than two people or of consolidating large groups (Freud, 1933, p. 104). As sexuality becomes more constrained and desexualized in the service of social solidarity—as we become, in effect, more civilized—we rebel at our loss of primitive self-expression. Apart from a small "natural aristocracy" who readily sublimate their libido, most of us remain manifestly in need of the discipline and constraint that only submission to a dominant elite or majority can provide. As Freud put it:

> It is just as impossible to do without control of the mass by a minority as it is indispensable to dispense with coercion in the work of civilization. For masses are lazy and unintelligent; they have no love of instinctual renunciation, and they are not to be convinced by argument of its inevitability . . . It is only through the influence of individuals who can set an example and whom the masses recognize as their leaders that they can be induced to perform the work and undergo the renunciation on which civilization depends.   (1927, pp. 7–8)

Moreover, he suggested, the resentment arising from the manifold injustices of class rule is mitigated by identification with the rulers and by semihypnotic, transferential ties between the masses and their leaders, in which they idealize the latter and put them in the place of their ego ideal. Freud's assertion that the majority of people—that is, normal individuals—inhabit a quasi-hypnoid state in relation to their political, military, and religious leadership is devastatingly frank (Freud, 1921). Coming from anyone else, it would be construed as a critique of mass society, a kind of call to arms. For Freud, however, it was merely a fact of life that justified his own elitist perspective (Fromm, 1959b, chap. 9).

For Freud, then, normality is doubly, perhaps trebly, problematic. Developmentally speaking, it is something to be accounted for in causal, scientific terms, and no less mysterious or complex than pathological phenomena. Sociologically, however, it involves massive cognitive distortion where social and political reality is concerned, even in the absence of manifest neurotic conflict. Finally (and perhaps inconsistently), normality considered as a product of historical development represents an achievement of almost tragic grandeur, whose ultimate shape and character are conditioned by (and subject to) all kinds of societal demands and instinctual vicissitudes. Through the transformation of sexual instincts, including homoerotic (or bisexual) components, nature ties the individual to the sphere of collective life, but at the expense of personal fulfillment. The resulting hostility to culture necessitates the emergence of class society and powerful elites to curb, contain, and coerce the mob and to furnish them with ego ideals that inspire identification and idealization and call forth acts of service and long-suffering, ostensibly on behalf of civilization as a whole.

Fromm and the New Critics

Freud's analysis of our civilized malaise and his critique of collective consciousness occupy a unique place in the history of psychology. Like Bacon, Freud claimed to have insight into the roots of collective delusions and possessed remarkable skill as a writer and polemicist. But Freud's social psychology combined a progressivist faith in reason with an unabashed elitism. For example, he prefaced *Group Psychology and the Analysis of the Ego* (1921) with a flattering assessment of Le Bon's *Crowd Psychology* and made no attempt to analyze its overtly reactionary ideological implications. Equally striking was his glorification of ascetic group leaders or intellectuals (for example, Leonardo, Prometheus, Moses), whose prodigious capacities for sublimation presumably gave them superhuman stature. This lionization of ascetic and charismatic leaders was rooted in peculiarities of Freud's own character (Fromm, 1935a, 1959b), but it also represented a partial return to the ascetic/elitist cast of pagan philosophy and metaphysics.

In *The Sane Society* (1955b), Fromm struck out on an independent path, with scarcely a glance at the formidable body of theory and conjecture Freud had marshaled in defense of his theory of civilization. In contrast, contemporaries such as Kardiner and Erikson prefaced their work with expressions of filial gratitude to Freud and articulated their ideas—which often paralleled Fromm's—in Freudian language, as far as reason would permit. Having dropped libido theory terminology, Fromm, however, focused on what he construed as specifically human or existential needs rooted in the very conditions of human existence, and not in specific tissue needs or somatic drives. Presumably, any society that fails to address these needs will produce defective people, regardless of the opportunities for drive satisfaction that same society affords its participants.

By redefining the source and nature of the needs that safeguard our sanity, Fromm transposed Freud's notion of the pathology of civilized communities into a different key. Freud had explained neurotic disability, and antipathy to constraints on sex and aggression, as inevitable products of historical development, which intensify and develop in a cumulative, unilinear, and probably irreversible manner. And although he was a believer in progress, it was progress with a heavy price tag attached. Fromm, on the other hand, insisted that the central problem was not the repression or sublimation of the instincts but how a society meets or disappoints the individual's existential needs for rootedness, transcendence, and solidarity with other human beings (1955b). Moreover, observing developments around him, Fromm saw no grounds for assuming that the repression and sublimation of sexual instincts follow some inexorable and unified historical progression; he felt that malignant aggression was as much created as constrained by the process of civilization (1973).

Despite their differences, Fromm most emphatically shared with Freud the notions that consensually validated versions of reality often belie the motive forces that give rise to a belief system, and that most people care very little about apprehending the truth. Neither of them had any monopoly on this kind of thinking: during the nineteenth century Kierkegaard, Feuerbach, Marx, Tolstoy, Nietzsche, and others concluded that the disinclination to face reality had something to do with a degeneration peculiar to the modern age (for example, Kierkegaard, 1846; Nietzsche, 1887). But whereas the critique of mass-mindedness in this earlier period had come from across the political spectrum, in the mid to late twentieth century the idea was taken up principally by independent thinkers on the left. Taken as a whole, their work might be termed a lament for the shattered dreams of the Enlightenment, and the promise of justice, peace, and reason in the midst of general prosperity. For whereas Bacon and his followers looked forward to an age of material plenty and linked that to the development of a sane and disenchanted public consciousness, in postwar America prosperity as such was no longer an issue. According to the new critics, the unprecedented rise in wage levels, the widespread availability of credit and consumer goods, actually covered up a deeper malaise. No one expressed the prevailing mood of disenchantment more pointedly than C. Wright Mills in *The Sociological Imagination:*

> ... it is not true, as Ernest Jones asserts, that "man's chief enemy and danger is his own unruly nature and the dark forces pent up within him." On the contrary: "Man's chief danger" today lies in the unruly forces of production, its enveloping techniques of political domination, its international anarchy . . .
>
> Science, it turns out, is not a technological Second Coming. That its techniques and its rationality are given a central place in society does not mean that men live reasonably and without myth, fraud and superstition . . . A high level of bureaucratic rationality and of technology does not mean a high level of either individual or social intelligence. From the first you cannot infer the second . . .
>
> It is no wonder that the ideal of individuality has become moot: in our time, what is at issue is the very nature of man . . . we must now raise the question in an ultimate form: Among contemporary men, will there come to prevail, or even to flourish, what may be called The Cheerful Robot? (1959, chap. 9)

The answer issuing from many quarters was a horrified but resounding "yes!" Similarly, Fromm remarked that speculation regarding the ostensible death of God is by now beside the point. What ought to concern us, what looms imminently on the horizon, is the death of man (Fromm, 1955b). Like Mills and others, Fromm was deeply concerned with what he regarded as accelerating and interrelated trends: the rise of consumerism, a deadening of spontaneity, an atrophy of conscience and sensibility, and, above all, a perversion or extinction of reason that coexists with the efflorescence of an unparalleled technical "know-how," evidenced, for example, in Cold War politics and propaganda and in the nuclear arms race (1955b, 1961c).

Fromm saw much of our cultural and political life as expressions of low-grade, chronic schizoid tendencies (1955b). In *Man for Himself* (1947) he observed that the passive registration of "facts," which is often confounded with "realism," is really a schizoid phenomenon. The productive, alive individual, though capable of passive registration and "monitoring," that is, a merely *reproductive* mode of perception, enlivens it with *generative* or affective currents drawn from deep in his or her psychic interior. When reproductive perception has atrophied completely, the person is indeed mad, estranged from actualities. When generative perception is absent, the person is an emotional cripple, lacking the ability to see beyond the surface of phenomena, to think critically and sympathetically about human reality (ibid., pp. 95–98).[3]

Commenting on the way in which subtle affective experiences are automatically debarred from consciousness owing to the cognitive and emotional templates of contemporary culture, Fromm observed that

> experience can enter into awareness only under the condition that it can be perceived, related and ordered in terms of a conceptual system and its categories. This system is in itself a product of social evolution. Every society, by its own practice of living and the mode of relatedness, of feeling and perceiving, develops a system, or categories, which determine the forms of awareness. This system works, as it were, as a *socially conditioned filter;* experience cannot enter awareness unless it can penetrate this filter. (1962, p. 114)

The Social Unconscious

Fromm's "social filters" mark a new and interesting departure in psychoanalytic social psychology. They ought not to be confounded with Freudian "censorship," which is an intrapsychic mechanism modeled along Herbartian lines that inhibits or distorts ideas in their struggle to gain access to consciousness. In Freud's model, censorship or repression involves *quantities* of excitation that adhere to various drive derivatives and their representations in a purely individual economy of reciprocally interacting energic impulsions that strive to engage our conscious attention. False consciousness is one aspect of censorship, in which material withheld from consciousness is replaced by convenient fictions in the service of maintaining a neurotic equilibrium. By contrast, Fromm's social filters are diffused throughout society and are *qualitative* rather than quantitative in character. They enable the individual to enter into consensually validated ways of interpreting natural, social, and interpersonal reality. Like Bacon's idols, they have the sanction of authority and collective prejudice. They screen out not only the derivatives of sexual and aggressive impulses but also more complex and differentiated emotional, interpersonal, or cognitive experiences from which the language, logic, and conventions of a given culture or class avert our attention in the interests of maintaining the status quo (Fromm, 1960d, sec. 4; 1962, chap. 9). The net result—a constriction of consciousness—is not unlike that of the Freudian censorship, except that the content of what is repressed is conceptualized differently, and the motive for such constriction is the fear of deviance and social isolation.

Approaching repression from an instinctivist standpoint, Fromm charged, Freud speculated that castration anxiety is the unconscious source of all dread and anxiety, whose subterranean springs feed other, derivative sources of conflict and repression. Fromm dismissed this as a fanciful supposition unwarranted by the clinical data and oblivious to enveloping social constraints (1962, p. 125). In reality, Fromm claimed, the main motive for repression lies in the need or desire to conform, to be related at any cost. For not to share in the prevailing consensus is to court ostracism, aloneness, and, quite possibly, madness (Fromm, 1935a; Fromm and Maccoby, 1970, p. 14).

Even so, Fromm recognized that there are circumstances that promote a "loosening" of social filters and favor a more critical and discerning attitude toward the prevailing ideology. Provided that the individual's judgment is not too impaired by social, economic, or personal insecurities, membership in a minority is one. Membership in a new, ascending class may be another, if the hegemony of the class in decline was buttressed by fictions that are beginning to wear thin. Drawing on the lessons of Marxist historiography, Fromm observed:

Decaying societies and classes are usually those who cling most fiercely to their fictions, since they have nothing to gain by the truth. Conversely, societies—or social classes—which are bound for a better future offer conditions which make the awareness of reality easier, especially if this awareness will help them make the necessary changes. A good example of this is the bourgeois class in the 18th century. Even before it had won political hegemony over the aristocratic class, it shed many fictions of the past and developed new insights into the past and present social realities. The writers of the middle classes could penetrate through the fictions of feudalism because they did not need these fictions—on the contrary, they were helped by the truth. When the bourgeois class had been firmly entrenched and was later fighting against the onslaught of the working class and, later, the colonial peoples, the situation was reversed; the members of the middle classes refused to see social reality, and the members of the forward moving, new classes were more prone to dispense with . . . illusions.   (1962, p. 130)

Fromm also recognized that the disposition to truth is not merely a function of broader social and historical conditions, but of familial and temperamental factors as well. The fact that, from Thomas Muntzer to Marx and Rosa Luxemburg, working-class leaders have often been drawn from the middle class did not escape him, and in such cases, he said, no generalizations were possible. Still, Fromm did not hesitate to describe the person whose judgment and humanity have not been compromised by social conditions as "the revolutionary character." The revolutionary character, he declared,

is one who is identified with humanity and therefore transcends the narrow limits of his own society, and who is able, therefore, to criticize his or any other society . . . He is not caught in the parochial culture which he happens to be born in, which is nothing but an accident of time and geography. He is able to look at this environment with the open eyes of a man who is awake and who finds his criteria of judging the accidental in that which is not accidental (reason), in the norms which are in and for the human race.   (1963f, p. 158)

But if, as Fromm maintained, we are all born with an innate disposition to develop our powers of love and reason, to relinquish idolatrous fixations, then it is to social conditions, and not to castration anxiety or an archaic inheritance of incestuous and parricidal impulses, that we must look for the source of repression. As Fromm himself put it,

man, in any culture, has all the *potentialities*: he is the archaic man, the
beast of prey, the cannibal, the idolater, and he is the being with the
capacity for reason, for love, for justice. The content of the unconscious,
then, is not just the good or the evil, the rational or the irrational; it is
both: it is all that is human. The unconscious is the whole man—minus
the part which corresponds to his society. Consciousness represents
social man, the accidental limitations set by the historical situation into
which the individual is thrown. Unconsciousness represents universal
man, the whole man, rooted in the Cosmos: it represents the plant in
him, the animal in him, the spirit in him; it represents the past back to
the dawn of human existence, and it represents his future to the day
when man will become fully human, and when nature will be humanized as man will be "naturalized." (1975, p. 404)

Only now can we survey Fromm's idea of the pathology of normalcy and uncover its sources in earlier traditions. In contrast to the
conformist, whose picture of reality is culture bound, the productive
or revolutionary character cleaves to what is universal—namely,
reason. The idea of the universality of reason, though Stoic in derivation, entered Fromm's world through the German Enlightenment
and thinkers such as Kant, Gotthold Lessing, J. G. Herder, Goethe,
and Hermann Cohen, whom Fromm studied in the company of early
mentors such as Nehemia Nobel (Fromm, 1966, p. 15; Funk, 1984,
chap. 2). His allusions to an indefinite future, when nature will be
"humanized" and humanity "naturalized," conjure up Marx's vision
of the postrevolutionary social order, which, as Fromm never tired
of repeating, represents a secularized embodiment of the messianic
kingdom (1960c, 1966). Fromm's emphasis on the universality of the
unconscious in this dual sense, as a repository of rational *and* irrational, social *and* antisocial impulses, incorporates concepts of the
unconscious traditionally associated with vitalism and the ideas of
Schelling, Lorenz Oken, Paul Carus, and Bachofen, among others.
Georg Groddeck, whom Fromm deeply admired, was a late heir to
this tradition (Fromm, 1935a). Although many of these thinkers were
frankly reactionary, elements of their vision were incorporated into
Fromm's concept of the unconscious, chiefly through the influence of
Bachofen and Groddeck.

Finally, Fromm's theory of social filters probably owes much to
Herder and Max Scheler. In the essay "On the Origin of Language"
(1772), Herder argued that language is a kind of cognitive template

that shapes and constrains what can be perceived, expressed, and represented in consciousness, and that the immense variety of human languages attests to the fact that our mode of adaptation to our surroundings is not, in fact, instinctive, but distinctively human and social, and capable of almost infinite variation. Herder's theory of language as a social filter was taken up by Wilhelm von Humboldt, and subsequently by Edward Sapir and Benjamin Lee Whorf, to whom Fromm was explicitly indebted, and whom he praised unstintingly (Whorf, 1956; Fromm, 1960d, p. 100n; Stam, 1980).

In "The Idols of Self-Knowledge" (1915), Max Scheler invoked a similar distinction between repression proper and the constriction of consciousness owing to linguistic convention. Like Fromm (1960d), Scheler argued that what we experience in our deepest psychic interior is seldom present to consciousness. Some of it is repressed in Freudian fashion, but much of it simply lacks adequate representation in the prevailing linguistic currency, or violates a widely shared taboo. According to Scheler, genuine self-knowledge requires more than the uncovering of pathogenic conflict in the clinical setting: a whole process of self-discovery involving the gradual but thoroughgoing emancipation from conventional social filters (Scheler, 1915, pp. 83–91).

Despite his illustrious forebears in linguistics and philosophy, Fromm showed questionable judgment in attacking so relentlessly Freud's dictum that castration anxiety is the source of all repression. Freud's discussion of repression as a social and historical phenomenon in *The Future of an Illusion* (1927) and especially *Civilization and Its Discontents* (1933) addresses processes and constraints that are conditioned by *the requirement of a minimum of social solidarity* in an otherwise antagonistic and potentially fragmented polity. By taking Freud at face value on the castration issue, Fromm overlooked a fertile contradiction in Freud's work, and scored some easy rhetorical points in a way that really does neither him nor Freud much credit. Freud's inventory of the various mechanisms or processes that unify an internally stratified society and buttress its reigning illusions includes idealization, identification, projection, displacement, sublimation, and reaction formation. In neglecting to discuss them, Fromm truncated a very rich field of inquiry and speculation.

On the other hand, in some respects, Fromm was probably a bit too Freudian. His indiscriminate use of the word *repression* is a case in point. In *Zen Buddhism and Psychoanalysis* (1960d), Fromm said that psychoanalysis pressed into the service of general emancipation transcends its mandate of mere symptom alleviation and attempts to "derepress" stereotypical habits of thought and perception rooted in the cognitive and emotional templates of the person's social milieus, as if the culturally conditioned unconscious were entirely a result of repression. But this is not always the case.

According to Freud, dynamic repression occurs when certain "contents" are excluded from consciousness because of the pain, anxiety, guilt, rage, or confusion they would occasion; and the process whereby they are excluded is also, necessarily, unconscious. The contents in question concern self, other, or environment but are deliberately withheld or distorted to maintain the subject's neurotic equilibrium.

However, as developments in linguistics, anthropology, as well as cognitive and social psychology suggest, there are modes of unconscious functioning that are equally pervasive, in which the bias and selectivity of thought, memory, and attention and our utter oblivion to the underlying process variables are routine but are rooted in the normal exigencies of biological growth and interpersonal communication, rather than in intrapsychic conflict (Piaget, 1972; Erdelyi, 1985; Burston, 1986a; Kihlstrom, 1987). Like the "unconscious repressed," they can be inferred or reconstructed only *ex post facto*, although, unlike them, they need not—indeed, cannot—be reintegrated or made conscious to facilitate optimal human functioning. These are processes that are part of the person's unconscious mental activity but are not disowned or "dissociated." A good deal, perhaps most, of the unconscious mind consists of processes of this nature. The question is whether the words *repression* and *derepression* are altogether appropriate here or whether we ought to evolve a more complex and discriminating vocabulary for handling the different modalities of unconsciousness.

The urgency of this need is underlined by the fact that in *some* instances social and political reality, prevailing definitions of gender, and selective inattention to intrapsychic and interpersonal issues *do* promote a socially patterned defect in which repression, in the proper sense of the word, is heavily implicated. Here culture pattern and individual neurosis are deeply intertwined. For example, the cult of masculinity in all its forms fosters and derives from infantile conflicts that have manifold social and political ramifications (Dinnerstein, 1976).

We are left with the practical and theoretical necessity of distinguishing between the "unconscious repressed"—in which certain contents and processes are deliberately thrust from awareness to avoid the experience of "unpleasure" (anxiety, rage, confusion, grief, and so on)—and equally unconscious processes that are inaccessible to normal introspection or retrieval, but not as a result of inner conflict. Fromm's theory conflates and confounds these diverse modalities of unconscious functioning (1960, sec. 4).

But if Fromm used the word *repression* in too sweeping and all-inclusive a sense, contemporary cognitivists tend to err in precisely the opposite direction. By and large, cognitivism treats unconscious mental processes as a welter of overlapping and interlocking automatisms designed to safeguard or increase *conscious* processing capacity, to minimize error, and so on, without probing the possibility that certain contents and perceptions are deliberately thrust out of awareness for very specific personal reasons, and sometimes with deleterious consequences (for example, Kihlstrom, 1987). Accordingly, cognitivists engage in research that is very sophisticated, but without exploring psychodynamic structure or the culturally specific automatisms that may regulate these processes; without discriminating between unconscious processes that are simple (or complex) automatisms, and those that actually do operate in the service of repression; and without determining why.

Consensus, Conformity, and Mainstream Social Psychology

Social filters and the pathology of normalcy might have endured longer as social psychological constructs had Fromm attempted to address the extant research in experimental social psychology on conformity and obedience. In that case, experiments on consensus and conformity might have continued to thrive within an expanded theoretical framework instead of becoming outmoded. But Fromm and his contemporaries used different methodological premises. From the standpoint of the experimental social psychologist, Fromm's ideas on conformity, though possibly very stimulating, seem somewhat speculative and impressionistic because they are not based on "hard" data. For as a rule, empiricists object, psychoanalysts do not test or cross-check their hypotheses in a rigorous or quantifiable fashion; therefore, both their clinical inferences and their subsequent application to the social domain remain intuitive and capricious in the extreme.

The analyst or psychodynamically oriented clinician might respond that interactions between an experimenter and his or her subject(s) might themselves be subject to unconscious processes that the experimenter simply cannot explain within a purely empirical framework; or that unless the experiment is understood as a specific kind of social interaction—albeit a somewhat anomalous one—it may be impossible to disentangle supposedly extraneous variables from the observed results or to generalize from these to the processes that determine the subject's behavior in her or his everyday life-world (for example, Fromm, 1973, pp. 70–76).

Given the extreme differences in these methodological positions and the practices from which they derive, the occasional similarities in results are all the more intriguing. The research and conclusions of two of Fromm's contemporaries serve as useful examples.

Solomon Asch

In the late 1940s and early 1950s Solomon Asch conducted a series of experiments to measure the social distribution of a trait he called "independence," that is, independent judgment. In his now-famous experiments, Asch brought a naive subject into a room of confederates who had been instructed to falsify their answers in response to a simple perceptual test, in which they were asked to say which of three lines on one graph corresponded in length to a single line on another, adjacent illustration. In short, Asch pitted his subjects against a unanimous majority. At first he kept the discrepancies between the various line lengths constant. Then he introduced some variation by widening or diminishing the perceptual discrepancies favored by confederates. Eventually he allowed the semblance of a monolithic consensus to diminish by allowing one or more confederates to differ from the prevailing view or even offer the correct answer. The results were startling: only 20 percent of Asch's subjects proved capable of independent judgment in the face of a monolithic consensus. Of these, many found the experience stressful and perplexing. By his own

account, Asch was not prepared for either the prevalence of conformist behavior or the degree of tension and conflict engendered by the
experimental proceedings, both among those who dissented and
among those who capitulated (more or less) to group pressure (personal communication, May 4, 1988).

Many of the assumptions that informed Asch's experimental research were convergent with Fromm's. Asch began with the premise
that—in the abstract, at any rate—consensus is not truth. In his own
words:

> Agreement cannot have validity if it is merely a pooling of unreliable
> and untrustworthy processes of individuals. The value and dignity of
> agreement rest on the value and dignity of individual observers and
> thinkers . . . Consensus is valid only to the extent to which each individ-
> ual asserts his own relation to facts and retains his individuality; there
> can be no genuine agreement about facts or principles unless each
> adheres to the testimony of his experience and steadfastly maintains his
> hold on reality . . . In this sense it follows that truth does not belong to
> groups or societies. The group and its consensus are not a criterion of
> truth; rather they themselves must submit to the requirements of valid-
> ity.   (1952, pp. 493–494)

Asch noted, furthermore, that the ability to maintain one's hold on
reality is not equally distributed in the population at large. Accordingly, he suggested:

> The task of investigation is first to describe the properties of those who
> are socially independent and of those who cannot maintain a stand
> under opposition and then to inquire into the conditions responsible for
> modes of action so different . . . Observation suggests . . . a broad hy-
> pothesis: that individual immunity to distortion by group pressure is a
> function of the person's relation to himself and others. Independence
> always requires some assertion about the self . . . It is therefore an
> expression of a certain confidence about the self and its relation to
> others. Yielding on the other hand is a sign of a lack of stability or
> confidence in these relations. It marks an inability to resist or reject
> others by an open assertion of one's dissident personal judgment. The
> independent person possesses certain sources of strength within himself
> that enable him to bear a brief ordeal, whereas the yielding person can
> find safety only by merging anonymously with the group. It would
> however be wrong to conclude that those who are not independent feel
> more deeply the need of close contact with others; the manner in which

they are willing to achieve this closeness casts doubt on this assumption . . .

If we reject, as I think we should, the assumption that the differences in question are constitutional, we shall want to inquire into the social and personal experiences that are responsible for them . . . In particular, it would be necessary to examine what social relations and demands further personal autonomy and what conditions hamper its development. The search for clarification will have . . . to start with the proposition . . . that social life makes a double demand on us: to rely upon others with trust and to become individuals who can assert our own reality . . . We may suppose that this aim can be achieved under favorable circumstances, but even then not without struggle . . . But there are conditions less favorable for development which, while encouraging individuals to live in a wider and richer world than the individual can encompass alone, also injure and undermine him. This happens when social circumstances stifle the individual's impulses and deny them expression . . . Since in the early years the individual is particularly dependent on consensus, he may come to define his self in terms of the evaluations others have of him and find a measure of safety in the procedure. To live up to the demands of others he may find it necessary to blunt his experiences, to develop a self that is shadowy, and to become superficial about the character of others. Such conditions impair the ability to trust; at the same time they injure one's capacity to do without support on those occasions that demand it. Those who yield act at times as if they had entered a compact which will guarantee them a minimum of safety at the cost of self-restriction. It is probable that self-limitation is achieved by a restriction of awareness and that the course of the process is largely unknown to its actors.

The present discussion converges in a difficult and intriguing problem: the relation between character and social action. Is there a describable relation between the event considered in its dependence on the individual and its social function? When extended beyond the present confines the question becomes one of the relation between the social import of action and its psychological foundations in the individual or of the relation between ideology and character.   (1952, pp. 498–499)

Indeed. And although he may not have been aware of it, in describing the yielding type Asch was also describing many of the features of Fromm's "marketing character": the simultaneous impairment of self-confidence and basic trust, an overreliance on how others perceive one, a symbiotic dependence on others that precludes genuine intimacy and a "shadowy" sense of self; all to the detriment of fundamental needs to relate oneself actively to the world and to express oneself truthfully without fear of reprisal.

Stanley Milgram

Milgram's best-known research was oriented not to conformity or perception, but to obedience. In a forceful, compelling, and deeply disturbing way, Milgram asked whether a nominally democratic American government during the Vietnam era could guarantee its own citizenry protection from the ravages of "malevolent authority." On the basis of his experiments and more or less contemporaneous events associated with the Vietnam war, Milgram ventured to answer in the negative (1974, p. 189).

Milgram's subjects were told that they were taking part in an experiment on learning. When the "learner"—a confederate of the experimenter's who was hidden behind a screen—gave an incorrect response to the "teacher's" (subject's) questions, the subject was instructed to administer electrical shocks of increasing intensity to the confederate, who, though not actually shocked in these proceedings, acted as if he were and, after escalating protests, pretended to lapse into unconsciousness.

Once again the results were startling. Only a minority of subjects refused to participate when the "learner" feigned protest and physical pain, and a considerable number "shocked" the experimenter's confederate into "unconsciousness." The willingness to obey, Milgram noted, was abetted by the experimenter's repeated insistence that he alone would take full responsibility for the proceedings. Milgram then drew a distinction between obedience and conformity:

> Asch's subjects *conform* to the group. The subjects in the present experiment *obey* the experimenter. Obedience and conformity both refer to the abdication of initiative to an external source. But they differ in the following important ways:
>
> 1. *Hierarchy.* Obedience to authority occurs within a hierarchical structure in which the actor feels that the person above has a right to prescribe behavior. Conformity regulates the behavior among those of equal status; obedience links one status to another.
> 2. *Imitation.* Conformity is imitation but obedience is not. Conformity leads to homogenization of behavior, as the influenced person comes to adopt the behavior of peers. In obedience, there is com-

pliance without imitation of the influencing source. A soldier does not repeat an order given to him but carries it out.

3. *Explicitness.* In obedience, the prescription for action is explicit, taking the form of an order or command. In conformity, the requirement of going along with the group often remains implicit. Thus, in Asch's experiment on group pressure, there is no overt requirement made by group members that the subject go along with them. The action is spontaneously adopted by the subject. Indeed, many subjects would resist an explicit demand by group members to conform, for the situation is defined as one consisting of equals who have no right to order each other about.

4. *Voluntarism.* The clearest distinction between obedience and conformity, however, occurs after the fact—that is, in the manner in which subjects explain their behavior. Subjects *deny* conformity and *embrace* obedience as the explanation of their actions . . . In Asch's experiments on group pressure, subjects typically understate the degree to which their actions were influenced by members of the group. They belittle the group effect and try to play up their own autonomy, even when they have yielded to the group on every trial. They often insist that if they made errors in judgment, these were nonetheless their own errors, attributable to their faulty vision or bad judgment . . .

In the obedience experiment, the reaction is diametrically opposed. Here the subject explains his actions of shocking the victim by denying any personal involvement and attributing his behavior exclusively to an external requirement imposed by authority. Thus, while the conforming subject insists that his autonomy was not impaired by the group, the obedient subject asserts that he had no autonomy in the matter of shocking the victim and that his actions were completely out of his hands. (1974, pp. 114–115)

Milgram then furnished a vivid illustration of how group pressure can undermine, rather than reinforce, obedience to authority; particularly when that authority is experienced as brutal or unjust. In a slightly altered experiment, three "teachers," two of whom were the experimenter's confederates, were instructed to shock a "learner" (another confederate) in regular succession in response to "wrong" answers. When the two teacher-collaborators refused to cross a certain threshold, the pressure on the naive subject to refuse obedience to the experimenter was correspondingly higher (Milgram, 1974, pp. 116–122).

If we grant Milgram's categorical distinction between obedience and conformity, then by implication, if not by conscious design, his study demonstrates the persistence of simple obedience in a nominally conformist milieu. However, Milgram overstated the differences between obedience and conformity. He allowed that both involve the abdication of "initiative" to an external source, but he did not emphasize sufficiently that both phenomena represent (contextually specific) choices to avoid being labeled as (or feeling like) an outsider or disruptive agent in the prevailing scheme of social relations.

This is not a trivial issue, since it raises the problem of false consciousness, which Milgram circumvents completely. Some of Asch's conformist subjects were doubly afflicted with false consciousness, first by falsifying their sensory experience, and then by making wildly irrational claims that they had exercised autonomous judgment throughout. By contrast, Milgram's obedient subjects *consciously* abdicated their responsibility and accordingly did *not* misconstrue or misperceive objects or events in their external surround. But—and this is crucial—Milgram's subjects *were not aware of having made a deliberate choice to avoid a certain outcome—namely, punishment or ostracism—at the expense of another person's physical integrity.* Does one really "abdicate" responsibility for such a choice, or does one merely repress the awareness of its implications? Milgram becomes even less convincing on this score when he speaks of "abdication of initiative" rather than of responsibility, but characterizes obedience—already described as "the abdication of initiative"—as being marked by a transition to an agentic state, when it is precisely the *lack* of personal agency that supposedly characterizes the obedient subject, since his sole responsibility—in his own mind, at any rate—is to the authority in question.

Milgram's concept of the agentic shift, though fascinating from a descriptive standpoint, is tied to a host of gratuitous cybernetic and evolutionary assumptions. Milgram observes that some measure of obedience or hierarchy is present in all human societies. He then assumes that the organism alternates between two ego-states: an autonomous or self-directed one, in which an instinctual drive toward indiscriminate aggression is checked in the interests of sociability; and another, agentic one, in which the individual's aggression toward others is aroused in deference to those in authority in the perceived interests of group hegemony. When the individual shifts from a sociable and autonomous to a heteronomous (or obedient/

aggressive) ego-state—whatever that may be—he supposedly undergoes an agentic shift and a corresponding change in the nature of his motivation and experience.

Like Freud, then, Milgram assumes that aggression is an instinct that is constantly operative, and not a product of social conditions or of the breakdown or perversion of our innate sociability. Moreover, like Freud, Milgram assumes an unbroken continuity between the domains of natural history and human history, as if hierarchy in human society were chiefly a result of natural selection. By assuming that dominance, authority, and obedience are endemic to all societies on *biological* grounds, Milgram overlooks one of the most important features of his own analysis, namely, that to compel obedience, an authority must be experienced as being a legitimate authority, as representative of society, or as both. Problems of social legitimacy and political representation have no analogue in the animal kingdom for the simple reason that these matters are not regulated by instinct, but by historic precedent and political culture, by considerations of language and faith, by (real and coerced) consent, and by the conflicting interests of various groups or classes, and the prevailing conceptions of property and human rights characteristic of each.[4]

Fromm and His Mainstream Contemporaries

Asch's views on the specious character of a forced or artificial consensus are identical in spirit with Fromm's. Like Fromm, he sees the role of group pressure on the falsification of judgment as a problem bearing on the relationship between character and ideology. Moreover, his experiments and conclusions lend plausibility to Fromm's characterization of contemporary social character and to his overarching contention that fear of isolation or ostracism is the cause of repression or "restriction of awareness" (Fromm, 1935a, 1962) and represents a problem we all confront—more or less successfully—at some point in our development.

Having made a heuristic distinction between conformity and obedience, Milgram thought that his studies of obedience addressed an entirely different phenomenon from the one studied by Asch. And as proof he cited the following circumstance: Asch's subjects often assumed responsibility for perceptual judgments they made, when in fact they had distrusted their own senses and deferred to the prevailing consensus. Milgram's subjects, by contrast, consciously disclaimed responsibility for their actions, but without falsifying their perception of events in their environmental surround.

However, Milgram's explanation of the observed phenomenon suffers from some serious oversights. In disclaiming personal responsibility—or in shifting to Milgram's hypothetical agentic state, in which their sole responsibility is to the person in command—Milgram's subjects disowned any meaningful responsibility for a personal choice, namely, the choice to avoid disrupting the experiment, or breaking the chain of command, by inflicting pain on another human being. Whatever moral construction one may attach to this act, this was *their* choice. If they chose not to own their choice and its consequences, both for themselves and for the victim, we are as entitled to speak of a false consciousness or falsification of judgment as we would be with many of Asch's subjects, although in Milgram's experiments it was internal rather than external reality that was falsified. To invoke a hypothetical shift in ego or mental states to account for subjects' behavior is utterly unnecessary and may be nothing more than an abject capitulation to the experimental subject's false consciousness.

Finally, despite his meticulous observations of behavior in the laboratory, Milgram's speculative biology was simply bad science and a transparent recourse to a reified naturalism. Along with our intelligence, of course, obedience and hierarchy may have secured our dominance in the food chain in the course of natural selection, as Milgram suggests. But experience suggests that it is precisely our lack of instinctual programming—the very thing that enables us to be so intelligent, in evolutionary and neurological terms—that makes this kind of obedience possible and effective. Leaving sociobiology aside, it is more economical to suppose that in the absence of a better solution, unquestioning obedience to a higher authority answers (in a perverse sort of way) to existential needs that emerge as a consequence of our rupture with the animal kingdom, and the terrors of emergent self-consciousness.

7 Appraisals of Fromm by Psychologists and Psychiatrists

Among the published responses of psychologists and psychiatrists who attempted an overall appraisal of Fromm's work, the earlier critiques tend to be the more thoughtful and substantive, probably because the critic is likely to have known Fromm personally. In the flurry of responses to Fromm's work in the 1940s and 1950s, it is clear that personal relationships with Fromm decisively colored his reception by psychologists and mental health professionals.

Otto Fenichel

Otto Fenichel knew Fromm at the Berlin Psychoanalytic Institute. Fromm, like Reich, participated in Fenichel's *Kinderseminar,* an informal gathering of left-leaning analytic trainees and staff (Jacoby, 1983, p. 67). Fenichel's published responses to Fromm's work reflect several years of acquaintance and private correspondence (ibid., pp. 107–110). For example, two years after Reich's vituperative "critique" of Fromm in 1934—to which Fromm did not respond publicly—Fenichel reproached Fromm for distancing himself from Reich and for minimizing the latter's pioneering contributions. Fromm explained his reluctance to cite Reich "on personal as well as factual grounds"; he found Reich's "pathological self-love and arrogance" insufferable and believed that Reich did not really understand Marx (ibid., p. 109). Evidently, Fenichel sympathized with Fromm at that time.

However, Fenichel did not sympathize with the direction Fromm's work took after 1935. In a review of *Escape from Freedom* in 1944,

Fenichel wrote: "Instead of studying the interrelations of erogenous zones and object relationships, they [Fromm and Kardiner] think statically, and are of the opinion that the insight into the role of object relationships contradicts the importance of erogenous zones" (quoted in Jacoby, 1975, p. 96).

This comment indicates that Fenichel was familiar with Fromm's early papers and perceived *Escape from Freedom* as an extension of them. And rightly so. Since 1934, Fromm had questioned whether the severity of clinical psychopathology could be gauged by situating a symptom, conflict, or character trait at some hypothetical point along an ostensibly preprogrammed ontogenetic sequence—an assumption that is axiomatic to orthodox theorizing. Today such reservations about the orthodox model of psychosexual development have become quite commonplace and are openly endorsed by mainstream psychoanalysts (for example, Kernberg, 1980, pp. 3–4). Still, Fenichel's charge that Fromm's discussion of drives, such as a drive to work or to "enjoy nature's beauty," were "very abstract, and in comparison with Freud's . . . analysis of the instinctual attitude, very vague" (quoted in Jacoby, 1975, p. 96), was perfectly just. In 1944, when the review appeared, Fromm had not yet articulated his philosophical anthropology or his concept of existential needs. Even if he had, however, Fenichel would not have been satisfied. As Fenichel had written earlier, in response to Karen Horney's work, "My conviction . . . is that the value of psychoanalysis as a natural scientific psychology is rooted in its being an instinctivistic and genetic psychology" (quoted in ibid., p. 97). Fenichel obviously had a great deal invested in the idea of psychoanalysis as a "natural scientific psychology." But he failed to acknowledge how tenuous the Lamarkian underpinnings of Freud's psychobiology actually were, and he was oblivious to its ideological subtext. Fromm, for all his faults, was not.

Patrick Mullahy

Patrick Mullahy's *Oedipus: Myth and Complex* (1948) presented the first synoptic overview of the various psychoanalytic schools in terms of their own inner logic and objective merits without indulging in sectarian rancor or name-calling. Like Fromm, Mullahy taught at the William Alanson White Institute, and it is therefore no accident that

Fromm wrote the introduction to this historic volume. Indeed, as Mullahy relates in the preface, Fromm and he initially intended to collaborate on the book. When that proved impossible, Fromm gave him access to an unpublished manuscript on Bachofen and the Oedipus myth to use (Mullahy, 1948, p. xvi). No doubt as a result, Mullahy's summary of Fromm's views was crisp, incisive, and sympathetic, and his discussion of Bachofen remains the best in the secondary literature.[1]

Mullahy's training in psychology and philosophy enabled him to discern dimensions in Jung, Rank, and Fromm that had been buried or dismissed by the orthodox. While this open-mindedness operated to the benefit of the dissident fringe (and Mullahy's readership), the chief beneficiary of Mullahy's broad scholarship was probably Fromm. In his concluding remarks, Mullahy noted:

> Fromm brings to his work a wide knowledge of sociology, anthropology and history. For this reason, if not for others, his writings have a profundity which those of most psychoanalysts lack. Fromm does not suffer from the illusion that all psychological knowledge began with Freud— or with Fromm. An Aristotle, a Spinoza, a Meister Eckhardt, a Kafka may not have known much about the so called libido, but they knew a great deal more about other matters—perhaps ultimately much more important matters—concerning what has traditionally been called man's spirit.   (1948, p. 331)

Clearly, Mullahy found Fromm's spirituality and ethical orientation deeply appealing. This fact registers in the mildness of his criticism. Nevertheless, Mullahy thought that Fromm made insufficient allowance for the role of science and technology in the development of modern capitalism, treating it as part and parcel of the economic sphere rather than as a causal force in its own right (1948, p. 332). Moreover, in Mullahy's estimation, Fromm was not sufficiently an "interactionist" in his description of social and psychological processes. Finally, Mullahy voiced what today would be termed a cognitive or cognitive-behaviorist objection to Fromm's theory of character; one anticipated in Sullivan's theory. Like most analysts, said Mullahy, Fromm took the patient's emotional attitude to be "primary" and regarded ideas, judgments, and so on as derivative manifestations of underlying emotional dispositions. (See, for example, Fromm, 1961c, pp. 3–4.) Mullahy, to the contrary, held that ideas affect one's emotional dispositions and that "ideas and judgments, for example, instead of being a result of character, are as efficacious in the constitution of character as anything else" (1948, p. 333).

Mullahy's criticism reflects Sullivan's influence. But it is interesting to historians of psychology because it harks back to a rationalist theory of the relationship between thought and affect that derives from Descartes, Spinoza, and Leibniz, in which affects are construed as false or mistaken ideas, or as the passions engendered by them. J. F. Herbart inherited this rationalistic bias from Christian Wolff, Leibniz' pupil and expositor. Freud was indebted to Herbart for his theory of repression and his insistence that all psychic activity is determined by lawful interactions among hypothetical quantities of mental energy (Ricoeur, 1970). But following Schopenhauer and Nietzsche, Freud reversed the terms of the equation by insisting on the primacy of affect, suggesting that ideas merely express unconscious volitions and fantasies that are adapted in varying degrees to existential actualities. Fromm's experience of human irrationality during the First World War made him inclined to accept this view of human affairs, and so he kept faith with Freud in this respect, without trying to disentangle or resolve these theoretical antinomies or put them in historical perspective.

Today the debate about the primacy of affect or cognition continues. Among cognitive theorists in particular, classical rationalism still has several respected representatives, although many theorists now emphasize that affect and cognition operate simultaneously in complex reciprocal interactions, with neither taking precedence (for example, Greenberg and Safran, 1984; Safran and Greenberg, 1987). Ernst Schachtel, who thought extensively about this subject, came to more or less the same conclusion (1959). Fromm's neglect of this issue, which is central to psychological theorizing, demonstrates his almost exclusive preoccupation with the ethical side of philosophy and his relative lack of interest in the relationship between affect and cognition, the mind-body problem, and the overarching problems and perplexities of Western metaphysics (Funk, 1984, pp. 46–47).

Clara Thompson

Clara Thompson was not a psychologist or a philosopher. Like Reich, Fenichel, and most other psychoanalysts at the time, she was a psychiatrist. Her *Psychoanalysis: Evolution and Development* (1950) was

notable because it discussed the ideas of Jung and Rank and rehabilitated two members of Freud's loyal opposition, Georg Groddeck and
Sandor Ferenczi. (Thompson had studied with Ferenczi and Fromm,
both of whom were admirers of Groddeck.) Like Mullahy, Thompson
was also close to Sullivan and taught at the William Alanson White.
Her exposition of Fromm was more schematic than Mullahy's with
respect to personality theory, but more explicit on clinical topics such
as character defenses and anxiety. For example, she noted that in
emphasizing respect for the patient, Fromm had much in common
with Jung and Rank (ibid., p. 204). Still, she warned:

> Freud has emphasized that the analyst must be free from any tendency
> to condemn the patient, that he must not have any emotional stake in
> what kind of person the patient becomes. Fromm agrees with this but
> points out that the analyst's convictions about what is good for man
> must play some part in his goal of therapy. He would use value judg-
> ments in choosing patients for treatment in the first place. A marked
> insincerity of attitude in a prospective patient, for instance, would point
> to the likelihood of unsuccessful therapy. There are certain dangers in
> this approach of Fromm's. A note of moral condemnation can easily slip
> in, and one may find oneself sitting in judgment on the patient, al-
> though I'm sure Fromm's attitude is far from this.   (Ibid., pp. 210–211)

Actually, according to Michael Maccoby and Herbert Spiegel (personal communications), what Thompson described as an incipient
danger was in fact the chief shortcoming of Fromm's therapeutic
posture. Thompson's fondness for Fromm and her respect for his
skills as a clinician may have made her reluctant to acknowledge this
in public. Or perhaps this characteristic weakness was not in evidence
at the time she wrote. Thompson's final remarks on Fromm and
Sullivan (1964, chap. 11) are a transparent attempt to mediate and
downplay what were by then strong personal and theoretical differences between the two men and their respective followers by emphasizing their essential complementarity. The result is stimulating reading in substantive terms. But it also reflects strongly Thompson's
conciliatory temperament and gifts and her peacemaking role in the
internal affairs of the William Alanson White.[2]

Rollo May

Rollo May's *The Meaning of Anxiety* (1950) appeared in the same year
as Thompson's *Psychoanalysis* and was followed in 1953 by *Man's*

Search for Himself. Though never a close friend of Fromm's, May was his analysand, and among the few psychologists to welcome Fromm's extensive scholarship and rigorous eclecticism without impugning his clinical credentials. This fact alone is remarkable. After all, Fromm's insistence that psychological phenomena be addressed in historical context—that problems and processes studied in economics, anthropology, sociology, theology, and ethics are not merely relevant but integral to a properly psychological understanding—would have struck a responsive chord in Wilhelm Wundt, Wilhelm Dilthey, or Max or Alfred Weber. But this outlook is anathema to those committed to a rigid division between psychology and other disciplines, and has contributed enormously to the widespread perception of Fromm as a dilettante or eccentric. By commending Fromm for the attributes that damned him in the eyes of his colleagues, May was indirectly passing judgment on many of Fromm's detractors, past, present and future.

However, elements of personal antagonism soon surfaced. John Kerr recalls Fromm's close friend Anna Gourevitch remarking that May cribbed the material for *Man's Search for Meaning* directly from his analysis with Fromm (personal communication, July 24, 1987). If Gourevitch in fact believed this to be the case, then Fromm probably did as well. Another factor in the estrangement between Fromm and May was that as May's involvement with existential and humanistic psychology increased, he became more anti-Freudian. Fromm, though a forthright critic of the psychoanalytic movement, continued to alternate between sharp criticism and celebrations of Freud's genius. The price Fromm paid for his continuing loyalty to Freud was that as humanistic and existential psychology movements burgeoned in America, the leading spokespeople for these movements—including May—increasingly ignored him.

From its inception, humanistic psychology in America declared psychoanalysis and behaviorism as its two chief enemies, calling itself "the Third Force" in psychology (Fuller, 1986, chap. 7). Although Fromm (among others) was cited as a precursor to the movement in a 1961 manifesto by Anthony Sutich (ibid., p. 151), he evidently refused the honor. In 1963, in an inaugural address for the new building housing the psychoanalytic wing at the Autonomous University of Mexico (reprinted as Fromm, 1975), Fromm also predicted the coming of a third force in psychology, psychiatry, and psychoanalysis.

However, he failed to cite a single American psychologist or to address the widespread perception among psychologists at that time that psychoanalysis is inimical to humanism. Indeed, Fromm argued that, despite its instinctivist limitations, Freudian theory is rooted in the same soil as Renaissance humanism and must be renewed and transformed, not discarded. From then on, Fromm refused to engage in dialogue with American humanistic psychology.

It is therefore not surprising that May's references to Fromm dwindled and became less flattering after the late 1950s. In *Power and Innocence,* for example, May criticized Reich and Fromm for oversimplifying the relationship between "the rebel" and society:

> Contemporary writers all the way from Reich to Fromm speak indignantly of society, venting their irritation with such words as "bureaucratic," "juggernaut," "supertechnocratic," implying all the while that it is society's fault that we are the way we are. On one hand, this arises from a utopianism—the expectation that when we develop a society which trains us rightly, we'll all be in fine shape. On the other hand, it is like a child wheedling his parents because they aren't taller or in some other way different from what they ought to be. All of which they cannot be expected to be . . . The rebel is a split personality in that he realizes his society nursed him, met his needs, gave him security to develop his potentialities; yet he smarts under its constraints and finds it stifling. (1967, p. 227)

Significantly, these remarks, which affect a tone of earthy common sense, describe Fromm as a writer rather than a psychoanalyst or social theorist and implicitly compare him to a spoiled, unreasonable child. Moreover, the phrase "all the way from Reich to Fromm" implies a breadth of perspective that did not exist, since the two were closely allied. Most important, there are no quotations from Fromm's own psychology of rebellion, which would have discredited May's attributions. In view of the ad hominem nature of the critique, the charge that Fromm did not really understand "the rebel" sounds suspiciously autobiographical.

In fairness to May, however, the dynamics between Fromm and him were inevitably complicated by the ideological warfare between Freudians and humanistic psychologists in the 1960s and 1970s. As the battle progressed, Fromm was stranded on the sidelines. He felt, no doubt, like a voice in the wilderness, with no allies or interlocutors in either camp. But he also thrived in his prophetic, outsider status.

Perhaps he preferred being ignored to the indignity of debating people
he perceived as posturing illiterates who did not understand Freud or
humanism deeply.[3]

G. S. Brett and R. S. Peters

R. S. Peters' abridged, one-volume edition of *Brett's History of Psychology* (1965) brought Brett's three-volume classic, published in 1912,
up to date with a concluding chapter written collaboratively by Peters
and various colleagues. (Consequently, it is hard to know precisely
whose opinion the contents represent.) The reference to Fromm is
perfunctory, but noteworthy in that it welcomes the kind of Freudo-
Marxist synthesis heralded by *Escape from Freedom* (1941), published
as *Fear of Freedom* in Britain. I quote in full.

> A "Neo-Freudian" who has suggested that psycho-analysis should have
> a social rather than a biological orientation is Fromm. In his *Fear of
> Freedom* (1942), for instance, he attempted to show the interaction
> between the psychological and sociological factors and to supplement
> the psycho-analytic interpretation of certain political and religious atti-
> tudes by a sociological theory of the economic determinants of social
> change taken from writers like Marx and Tawney. This attempt to work
> out the interrelation of the insights of Marx and Freud is most suggestive
> and welcome after the oversimplified theories of both. It is also charac-
> teristic of the twentieth-century trend away from the tendency to inter-
> pret social phenomena in exclusively psychological terms. (Brett,
> 1965, p. 715)

This brief mention of *Escape from Freedom* is followed by a somewhat lengthier description of Kardiner's theory of basic personality
structure and by the following caveat:

> These examples are sufficient to show the way in which social science is
> making its influence felt on psychoanalysis. It is only fair to Freud,
> however, to say that he was well aware of the differences between
> cultures and that his great importance lay in demonstrating the modi-
> fication of instinctive drives when they came up against normative
> pressures. No man was more conscious of the common saying that all
> psychology is social psychology . . . Freud started off with a predomi-
> nantly biological orientation. But he came to see more and more the

infinite plasticity of human beings and the determining influence of their social relationships. (Ibid., pp. 715–716)

Clearly, whoever wrote these passages had not read Fromm's German-language publications—notably "The Dogma of Christ" (1930a) and "The Method and Function of an Analytic Social Psychology" (1932a), in which Kardiner's idea of a basic personality structure is vividly prefigured. Kardiner did not present his theory of the basic personality until 1939, in *The Individual and His Society,* and the fact that Fromm's earlier work was not mentioned at this juncture suggests that Peters and his colleagues were simply ignorant of it. Though regrettable, this gap in their knowledge is scarcely surprising. *Escape from Freedom* was Fromm's first book in English, and most of Fromm's English-speaking evaluators begin with that work.

Ruth Munroe

Ruth Munroe, author of *Schools of Psychoanalytic Thought* (1955), was a psychologist who, like Fenichel, found Fromm's disregard of Freud's psychosexual theories cause for concern.

> I state the argument *ad absurdum,* but I am not very much impressed by casual acknowledgment of bodily needs as "obvious but psychologically unimportant." What does the infant know beyond the bodily needs? On what other basis does he learn than by elaboration and correction of what he already "knows"? Can we say, with Fromm, that the infant has biological needs, and so does the adult, but that human needs start where the biological needs leave off? This is true enough, but specifically human needs originate in infancy when the child *who wants to move his bowels* is already in human relationship with his parents, so that his handling of his anal impulses is "humanized" from the beginning. (1955, p. 418)

And again:

> One may criticize the libido theory of Freud as neglecting half or more than half the story; one may feel that the actual stages of development in these systems have not been perfectly delineated . . . Nevertheless . . . it seems to me quite simply wrong to make a positive point of ignoring the sexual systems as factors in the development of the human psyche. Any sensitive, unbiased study of the young child prior to gross cultural

intervention shows spontaneous concern with "sexual" areas—oral, anal and genital.   (Ibid., p. 419)

Overall, however, Munroe's response to Fromm—by contrast with Fenichel's—was positive. She acknowledged that the inescapable certainty of one's own death poses an existential problem. And like Fromm, she distinguished the class of existential problems from the manifold social and historical dichotomies that, in Fromm's estimation, are capable of transcendence in human history (such as poverty and war), and without dismissing him as hopelessly utopian (ibid., pp. 352–353).

Furthermore, Munroe grasped the role played in Fromm's system by the concepts of individuation and the need for relatedness to others, and she showed a keen appreciation for his analysis of Nazi psychology (1955, p. 390). She gave qualified endorsement to Fromm's notion of the marketing orientation, which she recognized as Fromm's distinctive contribution, with no analogue in Freud's ontogenetic schema and, by implication, no specific anchor in somatic organization (ibid., pp. 393–394). However, like David Riesman, Munroe argued that although the marketing orientation is endemic to contemporary American life, Fromm overlooked positive changes in social interaction that accrued with the demise of old-fashioned patriarchal authority (ibid., pp. 475–476).

However, the distinctive nature of Fromm's clinical contribution is not apparent in Munroe's assessment, and Fromm contributed to this failing. Munroe devoted an entire chapter to the concepts of pathology and treatment among Alfred Adler, Karen Horney, H. S. Sullivan, and Fromm. She showed insight and sensitivity about their differences concerning personality dynamics and other topics. But she had little to say about Fromm's views of the treatment situation; far less, in fact, than she said about any of his contemporaries. She explained the omission thus: "In a personal communication, Fromm remarks that his position on these matters is much closer to Freud's than to Horney's. Since he has not written much about treatment procedures as such, I shall not try to elaborate" (1955, p. 518). Furthermore, according to Munroe,

> Fromm himself does not intend that his philosophical analysis be used directly in psychoanalysis. I dwell on this because enthusiastic lay readers of his books and critical psychoanalytic colleagues often assume a

much more immediate connection between theory and practice than is at all justified. Fromm's special contribution does not lie in the area of refined analysis of the individual. Here, like any good practicing psychoanalyst, he uses the contributions of other people and would himself consider direct application of his philosophical orientation to treatment of the individual as a travesty upon psychoanalysis.   (Ibid., p. 474)

The problem with this passage is that it is not clear from the context whether what Munroe says about Fromm's attitude toward his ideas in the clinical context is based on his written or spoken communications, or whether the suggestion that philosophical formulations have little relevance in his clinical orientation is a gratuitous assertion designed to defend Fromm from harping critics or to defend an image of Fromm existing in her own mind. If Munroe's attributions stem from a statement by Fromm himself, then Fromm contributed directly to the widespread perception of himself as having nothing distinctive to say about treatment. On the other hand, if these assertions were merely conjectures by Munroe, however well intended, they illustrate how Fromm's reticence about treatment issues prompted people to imagine either that he did or did not use these ideas in treatment, since either scenario is equally conceivable in the absence of explicit statements to the contrary.

According to Benjamin Wolstein, a psychologist training with Fromm at the time, Fromm in 1955 endorsed a return to the "classical technique" of the years 1915–1917 by his trainees at the William Alanson White (Wolstein, 1981, p. 484). This account suggests that Fromm's response to Munroe reflected how Fromm saw his own conduct as a clinician. But clinicians who worked with Fromm after 1955 thought otherwise. In conversations with the author, Marianne Eckardt (1987), Maurice Green (1988), Michael Maccoby (1985), Herbert Spiegel (1987), and Paul Wachtel (1986) all recalled that Fromm's penchant for moralizing occasionally colored his formulations of clinical case material and could intrude in face-to-face interviews as well.

Wolstein observes that Fromm's long-promised book on technique might have clarified matters somewhat (1981, p. 484). But even if it had materialized, it would merely have presented Fromm's views on treatment, with no clear evidence about his practical conduct of an analysis. In the absence of a definitive answer, it seems plausible to suppose that Fromm himself was unclear on this issue, but that before

1955 he saw himself practicing in a (more or less) orthodox mold, notwithstanding his critique of neutrality (1935a) and public perceptions to the contrary.

Calvin Hall and Gardner Lindzey

Calvin Hall and Gardner Lindzey, in their first appraisal of Fromm (1954), described him as being "more influenced than influencing" (p. 174) on the American scene, and were ignorant of Fromm's early methodological papers—an omission that, to all appearances, they never made good. Hall and Lindzey based their evaluation on an extensive survey of current textbooks in social psychology. And indeed, my own survey of several textbooks from this period—*Theory and Problems of Social Psychology* (Krech and Crutchfield, 1948), *An Outline of Social Psychology* (Sherif and Sherif, 1948), and *Social Psychology* (Asch, 1952)—shows that Fromm is cited not at all or only perfunctorily. *An Outline of Social Psychology,* for example, briefly paraphrased Fromm's discussion of changes in social character from feudalism through the modern period in *Escape from Freedom* (1941) in connection with the effects of technology on collective behavior. Even the revised edition (Sherif and Sherif, 1956, pp. 712–713) contained no reference to the "marketing character," although Fromm's views on the subject had by then been in print for almost a decade. In short, if Sherif and Sherif are any indication it seems reasonable to conclude that after *Escape from Freedom,* Fromm was ignored by social psychologists. Apparently, Hall and Lindzey's characterization of Fromm's social psychology as derivative, though fundamentally mistaken, reflected an emerging consensus within the field.

Hall and Lindzey's *Theories of Personality,* published in 1957, was advertised as "the first objective and comprehensive review of the major theories of personality" and was addressed to students of personality theory rather than social psychology. It has gone through several editions and is still used extensively as an introductory text in most universities. As a result, and in sharp contrast to their neglect of Fromm's social psychology, Hall and Lindzey ensured that most personality theorists in North America became vaguely conversant with Fromm's ideas, although none attempted to apply those ideas empirically.

Given the air of studied neutrality that attaches to treatments of this sort, it is impossible to determine Hall and Lindzey's attitude toward Fromm's theory of personality. On the whole, it seems to have been quite positive. Within a mere four pages, they conveyed a tolerably accurate and sympathetic account of Fromm's concepts of individuation versus symbiosis, of existential needs, and of the impact of social and historical conditions and contingencies on the unfolding or alienation of the person.

But there are several areas in the first edition where Hall and Lindzey misguided their readers. For one thing, they classified Fromm along with Neal Miller, Gardner Murphy, John Dollard, Kurt Lewin, and Sullivan as a "field theorist," because of his emphasis on the environmental determinants of personality. This label misleadingly implies some underlying uniformity or consensus among these theorists on the nature of the "field." To Fromm the chief "field" determinants affecting personality were class origins and affiliations, prevailing methods of the production and distribution, the psychology of work, and so on. If class structure, the family milieu, and the working environment constitute "fields," then Fromm was a "field theorist." But calling him a field theorist without further qualification is apt to be misleading.

A more serious shortcoming is that Hall and Lindzey classed Fromm among "environmentalists," along with Horney, Sullivan, Lewin, and Carl Rogers, who minimize the impact of heredity on personality (1957, p. 542). This is simply a misreading. Fromm always emphasized the importance of innate disposition. Personality, for Fromm, consists of a combination of the innate and the acquired—or, in his own terminology, of "temperament" and "character" (1947, pp. 59–62). When acquired traits (character) conflict with one's innate dispositions (temperament), one becomes chronically neurotic and insecure, with a false or tenuous sense of identity. An important goal of therapy, according to Fromm, is to disentangle the real self from characterological trends that have been superimposed by socialization, and then to affirm and strengthen those features that promote health and happiness, even if they conflict with prevailing norms of conduct and belief (Thompson, 1950, p. 210; Fromm, 1980, pp. 65–66).[4]

Another serious misconception Hall and Lindzey fostered was that Fromm was an "intuitive" theorist, who never engaged in any empirical research (1957). Plainly, they were not aware of Fromm's pioneering research among the working class in Weimar Germany that Fromm undertook in 1929 and 1930, or the massive study of a Mexican village that commenced that same year.

Finally, in characterizing him as naively utopian, Hall and Lindzey utterly failed to appreciate the tragic dimension in Fromm. They noted that in Fromm's idea of a truly human social order, everyone would have an equal opportunity to develop his or her specifically human capacities. But they also made the further (unfounded) assertion that Fromm was a Pollyanna. According to them, in Fromm's "sane society" there would be no loneliness, no feelings of isolation, no despair. Fromm never said any such thing. On at least two occasions he stated expressly that a sense of the tragic side of human existence is a prerequisite for productive living and emotional literacy; that even without the misery, insecurity, and privation engendered by general want and social injustice, human existence is a sad undertaking (1941, pp. 270–271; 1955b, pp. 174–175). On balance, Fromm was much closer to Freud and existentialism than Hall and Lindzey implied.

To their credit, however, by the third edition of *Theories of Personality* (1978), Hall and Lindzey improved their reading of Fromm considerably. Although they still characterized him as a field theorist (p. 690), they clearly acknowledged his Marxist bearings and gave ample recognition to his empirical research in Mexico (ibid., p. 174).[5] The discussion of Fromm's theory of character was more concrete. The role of innate dispositions in Fromm's theory was emphasized (ibid., p. 173), and the attribution of radical environmentalism withdrawn (ibid., p. 198). Unfortunately, a small but noteworthy distortion crept into the new characterization. They correctly described *Marx's Concept of Man* (Fromm, 1961b) as "an unconditional eulogy to Marx" (ibid., p. 170). There Fromm ascribed the advent of Leninism and Stalinism to distortions of Marx's original message and praised Marx's broad humanistic background and aspirations. They failed to note that six years earlier, in *The Sane Society* (1955b), Fromm had reproached Marx for his economistic bias and his dogmatic, authoritarian behavior.

But this distortion was a small price to pay for the vast improvement in Hall and Lindzey's analysis. Most likely what generated this deeper understanding was their reading of *Social Character in a Mexi-*

can Village (Fromm and Maccoby, 1970). All that remained of their earlier errors was the unfounded notion that in Fromm's sane society, loneliness and despair would cease to intervene in human affairs. The image of Fromm as a benignly optimistic utopian environmentalist was modified but not entirely abandoned.

Harold Searles

Harold F. Searles is a psychiatrist known principally for his work with schizophrenics. Although he was never associated closely with Fromm, he acknowledged a deep personal debt to Fromm's first wife, Frieda Fromm-Reichmann, whose treatment philosophy he studied at Chestnut Lodge (Searles, 1965, p. 9). Searles provided no analysis of Fromm's contributions, but he referred to Fromm throughout his collected papers from 1959 on, perhaps most notably in an article in 1965. Commenting on the schizophrenic's (conscious and unconscious) fear and avoidance of developing an individual, autonomous identity, he observed:

> The invaluable work of Erikson concerning identity crises and other aspects of the struggle for identity has tended to highlight, by its very beauty and perceptiveness, the sense of ego-identity as something to be cherished so that we tend to underestimate how ambivalent are one's feelings—particularly, the psychotic individual's feelings—about this matter of identity . . . Fromm's comments in his *Escape from Freedom,* pointing out some of the psychological costs entailed in the development and maintenance of a sense of individuality, emphasize a fact of this subject of ego-identity not to be forgotten in our appreciation of Erikson's work.   (1965, p. 648)

Searles also drew on Fromm extensively in his book *The Non-Human Environment* to illustrate his thesis that

> in our culture, a conscious ignoring of the psychological importance of the non-human environment exists simultaneously with a (largely unconscious) *overdependence upon* that environment. I believe that the actual importance of the environment to the individual is so great that he *dare* not recognize it . . . That is . . . I hypothesize the existence . . . of an intrapsychic situation which is analogous to that situation which is well known to exist in neurotic and psychotic patients as regards interpersonal matters: the patient steadfastly denies the importance to him of

certain other persons on whom he is unconsciously extremely dependent and who constitute, via his unconscious identification with those
persons, important parts of his own personality.   (1960, p. 395)

Moreover, he insisted, in a remarkably prescient declaration, that
"man's impaired relatedness to his nonhuman environment may
contribute significantly to this threat with which mankind is grappling" (ibid., p. 394).

The threat to which Searles was referring is our simultaneous
tendency to dehumanize people (witness the Holocaust) and to treat
nature increasingly as part of the impersonal "it-world" to which we
have no meaningful connection as a result of our deeper fear of
dependence, which is subject to psychotic denial on a cultural scale.
According to Searles, Fromm's description of the universal human
conflict between the desire for symbiotic fusion and the contrary need
for mature relatedness is not only useful for understanding schizophrenia, but is characteristic of our culture as a whole, which dis-
guises its dependence on nature by reifying and degrading it. Searles
was one of the few clinicians who attempted to apply Fromm's more
philosophical concepts in the clinical situation, and subsequently to
his own cultural critique, in which schizophrenic psychopathology
represents merely a more overt and dramatic form of conflicts faced
by everyone.

Benjamin Wolman

Benjamin Wolman's *Contemporary Theories and Systems in Psychology*
(1960) presented a more accurate assessment of Fromm on minor
points than any other work. For example, unlike Hall and Lindzey in
the first edition of *Theories of Personality,* Wolman pointed out that
Fromm took cognizance of inherited constitutional factors in personality dynamics (1960, p. 362). Unlike Munroe in *Schools of Psychoanalytic Thought,* he noted the role of value and ethical judgments in
Fromm's theory and therapy (ibid., p. 366). And although discussions
of Fromm's social and historical views were not new in the secondary
literature, Wolman was the first to attempt an analysis of the relationship between clinical theory and the philosophy of history, and to give
explicit recognition to the conceptual interdependence and reciprocal
interaction between these two discourses in psychoanalytic inquiry.

In general, however, Wolman's analysis was blighted by muddled thinking and misinformation. For example, he made flatly contradictory assertions about Fromm's use of the "biogenetic principle," which Freud borrowed from Ernst Haeckel and applied to history and human development. At one point he stated that "Fromm shifted away from Freudian philosophy on several points. He discarded the biogenetic principle and attached more weight to the cultural heritage. In fact, he regards human behavior at any historical moment as a product of cultural influences at a given time" (1960, p. 355). Yet only six pages later he asserted that "Fromm follows in Freud's footsteps and applies the biogenetic principle. Childhood development presents a pattern similar to that of the history of mankind" (ibid., p. 361).

Other statements suggest an elementary incomprehension of the subject matter. According to Wolman, "Freud's philosophy of history was an addition to his psychological theory; Fromm's philosophy of history was the cornerstone of his psychological theory. The reason is apparent. Freud regarded history as man-made, while Fromm regarded man as history-made" (1960, p. 356).

Minor distortions are inevitable in a schematic and condensed account such as this. But this formulation is completely untrue. Freud himself would have vigorously denied that his philosophy of history was an addition to, rather than an expression of, his psychological outlook. Moreover, Wolman implied that Freud first engaged in a careful and deliberate examination of the clinical data, then framed the appropriate empirical generalizations regarding human behavior, and then—and only then—drew inferences about society and history. But Freud did not work in this manner. No one familiar with Freud's cultural environment and its impact on his thinking could entertain this image of him as some sort of plodding positivist or empiricist. And although Fromm regarded man as a product of history, as Wolman alleged, he also saw history as the product of human agency—of the unfolding of our "productive powers" and the inevitable alienation that dogs each new step toward freedom (Fromm, 1955b, 1961b). Like Marx, Fromm emphasized that history as such does nothing. Men make their own history, albeit seldom under conditions of their own choosing (Fromm, 1941, p. 28).

In his concluding remarks, Wolman declared:

> Though the discussion of Fromm's philosophy and ethics transcends the borders of a scientific study of true and false statements, it is good to point to this revolt of a psychologist against objective truth in favor of moral judgments. Thus Fromm's writings confront scientific truth seekers with the problem of right and wrong.   (1960, p. 368)

Implicit here is the view that science or "objective truth" stands in some sort of adversarial relation to "moral judgment"—that ethics are a matter of subjective preference or of cultural convention. This view is increasingly questioned by cognitive-developmental theorists studying moral development (for example, Kohlberg, 1971).

Of course, cogent and persuasive arguments can be adduced against Fromm and in favor of ethical relativism (for example, Birnbach, 1961, pp. 76–77, 83–89). But whether we agree with him or not, an essentially Kantian perspective on ethical conduct was integral to Fromm's normative humanism and to his views on social psychopathology. Fromm had criticized the tendency to relativize ethical issues in Freudian theory and therapy (1935a; 1947, introduction). He argued that the choice for or against a given ethical choice can be judged objectively as good or bad, as rational or irrational, to the extent that it is conducive to the full development of the human person, and irrespective of the degree of consensual validation that attaches to it one way or another. Given the centrality of this issue in Fromm's work, it was incumbent on Wolman—among others—to give this point explicit consideration, rather than treat it as a mere afterthought, declaring Fromm's views on ethics as tangential to "objective truth" by mere fiat. This he failed to do.

Duane Schultz

Duane P. Schultz's (1969) perfunctory description of Fromm in *A History of Modern Psychology* (1969) echoed those of Hall and Lindzey (1957) and Wolman (1960). According to Schultz, Fromm "believes that the prime motivating force in human existence is not the satisfaction of instinctual drives, but the desire to revert to a condition of dependence" (1969, p. 304). Schultz concluded his summary with the observation that "Fromm's descriptive analyses are not defined to the degree of precision required of scientific evidence" (ibid., p. 306). In the following section, in a critique of Jung, Adler, Horney, and

Fromm, Schultz chided all four for their portrayal of human beings as essentially rational, conscious, socialized creatures who are victims of debilitating social systems: "We are left with the paradox of man, an eminently rational, perfectible, socialized being, who has nevertheless developed an abundance of social systems inadequate to his needs" (1969, p. 306).

Let us take these assertions in order. First, Fromm did not in fact suggest that the primary motivating factor in human behavior is the desire to revert to a condition of dependence. At the very most he suggested, in *Escape from Freedom* (1941) and *The Heart of Man* (1964), that the desire to revert to a condition of dependence is an integral element of all clinical psychopathology. This reasonably modest and balanced assertion, which Schultz distorted, was balanced by the explicit recognition that, given proper conditions, this regressive longing is outweighed by the healthy individual's growing need and capacity to relate productively to others.

Shultz's distortion in the first passage seriously undermines his complaint in the second that Fromm's descriptive analyses lack the "precision required of scientific evidence." Like Wolman, Schultz takes the meaning or nature of science entirely for granted, as if it were something self-evident rather than something requiring definition and discursive elaboration. The cumulative effect is one of smugness. His global characterizations of Jung, Adler, Horney, and Fromm are equally trite and misleading. It is true that all four stressed man's *potential* sociability and his *relative* capacity for reason far more than Freud did. But the entire raison d'être of psychoanalytic psychotherapy is predicated on the assumption that the dark and irrational forces in us are outside our conscious control.

Still, the question *why* we develop social systems that do not meet our existential needs is a valid one. In all likelihood, Fromm's considered answer to this would have been that until relatively recently, there was a scarcity of material means to provide everyone with the basis for a decent and dignified life. This scarcity required the division of society into classes, and the use of force and deception to maintain class rule. The explosive development of productive forces in the nineteenth and twentieth centuries, which makes adequate provision for material needs possible—enabling us, potentially, to dispense with force and deception—has been carried out under capitalist auspices. Unfortunately, capitalism also fosters the widespread proliferation of alienation, mechanization, consumerism, and so on, which render it difficult to experience, much less address, our specifically human needs, and so implement social change that would make adequate provision for all. Indeed, now that we have the material means to do so, our ability to implement them is obstructed by the legacy of centuries of fear, greed, and oppression that are ingrained in our social character from preceding epochs (Fromm, 1937, 1955b, 1960d, 1968b).

Schultz's rendering of Fromm, though briefer than some, is typical of responses in the mainstream of academic psychology after 1960. It gives the impression that Schultz read Hall and Lindzey (1957) and Wolman (1960), without actually reading Fromm, or that he read Fromm indifferently, with a view to confirming preconceived ideas, gleaned secondhand from "authoritative" sources.

Robert Lundin

Robert Lundin's treatment of Fromm in *Theories and Systems of Psychology* was as flawed as Schultz's, though perhaps more sympathetic. Lundin recognized the role of inherited constitutional predispositions in Fromm's theory of personality (temperament), but like Hall and Lindzey in 1957 he categorized Fromm inappropriately, citing Fromm's theory as an example of "social learning" (1972, p. 284). In a sense this label is justified, given the mediation of family, school, and other social factors in the shaping of characterological traits. But it is more likely to confuse than enlighten, since Lundin offered no explanation about the enormous differences separating Fromm and the other theorists included in this designation. Moreover, and more important, Fromm explicitly repudiated the idea that behavior is chiefly a product of learning or imitation (Fromm and Maccoby, 1970, pp. 10, 19).

Lundin did take more care to grapple with some important fundamentals than several of his predecessors, however. Instead of suggesting that the primary motivation underlying all human behavior is the desire to revert to a dependent state, for example, he noted correctly that for Fromm the primary problem confronting all human beings is that of overcoming aloneness (Lundin, 1972, p. 284). This is a fundamentally different assertion, since the desire to overcome one's aloneness, characteristic of both health and illness, need not promote a reversion to dependence. Lundin followed this trenchant observation with a brief enumeration of the various "escape mechanisms" cited in *Escape from Freedom* (Fromm, 1941), the various character types delineated in *Man for Himself* (Fromm, 1947), and the existential needs described in *The Sane Society* (Fromm, 1955b). Though correct on the whole, the treatment is sketchy and appears designed (through its enumeration of, say, *three* escape mechanisms, *five* characterological orientations) as a simplistic aid to rote memory for undergraduates.

Like Wolman, Schultz, and others, Lundin stated that Fromm's attitude to the human species is "loving," but idealistic and lacking in realism. Echoing Wolman (1960, p. 367), Lundin argued that Fromm's attempts at describing the historical evolution of the modern psyche are in fact unhistorical, lacking empirical specificity (Lundin, 1972, p. 286). "Perhaps," he wrote, "we should not call him a psychologist at all, but rather a historical and ethical philosopher" (ibid.). But what manner of historical philosopher would Fromm be, if Fromm's historical theorizing is fundamentally unsubstantiated, as Lundin claimed? The overall impression conveyed is that Fromm is a nice fellow, but hardly worth attention as a *serious* psychologist.

Dieter Wyss

A notable exception to the prevailing trend after 1960 is Dieter Wyss's *Psychoanalytic Schools from the Beginning to the Present* (1973). Wyss is a psychiatrist practicing in Frankfurt, and his primary focus is philosophical. Consequently, perhaps, he commends Fromm for attempting to clarify the rather modest role of "instincts" in human behavior, and to substitute for them existential and humanistic concepts of human motivation. His analysis of Fromm's philosophical anthropology in connection with his views on love rivals or exceeds those of Mullahy and Thompson in breadth and acuity (Wyss, 1973, pp. 271–280). Unlike most psychologists and psychiatrists, Wyss appears to endorse Fromm's outspoken ethical views, and he argues for their relevance to the later phases of psychotherapy (ibid., p. 280); an interesting suggestion, which to the best of my knowledge has never been addressed by anyone since. His concluding remarks are confusing, however. He likens Fromm to Otto Rank in ways that Fromm himself would have rejected, adding that Fromm

> evaluates clinical symptoms as being of secondary importance only and accords them their proper place within the total phenomenon of "man." Like the other Neo-Freudians Fromm failed to recognize the problem posed by the instances and the difficulties which prevented Neo-Freudianism from establishing its independence from Freud in this respect. But then the clinical investigation and description of neurosis was not his primary concern. (Ibid., p. 524)

Coming from the vast majority of psychiatrists, the suggestion that the description, study, and cure of neurosis were not Fromm's primary concerns would constitute severe criticism. But for Wyss, the opposite appears to be the case. Indeed, he implies that neo-Freudianism— Fromm included—did not distance itself from Freudianism *enough*, but without saying why. Even if we grant that symptom remission or alleviation is not "the cure of souls," as Wyss and Fromm insist, this attitude vitiates the value of Wyss's evaluation considerably.

William Sahakian

William Sahakian discusses Fromm in two books, *Systematic Social Psychology* (1974) and *History and Systems of Social Psychology* (1984). Unlike Hall and Lindzey's efforts, however, Sahakian's show no noticeable improvement. Though mercifully free of simplistic enumerations of the various needs, character types, and so forth to assist undergraduates at examination time, it lacks both the depth and precision one would expect in a serious treatment. According to Sahakian, on coming to the United States Fromm "found himself under the sway of the sociologists John Dollard and Harold Dwight Laswell, the psychoanalytic anthropologist Abram Kardiner, as well as anthropologists J. Hallowell and E. Sapir" (1974, p. 173). This suggestion that Fromm's theorizing took shape under these convergent influences ignores the fact that Fromm's outlook took shape in Germany in the period 1927–1933. Fromm did cite these figures once, in *Escape from Freedom*, as providing convergent testimony regarding his critique of Freudian social psychology (1941, p. 28, n. 6). But when Fromm met them through Sullivan's "Zodiac Club" in the late 1930s, he was already a formidable intellect in his own right, and most accounts suggest that whatever influence there was flowed in precisely in the opposite direction.

Immediately after this false claim, Sahakian states that "Fromm and Horney are at odds with Freud, whose contention was that man is the product of his biological nature . . . instead of being generated by social learning." Yet the term *social learning* appears nowhere in Fromm's or Horney's writing. Moreover, Fromm never suggested that "man," or human nature, is "generated by social learning." According-ing to Fromm, human nature is a transhistorical constant, which is shaped or distorted in manifold ways according to prevailing social conditions.

Robert Fuller

Robert Fuller's *Americans and the Unconscious* (1986) gives an account of humanistic psychology's response to Freud and attempts to situate Fromm in a perspective on the unconscious mind that is ostensibly indigenous to America. For humanistic psychologists such as Abra-ham Maslow, Rollo May, Gardner Murphy, Ira Progoff, Carl Rogers, and Walter Weisskopf, the unconscious is more a repository of posi-tive, growth-oriented, and "higher" mental functions than of primi-tive or antisocial impulses. Nowhere is this more apparent than in Rogers, who characterized the

> human organism as a pyramid of organic functioning, partly suffused by
> an unconscious knowing, with only the tip of the pyramid being fleet-
> ingly illuminated by the flickering light of fully conscious awareness . . .
> some of my colleagues have said that organismic choice—the nonver-
> bal, subconscious choice of being—is guided by the evolutionary flow. I
> would agree and go one step further. I would point out that in psycho-
> therapy we have learned something about the conditions which are
> most conducive to self-awareness.   (Quoted in Fuller, 1986, p. 169).

Elsewhere, but in the same vein, Rogers argued that "when we provide a psychological climate that permits persons to be . . . we are tapping into a tendency which permeates all of organic life to become all the complexity of which the organism is capable. And on an even larger scale, I believe we are tuning into a potent creative tendency which has created the universe" (quoted in ibid., p. 171).

To situate Fromm historically, let us contrast Rogers' notion of the unconscious with the Freudian variety, and then with Fromm's. Except for certain portions of the ego, what is unconscious for Freud is chiefly the timeless, archaic id, which, by virtue of its conservative and perseverative character, resists adaptation to reality. Freud's emphasis on the conservative character of the instincts (1921) was rooted in the mechanistic materialism of Hermann Helmholtz and Ernst von Brücke. Although biology may lend a hand, in the final analysis the reality principle and the ego, which mediate the processes of adaptation to the environment, evolve chiefly through cultural constraints, not biological processes, and then only at the price of inevitable neurosis—a pessimistic view antithetical to Rogers' own.

And Fromm? According to Fuller,

> Of all the neo-Freudians, Erich Fromm has unquestionably been the most influential. Virtually every theme that distinguishes the "American psyche" from its Freudian predecessor appears in Fromm's writings: the importance of the present (or existential) situation of the individual rather than his or her past; consciousness and willed freedom rather than intrapsychic determinisms; the continuing openness of the personality and its responsiveness to new experiences . . . Importantly, Fromm's psychoanalytic orientation prevented him from following his social and environmentalist ideas to their logical conclusions. The unconscious became for him a psychological bastion defending the individual from total domination by outer forces . . . Describing this deeper mental life, he repeatedly draws upon such patently mystical language as the Zen account of satori, Meister Eckhart's depiction of union with the Godhead, and Paul Tillich's description of the psyche's participation in "the ground of being." (1986, p. 126)

This characterization suffers from several serious defects. But the real problem resides chiefly in how Fuller constructs the "American unconscious." With reference to Rogers, for example, he cites Emerson as an important influence, which, by Rogers' own account, is perfectly true (Fuller, 1986, p. 169n.). Elsewhere in his book Fuller correctly cites F. W. Myers—an English Romantic and parapsychologist—as a background inspiration for Americans. However, Fuller neglects to mention that the cosmic unconscious described by Rogers —though compatible, no doubt, with Emerson, Myers, and so on— emerges fullblown in the philosophy of Schelling and Carus, and subsequently in other varieties of vitalism (for example, Johannes

Müller, Henri Bergson, Samuel Butler, Pierre Teilhard du Chardin). A late representative of vitalism among Freud's followers, Georg Groddeck, was Fromm's friend and preceptor during his late twenties and early thirties.

Thus Fromm's affinity for the "American unconscious," though neither trivial nor accidental, is less an adaptation to the New World than a reversion to an older, pre-Freudian view of unconscious mental processes that has deep roots in his own cultural milieu. Schelling's and Bergson's views of the unconscious as a creative, forward-looking evolutionary principle are completely antithetical to the archaic, conservative character of the instincts as understood by Freud. But both are true in some measure. Like Reich, Fromm made allowance for healthy, prosocial strivings that are repressed or distorted in the process of socialization, but laid equal emphasis on the difficulties of altering the fixed and perseverative character of distorted patterns of human functioning. By focusing exclusively on the vitalist side of Fromm's concept of the unconscious, Fuller distorts Fromm's position to fit his preconceptions, an approach that enables him to reproach Fromm for not following through with his "social and environmentalist" ideas. And by treating this facet of his work as uniquely American, he engages in a double distortion that is very difficult to refute because of its surface plausibility.

Finally, Fuller's construal of Fromm begs the question of why Fromm avoided any dialogue or involvement with the burgeoning of humanistic psychology in the 1960s and 1970s. Fromm's policy of ignoring the movement becomes intelligible only if we understand the divergent meanings "humanism" has in the European and American contexts. Even among Europeans, the term has had diverse significations, depending on one's political persuasion. To the cultured conservatives, such as Tocqueville, Goethe, and Thomas Mann, "humanism" signifies an ivory-tower retreat from political life; for liberals and leftists, such as Camus and Sartre, the term is a clarion call for struggle against prevailing conditions that render a life of dignity and self-realization impossible for the broad mass of humanity. But regardless of political coloration, the sine qua non of European humanism is sustained reflection on philosophical and historical texts dating to the Renaissance (or before), in which one's intellectual ancestry is scrupulously authenticated through direct citation, paraphrase, or allusion to previous thinkers.

As a cultured, bookish European, Fromm inherited a culture of scholarship and the ancestral piety that goes with it. In contrast—if Fuller is any indication—humanistic psychologists in America tend to espouse the attitude of "self-reliance" found in Emerson, Thoreau, and Whitman and seldom look to Freud, Marx, Spinoza, or Meister Eckhart for inspiration, as Fromm did throughout his adult life. At its best, this self-reliance imparts an openness to new ideas and a willingness to question authority. But to Europeans, this attitude often appears to serve as a rationalization for avoiding the rigors of genuine scholarship; an eclecticism that lacks substance, discipline, and real social and political commitments.

Apart from the absence of rigor and ancestral piety, Fromm was suspicious of what seemed to him the self-indulgent quality of the human potential movement, which was aligned to humanistic psychology. Fromm was not opposed to sociability, sensuality, or "spontaneity." But to a cultured European, authentic self-expression is unthinkable in the absence of tact and reserve in appropriate circumstances. For an American, by contrast, "spontaneity" is almost synonymous with the deliberate rejection or flaunting of constraints— often in a perversely conformist way. As a consequence, what strikes the European as a "spontaneous" form of emotional expression often strikes the American as "uptight," premeditated, or downright deceptive. Conversely, the American's "spontaneity" strikes the European as exhibitionistic, shallow, self-indulgent, or forced. The kind of openness and spontaneity espoused by Fromm was of a decidedly European cast, which may be one reason some American students found him aloof.

Summary and Conclusion

From the preceding sample certain trends emerge with vivid clarity. Of the psychiatrists who evaluated Fromm, some, like himself, were transplanted Europeans, and therefore familiar with Fromm's earlier writings. For that very reason, they carried the sectarian squabbles of Marxism and psychoanalysis with them to the United States. Examples include Reich, Fenichel, and their followers here. The exception is Dieter Wyss. He clearly understood features of Fromm's thought that others failed to grasp. American psychiatrists such as Thompson and Searles, who knew Fromm through Sullivan and Fromm-

Reichmann, were unfamiliar with his early work but explored his English-language contributions sympathetically, and used his philosophical anthropology to the extent that they were able to. After Fenichel's withering comments in 1944, however, American psychiatrists of the orthodox Freudian persuasion simply ignored Fromm, as the paucity of references and lack of a single substantive analysis in the orthodox American psychoanalytic literature demonstrate.

In psychology as a whole, Fromm fared little better. With some notable exceptions, most secondary literature on Fromm after 1960 is mediocre or misleading. Even nominally sympathetic reviewers and critics could not refrain from labeling Fromm inappropriately, misrepresenting him on fundamental issues, and smugly repeating the pronouncements of earlier "authorities," without first checking their sources. Social and personality psychologists, and would-be historians of psychology—excepting Peters and his colleagues—have alternately classified Fromm as "intuitive," a "field theorist," a "social learning" theorist, or an "environmentalist," ignoring important features of Fromm's work that exempt him from these designations. They could not relinquish their image of Fromm as a fuzzy-headed utopian lacking an appreciation for the irrational and tragic dimensions of human life, even when they became enlightened on other scores (for example, Hall and Lindzey, 1957 versus 1978). In all likelihood, this persistent misattribution served a rhetorical function, suggesting, by example, the kind of theorizing the author thought best to avoid.

Given the extent and frequency of these errors, it seems almost pointless to blame individual authors. Something of a more global character is obviously at work here. Indeed, the grotesque distortions by Fromm's American critics and would-be expositors attest to the validity of Fromm's theory of social filters, in which experience and information are screened according to cultural preconceptions. Thus, for someone who bothers to read Fromm carefully, there is a comic irony and, in a sense, vindication in this sad and deplorable state of affairs.

Among clinical psychologists Fromm also had a poor reception. Wolman's formulation of Fromm's clinical theory and philosophy of history foundered in weak, misguided generalizations and contradictory accounts of Fromm's premises, methods, and conclusions. Mullahy's treatment, an obvious exception, was informed by a strong background in philosophy, religion, and comparative mythology and literature that made him receptive to the style and content of Fromm's work. But Fromm himself had a hand in *Oedipus: Myth and Complex,* so that this exception does not count for much. Ruth Munroe, the only analytically oriented psychologist here who did not know Fromm personally, generally combined clear-sighted, forthright criticism with a sympathetic and accurate understanding. Granted, she was unsure about the extent to which ethical and philosophical ideas entered into Fromm's clinical conduct, and assumed that his ideas on these lines were immaterial to his practical conduct in therapy. But so was Thompson, who was supervised by Fromm. Perhaps Fromm himself was more confused or ambiguous on this point than he cared to acknowledge, because he was sorting out conflicting intellectual loyalties and component parts of his own personal identity.

The two fields in which one would have expected Fromm to flourish are those of humanistic and existential psychology. But with the exception of some laudatory passages in Rollo May's first few books, and fleeting references here and there (for example, Stone, 1986), Fromm's distinctive combination of Freud and Marx, of humanism and existentialism, failed to gain a foothold. The sole exception here is Ernest Becker, whose book *The Denial of Death* was widely read and appreciated by existential and humanistic psychologists. Although he never attempted an overall assessment of Fromm's work, Becker showed a good understanding of Fromm and a keen enthusiasm for his ideas (for example, 1973, p. 134). But the exception proves the rule. For Becker was not a psychologist, but a cultural anthropologist with broad interests in philosophy, the social sciences, and literature, and his popularity among psychologists and psychiatrists seems to have done little to strengthen their understanding of Fromm.

The question then arises: why did Fromm receive such a sloppy and indifferent reception among psychologists? The answer is quite complex, involving a variety of factors.

Being a sociologist by training, Fromm apparently felt no need to justify the existence of psychology either within the psychoanalytic fold or even as a discipline in its own right. And while psychologists trained in the shadow of psychiatry continued to justify their precarious status in terms of a special competence for quantitative and statistical analysis, Fromm emphasized the *qualitative* features of individual and social psychology. Fromm's penchant for exploring the economic and cultural determinants of widespread phenomena such as anxiety, conformism, and the origins, history, and psychological ramifications of collective belief systems, and his refusal to succumb to the more commonplace varieties of reductionism commonplace in both the Marxist and Freudian camps (Brett, 1965), made him difficult to categorize. Moreover, his attempts to decipher the ideological subtexts of Freudian theory (for example, Fromm, 1935a, 1959b) rendered it practically disadvantageous for analytically oriented theorists doing clinical or social research to cite or apply his ideas, despite his protestations of fidelity to Freud. So long as Fromm was anathema, the practical constraints attaching to the use of his ideas were—and still are—quite formidable, involving the availability of funding, the esteem of one's colleagues, prospects for advancement, and so on. Thus, despite widespread public enthusiasm, reflected in numerous best-sellers, he had no tangible impact on analytically oriented psychologists beyond his personal sphere of influence at the William Alanson White Institute and at the Mexican Psychoanalytic Institute, where the majority of his trainees were psychiatrists anyway.

Of course, analysts account for a very small portion of psychologists in general, but many of the features that rendered Fromm unpalatable to analytically oriented psychologists estranged him from academic psychologists as well, even when their research interests were highly convergent (for example, problems of conformity and consensus). Fromm's Marxist and Freudian leanings, which were already a strike against him, were blended with an approach to psychological questions that was more akin to that of late nineteenth-century proponents of the *Geisteswissenschaften* than to prevailing ideas on scientific method. The impact of positivism on experimental, social, and clinical psychology, and the corollary tendency to approach problems of human behavior in a radically unhistorical way, rendered it all but impossible for most mainstream academic psychologists to grasp what Fromm was talking about, much less lend his assumptions and methods any credence. Here again, practical and intellectual constraints conspired to ensure that Fromm's influence remained peripheral at best. The fact that his name appears in numerous articles and textbooks on social and personality psychology does not alter this fact. In these contexts, Fromm's name usually appears as a testimony to the author's broad and inclusive scholarship, as a convenient straw man who vindicates the author's prejudices, or as a gesture of courtesy or cautious acknowledgment to other "experts" who saw fit to include him in previous treatments of the fields.

Of course, Fromm himself contributed to the widespread neglect he suffered. To see him simply as a victim is unfair to critics and expositors who made a genuine effort to puzzle him out. But given the prevailing intellectual climate, a measure of distortion was inevitable, no matter how much—or how little—Fromm contributed to it. Psychology under positivist and behaviorist auspices in America involved a radical devaluation of the qualitative aspects of human experience, and a corresponding valorization of what Fromm termed tendencies toward "quantification and abstractification" (1955b, pp. 103–111). Apart from his emphasis on the qualitative dimensions of psychology and its emancipatory, disillusioning function (Fromm, 1959a), his belief in the possibility of—indeed, in the logical necessity for—an objective ethics, grounded in laws of human nature, struck many psychologists as grossly unscientific. In psychology and psychiatry, the prevailing orientation was predicated—as it is today—on the belief in the reality of objective *knowledge,* but not on the possibility of an objective *ethics.* As a result of Hermann Cohen's influence, perhaps, Fromm refused to concede that ethics are merely a matter of arbitrary preference or consensual validation. And predictably, the Kantian insistence that valid norms for all humanity can be arrived at through "reason," irrespective of prevailing norms and practices, cost him dearly in terms of professional credibility, although it endeared him to sectors of the broader reading public.

8 *Fromm's Contribution to the History of Psychoanalysis*

The Freud Myth and Fromm's Critique

Popular misconceptions notwithstanding, the psychology of the unconscious did not begin with Freud. Indeed, it preceded him by at least two centuries, with many illustrious exponents. Nevertheless, the vast majority of people associate the word *unconscious* with Freud. One reason for this, no doubt, is that when Freud and his followers began to systematize and codify psychoanalytic theory, they wrote as if he had started the psychology of the unconscious *de novo*, deriving his concepts from his own self-analysis and rigorous inductive inferences about anomalies encountered in the clinical setting, and without prior acquaintance with J. F. Herbart, Schopenhauer, Nietzsche, Theodor Lipps, and others.

Since Freud's death, Freudians have tended to perpetuate this interpretation. And when Freudians do refer to pre-Freudian theorists, they often do so in a patronizing and partisan way. There is a valid analogy between mainstream psychoanalytic historiography and the Christian apologists of the second through fourth centuries. The church fathers were struck by the far-reaching parallels between Christian teaching and the earlier doctrines of Plato, Aristotle, the Stoics, Plotinus, and so on. Rather than deny them entirely, theologians such as Clement of Alexandria, Tertullian, Origen, and Augustine argued that the pagan saints and philosophers had had fragmentary, distorted premonitions of the truth. By contrast, they insisted, Christian revelation constitutes a unique, unprecedented, and unrepeatable event that gives a full and adequate disclosure of man's origin and fate, of his ground in Being and his relation to the Absolute. Accordingly, pagan philosophy was studied to prove the inadequacy of earlier belief systems and to extort corroborating testimony to give Christianity an uncontested monopoly on truth.

Similarly, when orthodox Freudians write the history of the psychoanalytic movement they tend to minimize earlier contributions or to praise Freud's predecessors ambivalently for coming close to the truth but invariably falling short in some respect. Along with this ahistorical approach to the history of ideas, they cherish a hallowed image of Freud the man. In their minds, Freud was a rigorous and impartial scientist laboring on behalf of suffering humanity, a devoted husband and family man, a loyal and ardent friend, and a blameless victim of duplicity and intrigue, who was deeply hurt by the betrayal of scheming, ungrateful disciples; a victim, it would seem, of his own generous and trusting nature.

Fromm was among the first psychoanalysts to break with this tradition. Born in 1900, too late to have been a member of Freud's intimate circle, Fromm nevertheless studied classical psychoanalysis under Freud loyalists such as Theodor Reik and Hans Sachs in his late twenties. At the same time, however, Fromm was developing intimate personal ties with non-Marxist members of Freud's loyal opposition, such as Georg Groddeck, Sandor Ferenczi, and Karen Horney, and in all probability learned much about Freud from his impact on *their* lives.

Fromm's first major contribution to psychoanalytic historiography came in response to Ernest Jones's biography of Freud (1953). *Sigmund Freud's Mission* (Fromm, 1959b) painted a portrait of Freud that conflicted with the one conveyed by most of the extant literature. Instead of the disinterested scientist, the devoted husband, the loyal friend and impartial administrator, the Freud that emerges from Fromm's characterization is a troubled and self-centered genius who was not entirely conscious of his real aims and objectives, whose personal happiness was blighted by overweening ambition, emotional coldness, pre-Oedipal anxieties, and a strong authoritarian streak. According to Fromm's portrait, alone, Freud's whole emotional life and dealings with others were colored by self-deception; the man who, as clinician, prided himself on being undeceived, understood himself little and, despite his celebrated self-analysis, was driven by the passions of ambition, thirst for revenge, and narcissistic anguish at his own personal losses, with no greater or finer depth of feeling underlying his neurotic equilibrium. However, Fromm's Freud also evinced a dauntless intellectual courage, an invincible faith in the emancipatory power of reason, and a prodigious scientific imagination, which generated a whole new way of understanding the irrational. Thus, according to Fromm, although Freud was emotionally impoverished and self-centered, Freud *the thinker* was a profound, prolific, and creative intelligence grappling with fundamental problems of human motivation and behavior.

On Fromm's reckoning, Freud's great merit lay in his attempt to reconcile contradictory currents of thought that were prevalent in his day, such as the problems of free will versus determinism, and Enlightenment versus Romantic thought. However, in Fromm's estimation, the power and depth of Freud's synthesis were underscored, and, to a certain extent, undermined, by his inability to reconcile the dichotomous threads of optimism and pessimism that ran through his philosophy of history, and by his abortive attempt to transcend the limitations of his earlier theory of the drives. His inability to follow through consistently, Fromm suggests, merely deepened the pessimistic streak in his nature, the consequence being that as he matured, Freud became more grim in outlook. But much as he criticized Freud, Fromm was by no means insensible to the tragic grandeur of Freud's vision. Although some critics construe Fromm as a Pollyanna, few writers have conveyed the spirit of Freud as faithfully in this regard as he did.

Freud's "Model of Man" and Philosophy of History

According to Fromm, psychoanalysis represents a (possibly unwitting) synthesis of Enlightenment and Romantic ideologies; its popularity owes as much to its reconciliation of these historically antagonistic perspectives as it does to any other factor. It is in light of this synthesis that Fromm interprets the first rival schools, those of Alfred Adler and Carl Jung. In "Freud's Model of Man and Its Social Determinants," Fromm declared:

> Although it is true that man is driven by irrational forces—the libido, and especially in its pregenital stages of evolution, his ego—his reason and his will are not without strength. The power of reason expresses

itself in the first place in the fact that man can understand his irrationality by the use of reason. In this way Freud founded the *science of human irrationality*—psychoanalytic theory . . . Because a person in the analytic process can make his own unconscious conscious, he can also liberate himself from the power of unconscious strivings; instead of repressing them, he can negate them, that is, he can lessen their strength, and control them with his will . . . Historically speaking, one can look at Freud's theory as the fruitful synthesis of rationalism and romanticism; the creative power of this synthesis may be one of the reasons why Freud's thinking became a dominating influence in the twentieth century. This influence was not due to the fact that Freud found a new therapy for the neuroses, and probably also not primarily because of his role as a defender of repressed sexuality . . . the most important reason for his general influence on culture is in this synthesis, whose fruitfulness can be clearly seen in the two most important defections from Freud, that of Adler and of Jung. Both exploded the Freudian synthesis and reverted to the two original positions. Adler, rooted in the short-lived optimism of the rising middle-classes, constructed a one-sided rationalistic-optimistic theory. He believed that the innate disabilities are the very conditions of strength and that with intellectual understanding of a situation, man can liberate himself and make the tragedy of life disappear.

Jung, on the other hand, was a romantic who saw the sources of all human strength in the unconscious. He recognized the wealth and depth of symbols and myths much more profoundly than Freud, whose views were restricted by his sexual theory. Their aims, however, were contradictory. Freud wanted to understand the unconscious in order to weaken and control it; Jung, in order to gain an increased vitality from it. Their interest in the unconscious united the two men for some time, without their being aware that they were moving in opposite directions. As they halted on their way in order to talk about the unconscious, they fell under the illusion that they were proceeding in the same direction.   (1970d, pp. 50–52)

In addition to synthesizing Enlightenment and Romantic thought in what was essentially a practical endeavor (that is, the therapy of the neurosis), Freud articulated a theory that mediated the opposite poles of free will and determinism but eschewed metaphysical abstractions. According to Fromm, "Freud was a determinist; he believed that man is not free, because he is determined by the unconscious, the id, and the superego. *But,* and this 'but' is of decisive importance for Freud, man is also not wholly determined. With the

help of the analytic method he can gain control over the unconscious" (1970d, p. 52).[1]

However, Fromm observed, Freud was not equal to reconciling
Enlightenment and Romantic positions in all spheres; a fact reflected
in his growing pessimism about the possibilities of individual and
social transformation, which eroded his Enlightenment faith in reason. As Fromm points out, in Freud's varying accounts of our social
origins

> we find man without culture, completely dedicated to the satisfaction of
> his instinctual drives, and happy to that extent. This picture, however, is
> in contrast to another, which assumes a conflict even in the first phase of
> complete instinctual satisfaction.
>
> Man must leave this paradise precisely because the unlimited satisfac-
> tion of his drives leads to the conflict of the sons with the father, to the
> murder of the father, and eventually to the formation of the incest taboo.
> The rebellious sons gain a battle, but they lose the war against the
> fathers, whose prerogatives are now secured forever by "morality" and
> the social order (here again we are reminded of Freud's ambivalence
> toward authority).
>
> While in this aspect of Freud's thinking a state of unrestricted in-
> stinctual satisfaction was *impossible* in the long run, he develops another
> thesis which is quite different. The possibility of this paradisiacal state is
> not denied, but it is assumed that man cannot develop any culture as
> long as he remains in this paradise. For Freud, culture is conditioned by
> the partial non-satisfaction of instinctual desires, which leads in turn to
> sublimation and reaction formation. Man, then, is confronted with an
> alternative: total instinctual satisfaction—and barbarism—or partial
> instinctual frustration, along with cultural and mental development of
> man. Frequently, however, the process of sublimation fails, and man has
> to pay the price of neurosis for his cultural development.   (1970d,
> pp. 58–59)

Fromm goes on to note that

> Freud's sympathies are on the side of culture . . . Nevertheless, his
> concept of history has a tragic element. Human progress necessarily
> leads to repression and neurosis. Man cannot have both happiness and
> progress. In spite of the tragic element, however, Freud remains an
> enlightenment thinker, though a skeptical one, for whom progress is no
> longer an unmixed blessing. In the second phase of his work, after the
> First World War, Freud's picture of history becomes truly tragic. Prog-

ress, beyond a certain point, is no longer simply bought at great expense, but is in principle impossible. Man is only the battlefield on
which the life and death instincts fight against each other. He can never
liberate himself decisively from the tragic alternatives of destroying
himself or destroying others.

. . . The skeptical enlightenment philosopher, overwhelmed by the
collapse of his world, became the total skeptic who looked at the fate of
man in history as an unmitigated tragedy. Freud could hardly have
reacted differently, since his society appeared to him as the best possible
one, and not capable of improvement in any decisive way.   (Ibid.,
pp. 59–60)

Fromm adduced several reasons for Freud's deepening pessimism.
On the one hand, Freud was essentially a liberal reformer and sought
to diminish sexual repression in his own society, without altering
its patriarchal and economically exploitative structure (see Fromm,
1959b, chap. 9). Inasmuch as he saw his own Viennese enclave of the
Austro-Hungarian empire as the epitome of culture and disregarded
its oppressive underpinnings—(or, indeed, embraced them)—he was
bound to see the collapse of his world in the First World War as the
definitive refutation of Enlightenment hopes for the victory of reason.

On the other hand, Fromm suggested, Freud was driven to this
conclusion by new conceptual developments that promised to transcend the mechanistic materialism that hobbled his earlier theories.
Although Fromm took issue with the death-instinct theory and the
tragic conundrum it poses for the human species (for example, 1980,
chap. 4), he also praised Freud for advancing to a more "vitalistic"
conception of the drives and for relinquishing his earlier and presumably less profound conjectures. Although the later drive theory became problematic, Fromm noted, it attested to a decisive deepening of
Freud's intellectual growth, so that there was a kind of personal
triumph amid the gathering despair that Freud shouldered with un-
flinching heroism.

But although Freud bore up bravely to the grim ramifications of his
new theory, Fromm emphasized, he remained insensible to the inherent contradictions between the earlier and later drive models; for
some mysterious reason, he could not cut loose from his previous
thinking. The mechanistic materialism that Freud derived from Ernst
von Brücke

was based on the principle that all psychic phenomena have their roots
in certain physiological processes and that they *can be sufficiently ex-*

plained and understood if one knows these roots. Freud, in search of the roots of psychic disturbances, had to look for a physiological substrate for the drives; to find this in sexuality was the ideal solution, since it corresponded both to the requirements of mechanistic-materialistic thought and to certain clinical findings in patients of his time and social class . . .

This theory of drives dominated Freud's systematic thinking until about 1920, when a new phase of his thinking began, which constituted an essential change in his concept of man. Instead of the opposition between ego and libidinous drives, the basic conflict now was between "life instincts" and "death instincts." The life instincts, comprising both ego and sexual drives, were placed in opposition to the death instincts, which were considered the root of human destructiveness, directed either toward the person himself or to the world outside. These new basic drives are constructed entirely differently from the old ones. First of all, they are not located in any special zone of the organism, as the libido is in the erogenous zones. Furthermore, they do not follow the pattern of the "hydraulic" mechanism: increasing tension → unpleasure → detension → pleasure → new tension, etc., but they are inherent in all living substance[2] and operate without any special stimulation; their motivating force, however, is not less strong than that of the hydraulically operating instincts. Eros has a tendency to unite and integrate; the death instinct has the opposite tendency to disintegration and destruction.   (1970d, pp. 46–48)

Fromm characterized the various efforts to harmonize the earlier and later drive theories as "theoretical patchwork," since their fundamental premises are basically irreconcilable. This judgment still seems justified.

In "The Social Limitations of Psychoanalytic Therapy" (1935a) and *Sigmund Freud's Mission* (1959b), Fromm attempted to trace the defects of Freudian theory to Freud's personal failings (such as his ambition, his lovelessness) and to the failings characteristic of his social class and time. These criticisms were also present in "Freud's Model of Man and Its Social Determinants" (1970d), but here Fromm emphasized the idea that Freud was held hostage by the need to reconcile contradictory currents in his cultural milieu (Enlightenment versus Romantic thought) and in philosophical anthropology (free will versus determinism), and by his successive (or simultaneous) adherence to different schools of thought (for example, mechanistic materialism, vitalism).[3]

With respect to the philosophy of history, Fromm noted contradictions in Freud's various accounts of our prehistoric estate. Sometimes Freud painted a scenario of unconstrained instinctual satisfaction, but bereft of progress. At others he depicted our primeval history as being marked by sharp social antagonisms, struggles with authority, and a pitiless environment. (Fromm might have added that this same ambiguity is reflected throughout the Enlightenment literature on this subject.) But although Freud may be classed as an Enlightenment figure in this regard, he did not represent the stream of Enlightenment thought that suffuses Fromm's work and comes to us by way of Rousseau, the utopian socialists, and Marx. In dramatic contrast to the Freudian outlook, this trend posits no inherent or necessary antagonism between the interests of the individual and of the species, between nature and culture, although collective life is now ordered in such a way as to render these interests conflictual (Fromm, 1975).

Freud, by contrast, saw conflict everywhere—a fact reflected in his vision of prehistoric social relations. In the wake of the "primal crime," or the slaying of the father, Freud envisioned a primordial pact to abstain from murder, and to effect an equitable distribution of women, breaking the father's monopoly on sexual chattels, as a kind of social contract or primitive precursor to civil law (1913, chap. 4). He was obliged to do so because he had no faith in the spontaneous sociability of the associated antagonists to prevent a recurrence of the same events in future. Quite the contrary. From Freud's perspective, it would seem, only the fear of murder or collective resentment could deter the average man from acting out primitive fantasies of domination and attempting to usurp the primal father's privileges.

The Death Instinct and Psychoanalytic Politics

Fromm's failure to note the divergent streams of Enlightenment thought does not invalidate his argument. On the contrary, in bringing these matters into focus, he provides us with an opportunity to put his own contribution and his differences with Freud into historical perspective. However, some significant omissions do weaken Fromm's characterization of Freud, specifically with regard to the death instinct.

By Fromm's reckoning, the death-instinct theory was occasioned by the First World War, both because of its unprecedented brutality, which shocked Freud deeply (see Freud, 1915), and because Freud's parochial investment in the Austro-Hungarian empire and Germanic culture, now badly shaken, left him culturally disoriented. Fromm's characterization would account for both the cosmopolitanism and the deepening pessimism that suffused Freud's later writings and gave them their resemblance to the work of Thomas Mann. In addition, Fromm suggested, the new theoretical tension between Eros and Thanatos involved an (unacknowledged) break with his earlier, mechanist drive theory and a deepening appreciation of the irrational in human nature.

Fromm's thesis is correct, as far as it goes. But it does not go far enough. For the death instinct can also be explained in ways that do not involve Freud's allegedly heightened realism or sensitivity or an abortive (but praiseworthy) theoretical breakthrough. Indeed, Freud's notion of the death instinct may attest to a cessation of growth (Suttie, 1935). Or it could be construed as a parting shot at Jung (Kerr, 1988). Pondering the etiology of schizophrenia, Jung had posited the existence of a primary regressive urge that attempts to reinstate a condition of undifferentiated oneness with the mother in the unconscious—the so-called incestuous libido. This primary regressive urge, Jung speculated, is not merely a feature of schizophrenic illness, but a basic part of our biological endowment, which "normal" individuals sublimate or transcend more or less effectively. In effect, Jung advanced a whole new theory of libido, in which the aim of the drive is merger or object-fusion, rather than drive tension reduction per se.

However, Jung's prescient forays into pre-Oedipal dynamics threatened to displace the conflict with the father that Freud deemed culture constitutive; they also imparted a regressive component to normal, adult libidinal strivings that was inconsistent with Freud's mechanistic conception of libido (Kerr, 1988). Accordingly, Freud found it expedient to posit an instinct that reduces biological tension/unpleasure to the absolute minimum that is nevertheless not libidinous—indeed, is antilibidinous. Here, then, was a primary regressive urge that, unlike Jung's, bypassed the mother and could be invoked as needed to account for various components of the Oedipus complex, including the (ostensibly) aggressive and destructive elements in male sexuality, the genesis of the superego, and the little boy's struggle with his own father. In this way, the essentially patricentric character of Freud's theory was preserved intact.

But the death instinct served an additional function for Freud. Freud's therapeutic optimism, such as it was, was sorely tried by the end of the First World War. In the death instinct, Freud found an airtight rationale for the intractable difficulties he and others employing orthodox technique routinely encountered in the clinical setting. Who can blame him? As Freud himself observed, psychoanalysis may disclose the roots of a repetitive, self-lacerating pattern of behavior without eliminating the compulsion to repeat it, or even ameliorating it to any significant degree (Freud, 1937). On the face of it, this candid confession contradicts the Enlightenment faith in the emancipatory power of reason, and with it, perhaps, the whole therapeutic raison d'être that presumably gave rise to analysis in the first place.

In other words, Fromm notwithstanding, the death-instinct theory was a gesture of resignation, an oblique admission that Freud had reached the limit in his ability to understand and activate the forces that might alter the inertia and perseverative quality that attaches to intractable cases (Suttie, 1935). But although Freud contrived a biological rationale for therapeutic failure and increasingly counseled analysts to have modest expectations of cure and recovery, not all the faithful followed suit. During the 1920s some disciples, including Reich, Rank, and Ferenczi, actually suggested that with appropriate changes in technique, the average analysis could be *shortened* to anywhere from six to eighteen months. This newfound optimism was based on diverse premises. Reich rejected the death instinct and stuck to Freud's early hydraulic model of the drives, hoping the orgasm theory would provide the key to unlocking the final mysteries of neurosis. In this way, he kept faith with Freud, in his fashion. Rank and Ferenczi adopted a more Jungian perspective, seeing genitality less as an avenue of drive discharge in the hydraulic metaphor than as a sublimated expression of the drive to restore the adualistic union of intrauterine existence (Ferenczi, 1924; Rank, 1924).

At first, Freud greeted these new developments with indulgent skepticism, if not with supportive encouragement. But it is no accident that, one by one, in the years that followed, each of these rising stars in the analytic firmament suffered a precipitous fall from grace and excommunication. And upstaging the master in therapeutic technique was not their only sin. Reich's forays into matriarchal theory challenged the patricentric assumptions of Freud's prehistoric musings. And by linking a primary regressive urge to the libido, Rank and Ferenczi revived a line of speculation that Freud had deliberately discarded in his quarrels with Jung, whose reformulated libido theory was influenced by Bachofen. Goaded by the factionalism of Ernest Jones, Karl Abraham, and Max Eitington, which he initially opposed (Fromm, 1959b, p. 133), Freud finally caught on. For if he had not been persuaded that the work of Rank and Ferenczi represented a radical departure from psychoanalysis—rather than its extension or a harmless digression, as he initially preferred to believe—they would never have been discredited so ruthlessly (Fromm, 1959b; Roazen, 1975).

Here, then, are two interpretations of the death-instinct theory and its reception. For Fromm, it was indicative of Freud's personal growth; a tentative, ambivalent, and ultimately abortive attempt to transcend the hydraulic detensioning model of the drives. And perhaps it was, up to a point. However, the death-instinct theory was also a gesture of resignation and a confession of impotence in the face of the baffling complexities of mental illness. Indeed, it may have suited Fromm to see the death instinct as evidence of Freud's growing maturity, despite abundant evidence to the contrary. It provided him with a platform from which to scold the majority of the faithful for lacking genuine appreciation of Freud (for example, Fromm, 1980, chap. 4). The unspoken proposition in Fromm's analysis seems to be that maturity and realism need not imply a deepening hopelessness about the human situation, and that Fromm himself—who made no attempt to reconcile the irreconcilable, and discarded the instinctivistic, drive-reduction framework that Freud inconsistently dragged along—was better off for it.

Fromm, Freud, and Ferenczi

One expression of Freud piety that recurs in Fromm's work is his tendency to exalt Freud at the expense of his followers. In *Sigmund Freud's Mission* (1959b), for example, Fromm characterized the majority of Freud's followers as insipid people who wished to avoid genuine political or religious commitment. Along similar lines, Fromm charged that most analysts and patients misused psychoanalysis as a palliative for middle-class alienation through a vicarious identification with Freud that precluded the kind of independent judgment Freud himself embodied (Fromm, 1962, chap. 10).

But in "The Crisis of Psychoanalysis" (1970b) Fromm considerably shifted his emphasis: he spent less time excoriating Freud's devoted followers, and laid more of the blame on Freud for the shape and character of his movement. In a similar spirit, Fromm chastised Freud once more for complicity in a bourgeois-patriarchal social order, arguing that it warped his clinical and scientific judgment (compare Fromm, 1935a and 1970b). Coming to Ferenczi's defense one last time, Fromm suggested that his attempt to resurrect the seduction theory was an attempt to reverse the prevailing policy of blaming the victim (that is, women, children, and adolescents subject to abuse and neglect). To buttress his analysis of the Freud-Ferenczi affair and his claim that Freud himself promoted conformism, Fromm adduced an open exchange of letters in 1958, occasioned by the publication of the third volume of Jones's biography, in the *International Journal of Psycho-Analysis* (Fromm, 1970b, p. 22, n. 10). Michael Balint, Ferenczi's friend, pupil, and literary executor challenged Jones's statement that Ferenczi's "deviation" from Freud was symptomatic of paranoid psychosis and "homicidal mania" toward Freud that surfaced fullblown shortly before Ferenczi's death. Moreover, Balint claimed, although Ferenczi's theories continued to be controversial, a more favorable climate than prevailed at present was necessary to evaluate the real worth of Ferenczi's contributions; posterity would have to judge. Jones responded with a feigned show of sympathy for Balint but reiterated his allegation that Ferenczi's psychosis was attested to by a reliable (but unnamed) eyewitness, and that his views of Ferenczi were shared by Eitington and Freud himself. Fromm's commentary on this episode was provocative. He noted hesitancies and contradictions in Balint's letter and reproached him for his timidity:

> If such a tortuous and submissive letter had been written by a lesser person than Balint, or if it had been written in a dictatorial system in order to avoid severe consequences for freedom or life, it would be understandable. But considering the fact it was written by a well known analyst living in England, it only shows the intensity of the pressure which forbids any but the mildest criticism of one of the leaders of the organization.

More important, Fromm put his finger on the central issue that Balint had avoided in the exchange with Jones, namely, *what* evidence Jones's anonymous source—if he existed—had brought forward. Given the gravity of Jones's "diagnosis," one cannot but wonder why there was not an outcry for this eyewitness to step forward. Whatever confidence may have been broken in the process, the reputation and life's work of a dedicated pioneer were at stake, and the interests of the dead, the living, and future generations outweighed whatever scruples this hypothetical party might have had for remaining silent.

Although it does not reflect well on Freud and his followers, the way Ferenczi's differences with Freud were handled in the analytic literature till recently illustrates the lengths to which the analytic leadership would go to settle a score and gratify their personal ambition, and how readily the rank and file acquiesced in the "official" version of reality.

Fromm's Freud: Alternative Construals

Fromm's portrait of Freud is both challenged and buttressed by psychoanalytic historians. For example, Mark Kanzer and John Glenn (1979) and Alexander Grinstein (1980) have amplified on Freud's oneiric disclosures and free associations in *The Interpretation of Dreams* (1900), which to the analytic eye (or ear) are more revealing than the most intimate autobiography. The Freud that emerges has some of the negative features mentioned by Fromm, but balanced and subdued by more positive ones, notably a thirst for truth, moral courage, and a deep and abiding love of humanity. For these authors, Freud's disposition to truth outweighed his tendency to self-deception, and his theoretical formulations—though in error or sometimes incomplete—are free of any ideological subtext. Their work must be read in conjunction with Fromm's—and, of course, *The Interpretation of Dreams*—before anything like a balanced assessment of Freud's personality will begin to be possible.

At the other extreme is the portrait of Freud drawn by Peter Swales (1982b, 1983, 1986). Like Fromm, Swales is keenly attuned to the burning urgency of Freud's personal ambition and the recurrence of religious motifs in his thought, although for Fromm, Freud's identification with Moses was paramount, while Swales stresses what appears to be an earlier imitation of Christ (Swales, 1982a). Moreover, in connection with the case histories, Fromm and Swales charge

Freud with colluding with parental perceptions and definitions of reality and minimizing the impact of parental pressures on the patient, invoking "psychic reality" as an escape hatch to avoid tangling with potentially explosive social issues that ramify throughout the structure of familial and social authority.[4]

Beyond this point the consensus breaks down, chiefly on the subject of Freud's honesty and reliability as a scientist. Fromm's Freud is flawed and engages in many varieties of self-deception, but he is fundamentally honest in other respects. By contrast, Swales's Freud often "cooks" theories and clinical vignettes to suit the occasion or theory of the moment and is thoroughly conscious of doing so (Swales, 1982b). But despite the shock and consternation he causes the orthodox, Swales, like Fromm, admires Freud deeply and sees him as a great cultural figure. This may be difficult to reconcile with the fact that Swales regards Freud's "psychology of fantasy as very largely the fantasy of a psychology" (personal communication, July 7, 1987). But Swales insists that "what I tend to take away from Freud, in terms of the claims for the clinical-empirical origins of psychoanalysis . . . I give back to him, perversely enough . . . in terms of the cultural-historical (humanistic) inspiration behind his theories, which does indeed invest them with some sort of claims to universality" (ibid.). Moreover, Swales continues,

> I am . . . strongly committed to a perception of Freud . . . as a vehicle for the transmission, transformation and transvaluation of virtually the whole history of human thought, but most particularly what is gleaned from the histories of culture and religion and humanistic literature . . . I tend to regard Freud as the living, larger than life embodiment, or personification, of all that has preceded him, and the seminal principle or "organic filament" behind so much that has come since—i.e., Sigmund Freud, an extraordinary renaissance figure, a child of twenty centuries and more, and one of the fathers of the twentieth.   (Ibid.)

Another Freud portrait that resembles Fromm's is Jeffrey Masson's (1984). Like Masson, Fromm felt that both Freud's break with Ferenczi and Ernest Jones's subsequent slander were precipitated by Ferenczi's revival of the seduction theory. However, Masson emphasizes the seduction theory far more than Fromm did. Instead of treating it as emblematic of deeper and more pervasive problems in psychoanalysis as a whole, Masson makes the validity of the whole edifice of analytic theory hinge on a single etiological issue. More-over, there is not a single reference to Fromm's work, published more than a decade previously, anywhere in Masson's study.

A third theorist whose approach to Freud resembles Fromm's on some points is Alice Miller (for example, 1986). Miller's interrelated discussions of poisonous pedagogy and the frequent retraumatization of the patient in analysis are vividly prefigured in Ferenczi's later work and in Fromm's first defense of Ferenczi (1935a). Miller de-clares that psychoanalysis went off the rails as a consequence of abandoning the traumatic theory of the neuroses circa 1896. Yet by the whole tone of her polemic—and her failure to cite Ferenczi, for example—Miller implies that no real progress or development has occurred since then; she thus invalidates nearly a century of alterna-tive theorizing both within and on the periphery of the analytic movement. In short, she leaves Fromm and Freud's loyal opposition to languish in theoretical obscurity. To the naive reader, this conveys the misleading impression that until Miller came along, the drive theory she so abhors held uncontested sway.

Swales, Masson, and Miller are merely three of the more controver-sial figures whose views on psychoanalysis Fromm anticipated to some degree. But in the vast, complicated, and constantly growing literature by scholars and practitioners from extremely diverse back-grounds, Fromm's contribution is seldom recognized. These psycho-analytic historians fall into four general groups. Some, including Henri Ellenberger, Robert Holt, Frank Sulloway, and L. L. Whyte, ex-plore the "prehistory" of psychoanalysis, linking it with broader cur-rents in the history of ideas. They combine intellectual and social his-tory, and, secondarily, biography. Others, such as William McGrath and Carl Schorske, explore the social and political environment in which Freud lived and its probable influence on his work. They share a desire to contextualize Freud's theories and to do away with the orthodox conceit that his ideas arose, so to speak, like Athena out of Zeus's head, as the unmediated response to his clinical experience and his own self-analysis.

Others, such as George Hogenson, Paul Roazen, François Rous-tang, and Paul Stepansky, tend to focus on people rather than ideas. Although they evince a deep and sympathetic grasp of analytic the-ory, they are more intent on illuminating the connections between "the thought" and "the life," and focus their attention on Freud, or on prominent figures in the early history of the psychoanalytic movement, and the vicissitudes of analytic discipleship.

A fourth group, the most heterogenous, ranges from psychiatrists to scholars in literature and the humanities, anthropology, political theory, and feminism. They combine social, intellectual, and biographical approaches to explicate the political content of psychoanalytic theory and to chart the course and meaning of the various schisms in the movement. They apply late twentieth-century perspectives in textual analysis and ideological critique—which owe so much to Freud—to Freud's case histories, his views on gender, therapy, and so on, or to the works of his followers. The interdisciplinary and hermeneutic orientation of this fourth group is not altogether surprising. When treating of Freud and his followers in any depth, the boundaries between biography, intellectual history, and social history are, if not irrelevant, then entirely artificial.

Where does Fromm stand in relation to this growing and heterogeneous scholarly community? Given the wide differences in temperament and training among practitioners of different disciplines, to expect a fully integrated approach from any single individual is no doubt unrealistic. Clinicians seldom have the time or training to be good historians or philosophers, and vice versa. Still, Fromm's historical musings, though meager from a quantitative standpoint, begin to approximate to this theoretical ideal, inasmuch as their historical and philosophical content are leavened with considerable clinical experience. Moreover, in Fromm's portrait of Freud, biography, intellectual history, and social history form part of a seamless continuum, with the emphasis determined by the topic. Perhaps the very breadth of his reflections, being scattered throughout his writings and seldom condensed around a single theme or topic, worked against him.

In the final analysis, Fromm's most enduring contributions to Freud scholarship are twofold. First, by his own example, Fromm showed that ideas deemed heretical by Freud and his immediate circle nevertheless make their way into the analytic mainstream. For example, during his own career Fromm endorsed the following propositions:

1. The Oedipus complex is not culture constitutive.
2. The tie to the mother is primary developmentally and clinically.

3. Freud's (and Abraham's) ontogenetic schema is too deterministic to account for all clinical psychopathology.
4. The therapist's "neutrality" can mask sadism, indifference, or a moralistic stance.
5. Human motivation and conflict exceed the exigencies of drive satisfaction.
6. Neurosis is a failure of individuation, of the ability to "live soundly against the stream."

Today all these propositions are quite acceptable within the analytic mainstream, whereas in Fromm's day, they were deemed heretical. And yet Fromm has not yet been rehabilitated, much less hailed as the pioneer he was. According to some authorities (for example, Gedo, 1984), a new ecumenical spirit prevails in analytic circles, which actively discourages the kind of sectarian squalls and schisms that marked the early years of the movement. The result is more theoretical openness than was possible twenty or thirty years ago. But if Fromm's case is representative, the new tolerance has not brought any increase in historical awareness. Indeed, in some respects it actually intensifies collective amnesia, since the theorists who originally propounded these ideas are still treated as marginal figures, while more fashionable theorists who are vetted by the establishment build flourishing careers based on inflated claims to originality.

Fromm's second contribution was his lucid demonstration that classical Freudianism is, among other things, a richly ambiguous philosophy of history. As such, it is more—or, arguably, less—than a scientific psychopathology or a therapy of the neuroses. Indeed, as Fromm was fond of noting, if that were all it is, or presumed itself to be, one could scarcely account for Freud's prophetic sense of mission, and of all the byzantine intrigues and persecutions that marked the development of psychoanalysis from the outset (Fromm, 1959b, chaps. 8–10).

In the absence of a consensus about Freud's character and accomplishments, and in a volatile and evolving field of endeavor, it is difficult to assign Fromm a fixed place, much less to speculate on how he will be heeded in future. Clearly, Fromm was not a disinterested observer. But no one committed to a specific tendency within psychoanalysis—whether as analyst or patient—can claim the objectivity that comes with complete detachment. And if anyone does, of course, the claim is automatically suspect. This is one reason why the efforts of competent historians with no analytic experience whatever are often a valuable corrective to the work of "insiders" in psychoanalytic historiography.

However, Fromm was not a typical insider. Unlike the analytic mythmakers, Fromm was intent on situating Freud historically, both as a thinker and as a human being, and not on elevating him to the status of a semidivine being. He approached this task with a level of humanistic scholarship, and of historical and sociological sophistication, that are rare in psychoanalytic circles. Moreover, his leanings toward Marxism and religion ensured a critical distance in relation to some of Freud's ideas. And although he became involved in many theoretical debates and witnessed many political power plays, he did so mostly at a distance. Having no status and little esteem in the analytic mainstream, despite his public popularity, Fromm had very little to lose and could afford to be candid about what he saw.[5]

Ultimately, the enduring merit of Fromm's portrait of Freud and of his various contributions to the history of psychoanalysis are a result of his paradoxical situation as an insider on the outside. Fromm shared this strange status vis-à-vis the analytic mainstream with other members of Freud's loyal opposition, including many non-Marxists, but he was better equipped than they to try to contextualize Freud, and to do the kind of searching historical, textual, and political analysis that his work calls for. Perhaps future historians will be more generous in their acknowledgment of Fromm's Freud. And perhaps they will not. Either way, his contribution to the history of psychoanalysis stands up as a creditable and far-sighted offering.

9 Oedipus, Instinct, and the Unconscious in the Fromm-Marcuse Debate

Although much has been written by others about Fromm's quarrels with the Frankfurt Institute for Social Research and the long, acrimonious debate between Fromm and philosopher Herbert Marcuse, there are still some important issues that have not yet been addressed in the secondary literature.

The Common Ground

The 1920s and 1930s were a time of crisis for the German left. Not only was the proletariat incapable of effecting the revolution Marx had predicted, but the self-appointed representatives of the working class—namely, the Communist party—were deficient in their grasp of social and political reality because of their exclusive emphasis on economic factors and their stubbornly rationalistic approach to human cognition and motivation. Despite some exemplary thinkers and activists in their midst, they were conformist, authoritarian, and out of touch. But they were also the most powerful and well-organized obstacle to a seizure of power by Hitler and his followers. Like many others, Wilhelm Reich joined the Communist party to fight the fascists, and in the hope that his efforts to synthesize Marx and Freud would help ameliorate the party's narrowness and dogmatism. Reich's efforts, though brave and commendable, were doomed from the start. Apart from his inability to conform with the unwritten rules of party etiquette and his well-known personal intransigence, party leaders were simply too threatened by Reich's frank and clear-sighted criticism and by the growing popularity of his German National Association for Proletarian Sexual Politics, which boasted a membership of 40,000 at its height in 1932 (Boadella, 1973, pp. 82–83). Reich was expelled from the party in 1933 more or less concurrently with his expulsion from the International Psychoanalytic Association.

Meanwhile, a more constructive dialogue between psychoanalysis and Marxism was slowly taking shape in the scholarly arena. The Frankfurt Institute for Social Research was founded in 1923 through the efforts of Felix J. Weil, a left-wing political scientist. (Weil's father, a German-born grain merchant in Argentina, endowed the Institute and its facilities at the University of Frankfurt.) Weil was interested in researching subjects such as trade union history and the origins of anti-Semitism but favored a nondogmatic approach to theory. Although he managed and controlled the Institute's financial affairs, Weil avoided taking on the directorship for fear it might compromise the work or reputation of this scholarly enclave.

The first director of the Institute was Carl Grunberg. Grunberg cultivated close ties with Moscow, and many of his associates and coworkers, such as Henryk Grossman and Karl Wittfogel, were members of the Communist party. However, a faction clustering around Max Horkheimer consisted of independent left-wing scholars pursuing philosophy and cultural studies. This small group, which included Theodor Adorno and Leo Lowenthal, had the growing sympathy and support of Horkheimer's friend, economist Friedrich Pollock, who was increasingly disenchanted with the orthodox political line of Grunberg and Grossman.

In 1927 Grunberg suffered a stroke, and Pollock became interim director till 1931, when Horkheimer was officially installed. Horkheimer coined the term *critical theory* to describe the Institute's new direction and efforts. Like Fromm and Marcuse, he was an admirer of Rosa Luxemburg and was very critical of Leninist centrism. Being a specialist in Kant and Hegel, he imparted a more interdisciplinary and philosophical complexion to the Institute's work. Horkheimer also studied psychoanalysis briefly with Karl Landauer, Fromm's former supervisor, and was in agreement with Fromm on the need to integrate Marxism and psychoanalysis.

Among the many cultural and intellectual influences in the Institute's evolving research agenda was the emergence of a new "Hegelian" Marxism. Thanks to David Ryazonov, head of the Marx-Engels Institute in Moscow, copies of Marx's early and as-yet-unpublished manuscripts were in circulation in prewar Europe. As a result, Marxist philosophers such as Karl Korsch, Georg Lukács, Lucien Goldmann, Alexander Kojève, Jean Hippolyte, and Herbert Marcuse were analyzing and debating the implications of Marx's early manuscripts in German, French, and Hungarian books and periodicals long before English-speaking scholars were even aware of their existence. The most important texts Ryazonov made available were Marx's *Grundrisse* and *Economic and Philosophic Manuscripts of 1844*. They proved how important Hegel's philosophy was to Marx, and how the young Marx's theory of alienation was rooted in a lucid critique of Hegel's *Phenomenology of Spirit*. Marcuse and, subsequently, Erich Fromm were deeply impressed by the humanism and radicalism of Marx's early work and struck by the strong degree of continuity between the earlier and later Marx, which vulgar Marxism energetically repudiated. However, as Martin Jay points out, not all Institute members shared their enthusiasm. Grunberg's orthodox enclave was largely unmoved by these new discoveries and debates and continued its economic research as before. But Horkheimer, Adorno, and Walter Benjamin were openly unsympathetic to Marx's theory of alienated labor, which became central to Fromm's work in the 1950s and 1960s. Indeed, Horkheimer once complained that the young Marx's tendency to regard labor as "a transcendent category of human activity" was a return to an ascetic, bourgeois ideology, while Adorno charged Marx with wanting to transform the entire world into a gigantic factory (Jay, 1973, p. 57).

Still, although many Marxists repudiated specific features of the new Hegel and Marx scholarship, the fact that some left-leaning intellectuals sought to integrate Hegel and Freud into a deeper, less doctrinaire kind of Marxism was certainly no coincidence. For in their various ways, Hegel, Marx, and Freud were all followers of the Enlightenment. They were persuaded of the reality of progress but waxed eloquent on the continuing prevalence of collective illusions. In admittedly different ways, they all saw progress as resulting from the resolution of conflict and contradictions in society, and regarded the origin and nature of these conflicts, and their effects on human motivation and cognition, as being largely unconscious to those affected by them. Finally, they regarded collective illusion as a reflection of our simultaneous participation in and estrangement from ontological verities they were striving to elucidate in the interests of general emancipation. For Marx and Freud—more so than for Hegel—enlightenment consisted less in the acquisition of positive knowledge than in the act of shedding or relinquishing illusions, and accordingly, they regarded their theoretical systems as weapons in a struggle to *disillusion* humanity. As Fromm later pointed out, it is in this sense that theory is—or should be—critical (Fromm, 1962).

Given the obvious incompatibility between Marx and Freud on other levels, it is also not surprising that during the 1920s and 1930s most Marxists rejected Freud's theories as irredeemably bourgeois. However, for critical theory—initially, at any rate—the integration of psychoanalysis did not involve a wholesale endorsement of (or capitulation to) Freud's cultural and historical pessimism. Rather, it was an attempt to understand the irrationality of mass behavior in light of analytic theory, and to evolve a research methodology appropriate to that task in the interests of general emancipation, but without adhering to the party line. During that phase, features of Freudianism that minimized the impact of social and economic conditions on collective psychology, that lapsed into reification, ahistorical thinking, or crude anticommunist rhetoric, were deemed expendable. At the beginning of the Institute's existence, there was a genuine interest in and openness to Freud, but no particular premium on adherence to any particular article of the Freudian credo. For despite the theorists' interest in grim topics such as authoritarianism and the psychology of anti-Semitism, there was a strong element of optimism in the first phase of critical theory's development—a faith in the possibility of widespread change in keeping with the spirit of Hegel's and Marx's sublimated messianism.

The Great Divide

This phase did not last. By the end of the Second World War, Horkheimer and his associates—with the possible exception of Marcuse—were exceedingly pessimistic about the prospects for social change. The power and prestige that came with defeating Hitler and Japan, together with the escalating tensions of Cold War politics, rendered the American working class deeply suspicious of socialism, and less interested in changing the system than in tasting the pleasures of the emerging consumerism. And as Europe slowly rebuilt with American aid, its citizens were succumbing more and more to American cultural influence—something Horkheimer and Adorno openly detested. World politics promised increasingly to be a never-ending series of skirmishes between two military juggernauts posing as the liberators of humanity, with atomic weapons that could—and probably would—utterly destroy us (Adorno, 1979; Horkheimer, 1978).

This shift from a sober, realistic, and even skeptical optimism to a despairing and angry pessimism was integral to the development of critical theory. No one has depicted this transformation more faithfully than Albrecht Wellmer:

> For Horkheimer, the rediscovery of Marx the dialectician (meant) . . . the rehabilitation of a significant concept of reason, which, originating in the philosophical tradition, came to its own only with Marx . . . This notion implied the immanent direction of the historical process towards men's autonomy in relation to the history they have made; towards the freedom of every individual and the acknowledgment of each man by every other man as a person; and, in short, towards the transcendence of the historic relationship of coercion by a joining together of all men in dialogue and common action without constraint.   (1974, p. 12)

With the passage of time, however, Horkheimer and Adorno came to see critical theory as

> a protest, impotent in practice, against the apocalyptically self-obturating system of alienation and reification; and as the spark whose preservation in a self-darkening world will keep alive the memory of something quite different. The eventual irruption of this "something else" became the object of a hope that grew in wisdom but . . . was touched by despair.   (Ibid., p. 52)

Although we cannot date this transition with any precision, the break between Fromm and the Frankfurt Institute at Columbia in 1938 was probably affected by it. For though given to some very pessimistic utterances in later life, Fromm clung stubbornly to the optimism and sublimated messianism that accompanied the Institute's inception. Meanwhile, however, their disagreements were probably more concrete. To begin with, there was Horkheimer's refusal to publish the study of German workers that Fromm had undertaken with his initial approval. And in 1935 Fromm wrote an article defending Georg Groddeck and Sandor Ferenczi, whose reputations were being savagely attacked by Freud's inner circle. Following Ferenczi, Fromm attempted to show that the classically oriented analyst partakes in a socially patterned defect endemic to the modern world; that an (unconscious) attitude of indifference or deprecation masked by a (conscious) show of tolerance and neutrality reproduces childhood traumas and reinforces the status quo. In contrast to classical detachment, Fromm endorsed an analytic posture that is actively engaged and affirms the patient's right to happiness (1935a). In this respect Fromm's critique resembled Ian Suttie's support of many of Ferenczi's ideas about treatment in *The Origins of Love and Hate* (1935). Unlike Suttie, however, who was not a Marxist, Fromm insisted that there is something quintessentially *bourgeois* about the attitudes and unconscious contradictions that suffuse Freud's various treatment recommendations.

In short, from 1934 to 1938 and probably for some time thereafter, Fromm was actively divesting himself of a portion of his Freud piety out of sympathy for Groddeck and Ferenczi. This fact is not simply reflected in his writings at that time. It is reflected in everything he wrote subsequently. From that point on, he lost no opportunity to unmask any bourgeois, authoritarian, or patriarchal features in Freud's character that crept into his work or correspondence. Horkheimer, Adorno, and Marcuse, by contrast, had no real familiarity with psychoanalytic politics, and no personal investment in Freud's loyal opposition, but were beginning to *assert* their Freud piety for the very first time. This dramatic polarization in perspectives and the tendency among Horkheimer, Adorno, and Marcuse to idealize Freud defensively are reflected in Fromm's recollection that as he was leaving the Institute—still bristling with indignation about Ferenczi and Groddeck's treatment, no doubt—his erstwhile colleagues had suddenly discovered a more "revolutionary" Freud (Jay, 1973, p. 102).

The first Institute member to attack Fromm publicly was Theodor Adorno, in an article delivered in Los Angeles on April 26, 1946. According to Martin Jay's analysis,

> Adorno objected to the stress on love in the revisionists' work. Fromm had attacked Freud for his authoritarian lack of warmth, but true revolutionaries are often called hard and cold. Social antagonisms cannot be wished away; they must be consummated, which inevitably means

suffering for someone: "It may well be that our society has developed itself to an extreme where the reality of love can actually be expressed only by a hatred of the existent, whereas any direct evidence of love serves only at confirming the very same conditions that breed hatred." Adorno finished the article with a phrase reminiscent of Walter Benjamin's often quoted remark from his study of Goethe's *Elective Affinities*, "It is only for the sake of the hopeless that we are given hope." "I suspect," Adorno wrote, "that Freud's contempt for men is nothing but the expression of such hopeless love, which may be the only expression of hope still permitted to us." (1973, p. 105)

Adorno's critique showed an elementary incomprehension of the clinical issues addressed in Fromm's 1935 article. Leaving aside the reality of social antagonisms and the inevitable suffering that accompanies their resolution, Adorno's perverse logic suggests that under present circumstances, a cold, hard exterior is the only adequate expression of love, while love overtly felt and expressed merely confirms and consolidates the hateful reality of oppression all around us. Moreover, Adorno ignored the fact that what Fromm regarded as chiefly inimical to the patient's sanity and prospects for recovery was the analyst's tendency to disguise and disown judgmental attitudes regarding the patient's emerging complexes; the fact that neutrality, so called, often masks fear and hostility or a deeper indifference to the happiness and well-being of the patient. Surface coolness and detachment may mask a deeper hypocrisy, and it is this hypocrisy, and the discrepancy between the analyst's conscious and unconscious attitudes, that are really pathogenic for the patient. Finally, Adorno overlooked the fact that Freud's attitude to the resolution of social antagonisms toward the end of his life was openly reactionary (Roazen, 1973, 1990). Far from wanting to see social antagonisms "consummated" in a revolutionary struggle, the elderly Freud actually commended Mussolini for imparting "discipline" to the masses (Roazen, 1973, p. 534). Accordingly, it comes as no surprise that Adorno offered no evidence for his assertion that Freud's "contempt for men" was a tortured expression of a kind of "hopeless love" engendered by the oppressive reality of contemporary social conditions. Evidence for this assertion is extremely hard to come by. True, in his correspondence with Martha Bernays, Maria Montessori, and Romain Roland, Freud movingly declared his intention of laboring selflessly on behalf of all humanity. But if actions speak louder than words, then the burden of evidence gathered by diligent historians suggests that Freud's coldness or hostility toward independent-minded friends and supporters—Joseph Breuer, Victor Tausk, Herbert Silberer, Reich, Groddeck, Ferenczi, Paul Schilder, and many others—was often the expression of wounded vanity or a coldly calculating egoism, rather than of strangulated altruism or fellow feeling, as Adorno implied.

Adorno's critique, then, was somewhat obtuse politically, and tangential to the clinical issues Fromm was addressing, and he did not reply to Adorno publicly. Marcuse's critique, published nine years later, was in some ways more thoughtful and circumspect, and Fromm was deeply stung by it. The vituperative remarks traded and the chronology of polemical thrust and counterthrust have been ably discussed elsewhere.[1] But it is worth noting that in this quarrel, as in the earlier one with Reich, fidelity to Freud was again at issue, although Marcuse's support of nongenital sexuality shifted the terms of the debate considerably.

Instinct and the Unconscious in Freud, Fromm, and Marcuse

In a paper published first as an article in *Dissent,* then as the epilogue to *Eros and Civilization,* Marcuse acknowledged the merit of "The Social Conditions of Psychoanalytic Therapy" (1935a) and commended the papers preceding it as exemplary embodiments of radical psychoanalytic theorizing. However, he dismissed Fromm's work after 1935 as a radical revision of Freudian theory. According to Marcuse, like other revisionists Fromm had abandoned Freud's most important concepts, including the primacy of sexuality, the death instinct, the archaic inheritance, and primary narcissism. But unlike Reich, who regarded sadomasochism and the authoritarian character as the products of repressed genital strivings, Marcuse argued that the dominant cause of repression is the primacy of genital sexuality, which thrives at the expense of polymorphous or pregenital drives. According to Marcuse, monogamy and "procreative sexuality," which buttress the primacy of genitality, are generated and sustained by a historic dynamic called the "performance principle." As an alternative to the repressive strictures of the performance principle,

Marcuse commended what he termed "the Orphic-Narcissistic Eros," which he linked to homosexuality, to the death instinct, and to the yearning to restore a predualistic sense of unity with the environment characteristic of intrauterine existence, or the state of primary narcissism the infant supposedly inhabits briefly after birth. Marcuse wrote:

> The narcissistic phase of individual pre-genitality "recalls" the maternal phase of the history of the human race. Both constitute a reality to which the ego responds with an attitude, not of defense and submission, but of integral identification with the "environment." But in the light of the paternal reality principle, the "maternal concept" of reality here emerging is immediately turned into something negative, dreadful. The impulse to re-establish the lost Narcissistic maternal unity is interpreted as a "threat," namely the threat of "maternal engulfment" by the over-powering womb. The hostile father is exonerated and reappears as a savior who, in punishing the incest wish, protects the ego from its annihilation in the mother. The question does not arise whether the Narcissistic-maternal attitude toward reality cannot return in less primordial, less devouring forms under the power of the mature ego and in a mature civilization. Instead, the necessity of suppressing this attitude once and for all is taken for granted. The patriarchal reality principle holds sway over the psychoanalytic interpretation. (1955, pp. 210–211)

In short, like Fromm and Reich before him, Marcuse criticized the patriarchal bias of classical analytic theory and invoked matriarchal theory to buttress his ideas about history and civilization. At the same time, however, he trivialized the nature and intensity of the morbid fear of engulfment that is characteristic of pre-Oedipal fixation by treating it as an artifact of patriarchal civilization rather than a frequent factor in the etiology of psychosis and related, borderline disturbances. Fromm later attributed this distortion to Marcuse's lack of clinical experience and to his lack of interest in and respect for clinical data (1970b, pp. 25–31).

Nevertheless, Marcuse did argue in a troubling and insistent way that advances in analytic "technique" ought not to be tied to fundamental issues in analytic theory. The real point of Freud's writings, he asserted, was to show that the individual's fate, as interpreted clinically, is only emblematic of the deeper, collective dynamic of historical development. (This is actually a self-defeating argument. For the fact that clinical concepts and case material allegedly illumine collective dynamics is scarcely grounds for dismissing or detaching them.) Far more compelling was Marcuse's complaint that theory and practice should be divorced because effective therapy in present circumstances involves strengthening conformist tendencies in the patient that enable the latter to adapt to the prevailing system of domination—then disguising this conformist undertaking with idealistic verbiage about maturity, "productive love," and so on.

Fromm's first response to Marcuse came in two installments in the fall and winter issues of *Dissent* in 1955–56 (1955a, 1956b). According to Fromm, Marcuse underestimated the extent to which Freud was a prisoner of nineteenth-century mechanistic materialism, and the way this is reflected in Freud's theory of the drives. Fromm also emphasized that genuine love, far from being merely "ideological," as Marcuse and Adorno alleged, is actually quite rare in contemporary society, because it is out of step with the prevailing character of social relations, which imposes market patterns on human relationships. Moreover, Marcuse failed to appreciate to what extent certain pregenital strivings are inimical to any civilized social order (Jay, 1973, p. 111).

At this time, in the mid-1950s, Fromm was somewhat overwhelmed by the ferocity of Marcuse's onslaught, and accordingly failed to expose some weaknesses in Marcuse's position that occurred to him only subsequently (1970b, 1973). But Marcuse's attack on the conformist implications of the revisionists' ideas and his attempt to resurrect and redefine the "death instinct" probably contributed to Fromm's odd and inconsistent avowals of practicing "classical technique" in the mid-1950s, and to his own confused attempts to translate Freud's ideas of the life and death instincts into existential idiom. Thus, Marcuse's critique was undoubtedly a powerful stimulus to Fromm's intellectual development after 1955, although he was too proud and too angry to admit this in public—or perhaps even to himself.

Marcuse's *Eros and Civilization* combines great scholarship and imagination with a creative but cavalier misreading of Freud. But in some important respects its criticism is sound. Fromm's revision of Freudian theory does involve a devaluation of sexuality as a formative and disruptive force in human development. Marcuse was also justified in chastising Fromm for ignoring the specifically sexual component of the Oedipus complex (1955, pp. 246–247). For although they may not represent the "core complex" behind the great variety of cultural patterns or the most profoundly repressed strata of the psyche, as Freud frequently alleged, Oedipal phenomena are so commonplace in our culture that one cannot ignore their existence altogether.

Contrary to what Otto Rank, Erich Fromm, and several object-relations theorists appear to believe, Oedipal phenomena are not always a defense against a deeper symbiotic fixation or a derivative of pre-Oedipal conflicts. Viewed developmentally, the more benign and transient varieties of Oedipal feeling in later childhood and adolescence actually represent a *progressive* rather than a regressive orientation; a desire to grow up and assume adult prerogatives and relationships. Indeed, in many instances, an Oedipal orientation in a developing young person may also represent a compromise in the struggle between progressive and regressive tendencies; between the desire to grow up, individuate, and leave the nuclear family, and the desire to perpetuate parental attachments. In effect, it is a wish to have it both ways—to be a child and an adult at one and the same time. Though inappropriate, embarrassing, and painful in an adult, such a paradoxical position mirrors the actual situation of young people in the nuclear family. And although nonsexual aims and aspirations—such as the desire to mature or the fear of regression—often color Oedipal strivings, and the guilt they give rise to, the sexual desire for the parent of the opposite sex—though frequently repressed, sublimated, or displaced onto a more suitable object—is too real and too frequent an occurrence to be dismissed by a thoughtful and sympathetic observer.

Unfortunately, Marcuse attempted to argue otherwise: though insisting that the Oedipus complex has a sexual component, he did so in a way that emphasized and endorsed its regressive rather than its progressive or ambiguous aspects. According to Marcuse, Oedipal attachment to the mother (he is silent on female Oedipal striving) is indicative of the desire to reinstate the adualistic world of intrauterine life, with its effortless gratification of all wishes and desires. In his own words:

> Fromm's ideological interpretation of the Oedipus complex implies the acceptance of the unhappiness of freedom, of its separation from satisfaction; Freud's theory implies that the Oedipus wish is the eternal

infantile *protest* against this separation—protest not against freedom, but against painful, repressive freedom. Conversely, the Oedipus wish is the eternal infantile desire for the prototype of freedom: freedom from want. And since (unrepressed) sex instinct is the biological carrier of this archetype of freedom, the Oedipus is essentially "sexual craving." Its natural object is, not simply the mother *qua* mother, but the mother *qua* woman—female principle of gratification.   (Marcuse, 1955, p. 247)

Here Marcuse overlooked the fact that for Freud, Oedipal desire is characteristic of only the genital phase of development, and that it therefore presupposes a high degree of individuation from the symbiotic matrix of pre-Oedipal attachment. Moreover, as we saw in the previous chapter, in his quarrels with Jung, Rank, and Ferenczi, Freud went to great lengths to deny the etiological importance of pre-Oedipal ties to the mother and never linked them explicitly to Oedipal symptomatology. Indeed, he and his intimates excoriated those who attempted to forge a link between the oral and Oedipal levels. Had he lived long enough, Freud might have accorded Marcuse's "defense" of the Oedipus complex the same reception.

To judge from his handling of the Oedipus complex, Marcuse's fidelity to Freud, which was a source of fierce sectarian pride, was actually far from perfect. In retrospect we know that Oedipal strivings are not pathogenic unless they are needlessly intensified or prolonged as a result of parental psychopathology—notably, by unconscious desires to seduce, infantilize, and/or control offspring emotionally. Such circumstances are by no means rare, but these problems are not culture constitutive. But Marcuse's oversights in this area pale in comparison with his naive and seemingly willful derelictions elsewhere.

As Fromm pointed out in "The Crisis of Psychoanalysis" (1970b), one of the odd and astonishing things about *Eros and Civilization* was the way Marcuse used the word *repression*. In his introduction Marcuse boldly declared that throughout his book, " 'Repression' and 'repressive' are used in the non-technical sense to designate both conscious and unconscious, external and internal processes of restraint, constraint and suppression" (1955, p. 7). This explanation makes it clear at the outset that *Eros and Civilization* is not a psychoanalytic treatise. Repression in the dynamic sense refers to an *unconscious* mental process whereby certain mental contents—be they thoughts, feelings, memories, fantasies, or wishes—are deliberately thrust out of awareness and rendered inaccessible to conscious retrieval or introspection (Burston, 1986a, 1988). Not only is the mechanism itself unconscious—as J. F. Herbart stipulated as early as 1825—but, as Freud later noted, so is the *motive* for repression.

Fundamentally, Freud's stature as a theorist of false consciousness rests on his notion of dynamic repression, and the whole meaning of the word is lost once the term is used to designate both conscious and unconscious, internal and external processes. Therefore, Marcuse's promiscuous use of the term *repression* violates both the spirit and the letter of Freud's work.

Classical Freudianism represents a synthesis or integration of (1) the theory of repression and the defense mechanisms, which describe and explain how we distort or falsify our awareness and limit our conscious experience and desires in accordance with external or internal constraints; and (2) the instinct and libido theories, also known as the drive theory, which gives a causal-deterministic account of human behavior. In Freud's mind, these two facets of his theory were inseparable, and the truly orthodox continue to attempt to perpetuate this point of view.

Recently, however, more and more analysts have come to believe that Freud's insights into unconscious mental processes are not capable of standing on their own, without being attached to, supported or qualified by an outdated and untenable biological theory. Fromm aside, the list of clinicians who have adopted this position is now quite considerable, and includes theorists as diverse as W. R. D. Fairbairn, Harry Guntrip, John Sutherland, John Bowlby, Charles Rycroft, Peter Lomas, R. D. Laing, Jacques Lacan, Heinz Kohut, Roy Schafer, Donald Spence, Edgar Levenson, and Morris Eagle. On the whole, these theorists do not aim at a simple divorce between the dynamic unconscious and Freud's theory of instinctual drives, but attempt to buttress their inferences about unconscious mental processes with more up-to-date biological assumptions or theories of language and language production, intersubjectivity, and so on.

In short, many creative theorists consider Freud's psychobiology and theory of the drives completely expendable. Marcuse, in contrast—and quite *unlike* truly orthodox Freudians—disregarded Freud's theory of dynamic repression while embracing his psychobiology and metapsychology—or an idealized and distorted version of it, as I will show below. Yet Freud's formulations on instinct were meant to illumine the workings of the unconscious mind, rather than vice versa. Surely even the orthodox would agree that without the dynamic unconscious as the central core, the whole edifice of Freudian drive theory—including the Oedipus complex—is really quite superfluous and absurd.

What is lost in Marcuse's use of *repression* as something involved in *all* processes of constraint, restraint, and suppression—conscious and unconscious, internal and external—is a historical understanding of what these terms actually meant to Freud. According to Freud, conscious, voluntary restraint exercised autonomously to regulate the play of internal impulses has nothing to do with repression and, though painful at times, is by no means necessarily pathogenic. Indeed, insofar as it is congruent with the demands of reason and reality, it helps us manage life's inevitable frustrations and hardships, and aids us in the struggle to survive.

Reason, Fantasy, and Desire in Freud and Marcuse

According to Freud, even the most mundane reality-testing, and, by implication, our very survival, is contingent to some extent on our capacity for purposive inhibition, as expressed, for example, in his notion of *secondary process thought,* which can be described as the temporary deferment of drive gratification in the interests of securing more realistic sources of pleasure and satisfaction in reality. Common sense indicates that a deliberate delay in the satisfaction of an impulse, much as it may frustrate or disappoint us momentarily, does not diminish our actual *capacity* for pleasure, nor does it block the entry of a specific thought, feeling, or fantasy into consciousness. In short, it has nothing to do with repression proper. Moreover, this kind of purposive inhibition is not to be confused or conflated with repression or with *neurotic inhibition,* which is not biologically adaptive, and which leads to a decrease in the capacity for pleasure in both the short and the long term.

Unfortunately, all of this was lost on Marcuse, who attempted to resurrect and defend the claims of fantasy, or *primary process thought,* against the overweening demands of reason and reality. In doing so he interpreted Freud in a starkly dualistic way that omitted, repressed, or merely failed to acknowledge key elements of Freud's thinking. According to Marcuse, for example,

The establishment of the reality principle causes a division and mutilation of the mind which fatefully determines its entire development. The mental process formerly unified in the pleasure ego is now split: its main stream is channeled into the domain of the reality principle . . . Thus conditioned, this part of the mind obtains the monopoly of interpreting, manipulating and altering reality—of governing remembrance and oblivion, even of defining what reality is and how it should be used and altered. The other part of the mental apparatus remains free from the control of the reality principle—at the price of becoming powerless, inconsequential, unrealistic. Whereas the ego was formerly guided and driven by the whole of its mental energy, it is now guided by that part of it that conforms to the reality principle . . . Phantasy as a separate mental process is born and at the same time left behind . . . Reason prevails; it becomes unpleasant but useful and correct, phantasy remains pleasant but becomes useless, untrue—a mere playing or daydreaming. (1955, pp. 128–129)

According to Marcuse, then, the growth of the reality principle—equated with reason—progressively impoverishes fantasy, monopolizing psychic energy and leaving the pleasure principle—equated with fantasy—powerless and inconsequential. And arguably, perhaps, this is actually the case. But it is not Freud. By Freud's account, the emergence of the reality ego supposedly involves the introduction of *structure* or organization to the hitherto inchoate id. Indeed, it is the emergence of this structure that marks the psychological birth of the individual, since before acquiring some voluntary control over its impulses and musculature the newborn infant is nothing but a bundle of reflexes. To see structure characterized so one-sidedly as a "division" and "mutilation" is a little alarming, when we consider that the development of said structure was conceived of in broad evolutionary terms as something absolutely necessary for organismic survival, rather than as a punitive regime imposed from without (Fromm, 1970b).

Moreover, Marcuse alleges that "reason" (or the reality principle) monopolizes mental energy, channeling it greedily to its own domain, whereas Freud stipulated that the ego (or "reality ego") is really just a differentiated layer or an appendage of the id. And although the ego may indeed *guide* the organism—under optimal conditions, at any rate—it is presumably the vast reservoir of instinctual impulses that exist beneath the surface of consciousness that continue to *drive* the organism throughout life—by Freud's reckoning, anyway.

In short, Marcuse confused a tendency inherent in ego function-ing—namely, to appropriate more and more instinctual energy to itself—with an ability to dominate and impoverish unconscious in-stinctual life, and then hypostatized this into a "fact" of historical development. By contrast, Freud, writing in the first half of our century, thought that it would take at least several more centuries to tame and domesticate the collective id, something Marcuse described as a disastrous and debilitating *fait accompli* a mere two decades later; a curious incongruity in historical perspective that Marcuse never explained. Freud's motto "Wo es war, soll ich werden" (where the id was, there shall ego be) and his repeated warnings on the power of the instincts and their sustained defiance of civilized "reason" do not accord well with this lament for the decline of fantasy.

Another problem with Marcuse's characterization of the reality principle is that, as Freud conceived it—and as Fromm pointed out (1970b, p. 27)—the reality principle is not really bent on the denial of desire. As the differentiated portion of the id, the ego, which operates on secondary process thought, nevertheless derives its energy and aims from the pleasure principle. For though subject to the constraints of external reality, reality testing or secondary-process thought is wedded to the program of the pleasure principle, which seeks to provide pleasure and to avoid pain, and denies pleasure only in the interests of survival (that is, the ego instincts). A suitable description of the reality principle might be that it is a kind of felicific calculus, which determines the probable yield of pleasure and pain contingent on any given course of action, then weighs the short- and long-term benefits that are likely to accrue, and then empowers the organism as a whole to act accordingly. But in Marcuse's rendering, as Fromm rightly noted, the reality principle is not an agent or a rational extension of the pleasure principle, but its open antagonist.

Finally, in Marcuse's lexicon, as Fromm again pointed out, the reality principle is something that is socially determined and socially constructed, and therefore susceptible to deconstruction in the inter-ests of fashioning a reality principle that is not antagonistic to the interests of pregenital sexuality; Marcuse's "sensuous reason." But this deconstructionist analysis makes sense only if we have already lost the original sense and intention of Freud's formulations, in which the reality principle is a biological or evolutionary given, rather than a social and historical artifact, and by no means necessarily opposed to the promptings of desire.

The Orphic Eros

Because of its discursive style and sustained level of theoretical abstraction, Marcuse's *Eros and Civilization* is susceptible to many different interpretations. But one clear conclusion his readers draw is that political liberation must be accompanied by sexual revolution if it is to effect a lasting transformation of society, and to allow human potential its optimal and unfettered expression. Fromm's characterization of Reich as "a sexual anarchist" in *Greatness and Limitations of Freud's Thought* (1980) suggests that, with advancing age, he greeted any call for sexual revolution—including Marcuse's—with considerable skepticism.

Still, as Fromm himself pointed out, Reich and he were actually closer in many respects than Reich and Marcuse. Marcuse's theory did not focus on the vicissitudes of genitality, nor did it see the widespread achievement of genitality as a condition of collective well-being, or even as something desirable in its own right as an antidote to fascism and patriarchal-authoritarian power relations (Fromm, 1970). In Marcuse's utopia, there would be greater scope for the efflorescence of narcissism and for (unspecified) features of pre-genital or component instincts that Reich, Fromm, and Freud himself would have deemed deeply injurious to individual and collective well-being. Marcuse began reasonably enough, stating that some activities and impulses deemed perverse are not necessarily incompatible with civilization per se, although they may be incompatible with the ideal of regulating sexual activity within the framework of monogamous heterosexual commitments. Of many possible candidates for rehabilitation here, Marcuse named three: homosexuality, coprophilia, and sadism. The compatibility of homosexuality with "civilized" life is no longer seriously disputed in enlightened circles, although because of AIDS many homosexuals are now inclined toward the monogamous ideal—something Marcuse could not have anticipated.

Leaving homosexuality to one side, however, Marcuse also insisted that certain unspecified components of sadism and coprophilia have an "instinctual substance" that is distinct from their overly civilized (and hence distorted) expression; that the general perversion of human life under the sway of the performance principle dictates that they acquire "inhuman, compulsive, coercive and destructive aspects" that are not intrinsic to their "instinctive" character. Unfortunately, he did not specify which elements of sadism and coprophilia warrant inclusion in a civilized social order, and which are beyond the pale, leaving us to rely on our own imaginations.

Unfortunately, this is not an inviting prospect. Coprophilia, as defined in Rycroft's *A Critical Dictionary of Psychoanalysis,* consists of "pleasure in touching, looking at or eating feces" (1972, p. 25). Curiously enough, this brief definition omits the specifically *olfactory* component of the coprophilic interest in excrement, to which Freud repeatedly drew attention (for example, 1930, chap. 4). But regardless of whether we emphasize smell, touch, or other sensory modalities, people who are sexually excited chiefly by contact with excrement are morbid and unbalanced. Clinical experience suggests that in such cases, other areas of human and interpersonal functioning besides sexuality are subject to pathological distortion as well. So perhaps Marcuse's lapse into silence here was prompted by the fact that he had nothing particularly cogent or believable to say in this regard.

To give Marcuse the benefit of the doubt, we can turn our attention to sadism, bearing in mind his assurance that the sadism of the SS troops, for example, is utterly unlike that found in a "free libidinal relation." And admittedly, on reflection, it is a well-known fact that in most varieties of sexual sadism, the victim's suffering is not inflicted without his or her agreement, but is a part of a consensually agreed-upon arrangement between two (nominally) free and equal adults. The element of external coercion—if not of unconscious compulsion—is absent by definition. But does that really settle the matter?

On the issue of civil liberties, which have occupied the foreground in recent debates, society has no right to proscribe *any* form of sexual play between consenting adults provided it does not result in serious or irreparable injury to either party. But this legal point scarcely exhausts the *psychological* side of the equation, which Fromm summed up in *The Anatomy of Human Destructiveness.*

> The problem is quite complex. If one defines as perversion—as has been done—any sexual practice that does not lead to the procreation of children, i.e., which only serves pleasure, then of course all those who are opposed to this traditional attitude will arise—and justly so—in the defense of "perversions." However, this is by no means the only definition of perversion, and in fact, it is a rather old fashioned one.
>
> Sexual desire, even when no love is present, is an expression of life and of mutual giving and sharing of pleasure. Sexual acts, however, that

are characterized by the fact that one person becomes the object of the other's contempt, of his wish to hurt, his desire to control are the only true sexual perversions; not because they do not serve procreation, but because they pervert a life-serving impulse into a life-strangling one.

   If one compares sadism with a form of sexual behavior that has often been called perversion—i.e., all kinds of oral-genital contact—the difference becomes quite apparent. The latter behavior is as little a perversion as kissing, because it does not imply control, or humiliation of the other person.   (1973, pp. 314–315)

Fromm goes on in this vein a little longer, but the gist of his argument is that the *desire* to control, injure, degrade, or humiliate another human being—or to be so treated—is sick, not the specific features of the sexual act in question. Accordingly, where fantasies of degradation, injury, and control figure prominently in people's sexual activity, it is naive to describe their impulses or activities as being "freely chosen." Many people laboring under unconscious compulsions prefer to think that they are not so driven, but have chosen their conduct "freely." If it is not infused with a feeling of tenderness and an attitude of respect—even in the absence of deep and abiding love— eroticism becomes degraded and degrading, and hence, perverse, regardless of whether the partners are of the same or of different sexes.

Fromm and Marcuse in Retrospect

In view of his handling of the Oedipus complex, repression, and the primary and secondary processes, Marcuse's critique of Fromm and the neo-Freudians is obviously somewhat suspect. Nevertheless, Marcuse enthusiasts still argue that Marcuse kept faith with Freud by continuing to emphasize the (apparently) irreconcilable claims of the libido and society, and the role of instinct as the primary motive for all human behavior, while Fromm betrayed him on this score. For reasons adduced below, this matter probably cannot be resolved by rational discussion, and to those unversed or uninterested in the relationship between psychoanalysis and critical theory, it is really a nonissue anyway. Nevertheless, students of Fromm and of the history of psychoanalysis generally should examine this unpleasant episode for what it reveals about Fromm personally, and about the whole intellectual climate that prevailed in psychoanalytic debate till the more recent wave of ahistorical ecumenicalism prevailed in North America.

Fromm (1959b), Paul Roazen (1974, 1990), and François Roustang (1982) all provide solid evidence that, in addition to his great intellectual courage and gifts, Freud had an uncanny gift for fostering a fractious loyalty among his followers, so that they vied jealously for his favor. In the interests of spreading his ideas and fame, Freud cultivated an atmosphere of sibling rivalry among his intimates and manipulated these emotional currents and conflicts in ways that tended to obscure or override the truly scientific content and dimensions of analytic theory. And although Freud paid ample lip service to the intellectual autonomy of his followers, in the long run he demanded unquestioning agreement on any idea that mattered to him. *This* kind of fidelity to Freud is usually worthless, scientifically speaking, and often quite contemptible in human terms because of the needless dogmatism and suffering it engenders. And as Fromm himself pointed out in connection with Rank and Ferenczi (1959b), the unwavering loyalty Freud required of his disciples produces historiographic oversights and falsifications of truly Stalinist proportions; so much so, in fact, that even today orthodox Freudian historiography can scarcely be trusted (Roazen, 1990).

Freud's loyal opposition differed from the rank and file in maintaining a greater measure of intellectual independence from the master. But even here debate was colored by fratricidal elements. Among the Freudo-Marxists, the fractious and competitive ambience that pervaded the Freudian establishment usually took the form of rival claims to have distilled and preserved the radical or revolutionary core of Freud's thought, or to have developed it to its ultimate logical conclusions. Perhaps on some symbolic level what was really at issue between Marcuse, Fromm, Reich, and Fenichel was the need to establish who was the true son and heir to Freud, or at any rate to the radical Freud that presumably gave way to the aging conservative theorist Freud eventually became.

To the extent that this is the real bone of contention beneath or behind the theoretical debates among the Freudo-Marxists, rational discussion is probably of very little use in sorting them out. Scanning the literature and pondering the arguments on all sides, one cannot help but suspect that what divided this tiny analytic enclave was really a kind of sibling rivalry that resembled the more obvious and pervasive variety endemic to the analytic establishment that scorned and rejected them, compounded by the characteristic sectarianism of left-wing politics. However, at the risk of making invidious comparisons—given that all the Freudo-Marxists were implicated in this historical process—there are certain points that speak in Fromm's favor.

Fromm began his career claiming to effect a consequent application of the principles of Freud's psychology of the individual to myth, religion, and other sociological and historical subjects. Nevertheless, from the outset his emphasis on the primacy of the ego instincts in the formation of social character sounded a note that was discordant with Freud and Reich's emphasis on the primacy of sexual problems in the historical and sociological arena, and with the passage of time he was increasingly frank and outspoken about the fact that his evolving perspective was a revisionist one.

In dramatic contrast with Fromm, Reich, Fenichel, and Marcuse were always more mindful of the fact that Freud insistently identified the core of his system with sexuality and the instincts; that—in the wake of his break with Jung—Freud warned that future theorists would try to dilute or indeed destroy his teaching by desexualizing the libido and minimizing the role of instinct in human behavior. Fromm was not impressed by this kind of rhetoric. He thought Freud's emphasis on sexuality, though controversial and addressed to deep-seated problems and hypocrisies, was actually quite ethnocentric; that the pivotal role Freud accorded it as a source of conflict in human affairs was a reflection of Victorian society, and not of conflicts inscribed in the heart of civilization as such (1970d). For Fromm, the radical component in Freudian theory was not the theory of the instincts and sexuality per se, but Freud's idea of the dynamic unconscious, and his ability to expose false consciousness or deception and self-deception both clinically and sociologically (ibid). In this, as he protested to historian Martin Jay, Fromm did indeed keep faith with Freud (Jay, 1973, pp. 89–90). But although he saw Freud as radical in his challenge to conventional pieties, he portrayed him consistently as a bourgeois, liberal reformer with strong conservative leanings that deepened increasingly with age.

In view of Freud's urgent admonitions to beware false prophets, one sympathizes somewhat with the emphasis most Freudo-Marxists put on the primacy of sexuality and instinct. But the attempts by Adorno and Marcuse to discover or defend a "revolutionary" Freud against Fromm's revisionist critique lack realism and perspective. Freud was indeed a radical thinker, in that his thinking went to the roots of phenomena, penetrating beneath surface appearances. He possessed the ability not to be deterred or disquieted by the character and conclusions of his pioneering research, and to defy prevailing prejudice; a trait often found in revolutionaries. Outside his chosen field, however, there was nothing particularly radical about Freud. Artistically, philosophically, and politically he was quite conventional, and despite his youthful flirtation with socialism (Fromm, 1959b) he was never a revolutionary in the sense of advocating sweeping political measures to redress the injustices of class society.

Moreover, despite Freud's anguished concern for the eventual fate of his theories, from a scientific standpoint there is actually nothing wrong with revising Freud's ideas about instinct, sexuality, and human motivation. Indeed, unless it claims the same status as revealed or religious truth, analytic theory requires continual revision and reformulation if it wishes to enjoy credence among serious intellectuals. As Charles Rycroft points out, for example, Freud's notion that the newborn infant possesses no innate structure or preprogrammed adaptive mechanisms at birth—that is, no reality ego—makes no sense in biological terms, and his idea of an instinct as a drive for the peremptory release of dammed-up bodily excitation is radically disjunctive with what contemporary ethologists understand by instinct (Rycroft, 1972, 1981). Continued adherence to Freud's notion of the drive, and of primary and secondary process, is an act of misplaced loyalty that condemns us to scientific sterility and obsolescence. In addition, if we consider the specifically Lamarckian dimension of Freud's psychobiology (Gould, 1977; Sulloway, 1979)—which Marcuse zealously championed along with the "archaic inheritance"—we soon realize that the biological underpinnings of classical Freudianism are radically unsound, and that we would do better to scrap them entirely and to start again at the beginning, bearing in mind the reality of repression and defense and the ubiquitous character of unconscious mental conflict, which is repeatedly attested in clinical work.

Another problem with depicting Freud as some sort of revolutionary as Adorno and Marcuse did lies with the specific connotations that they attach to the meaning of the word *revolutionary.* On the whole, it is an essentially negative connotation, implying a total rejection of the world as it is, and a profound despair about changing it for the better (Fromm, 1970b). Martin Jay notes that the late-blooming Freud piety evidenced by Horkheimer and his circle reflected deep pessimism about the possibilities for social change. According to Jay's account, their defense of a "revolutionary" Freud was prompted in part by their continuing need to see themselves as radicals or revolutionaries even as they changed from being politically engaged intellectuals into detached cultural mandarins (Jay, 1973). But if we allow them to color our social and political judgments, the sense of impotence, disconnectedness, and cultural dislocation that Horkheimer, Benjamin, Adorno, and Marcuse all experienced and expressed so eloquently in the course of their collective development can be so overwhelming and categorical that they damage our capacity for hope and contribute to a mood of paralysis and inaction. As Paul Wachtel pointed out in connection with Marcuse and Jacoby, their writings

> tend to be totalistic. The present society is not just badly in need of change; it is so utterly antithetical to all human needs that the possibility of genuine fulfillment . . . indeed even of genuine personhood, is denied. Such rhetoric is bracing, but its consequence is that nowhere is seen even a toehold for launching effective action. All that can be done is dialectical kvetching . . . If we are serious about change, as therapists or as social critics, we have to see not only what is wrong but what there is to build on. (1987, p. 91)

Epilogue

An unfortunate consequence of most criticism of Fromm emanating from the mental health professions and, in a different way, from Marcuse's intellectual orbit is that the real tensions and contradictions in Fromm's work are routinely obscured through thoughtless, superficial, or polemical readings. As a result, the real strengths and weaknesses in his work seldom come up for serious discussion, and whatever debate there is centers on a one-dimensional caricature of the man and his ideas. Nevertheless, real tensions and contradictions do exist in Fromm's work, and the evidence indicates that Fromm was unconscious of most of them. Moreover, many of these problems appear to relate to his attitude toward Freud, both as a theorist and as a clinician. To an orthodox Freudian, such attitudinal ambiguity suggests an underlying emotional ambivalence, and some Freud zealots would probably still insist that the fact that Fromm disputed the universality and irreducibility of the Oedipus complex constitutes an unconsciously motivated assault on Freud, and a resistance to confronting his own Oedipal difficulties.

However, there are serious methodological problems with interpreting Fromm's relationship to Freud purely or primarily in Oedipal terms. As a creative theorist whose work was undergoing continuous transformation and renewal, it was probably impossible for Fromm to think through the implications of the different trains of thought that surfaced spontaneously from the different regions of his soul at different times in his life. This problem is extremely common in the history of ideas, and Freud himself furnishes us with some remarkably vivid examples of this phenomenon (Fromm, 1962, 1970d). Besides, the scope of Fromm's intended synthesis was exceedingly broad, embracing not only Marx, Freud, Bachofen, and the legacy of Kant, the German Enlightenment, and German sociology, but also numerous religious and philosophical thinkers from antiquity and medieval times. If his synthesis was not entirely successful, and if he betrayed some ambivalence toward Freud in the process, the problems of reconciling different loyalties, enthusiasms, and philosophical and scientific perspectives in a coherent intellectual framework probably took precedence over any transferential process.

Of course, Freudians would not find such reasonings—which are commonplace and compelling for intellectual historians—very convincing. But then it is impossible for all but the most orthodox to regard Freud without mixed feelings. Yet even orthodox analysts may concede that whereas a malignant or pathological ambivalence impairs our judgment and precludes a constructive engagement with another person, a benign or creative ambivalence balances tendencies toward idealization with increasingly realistic and balanced appraisals of another's inevitable imperfections. Fromm's ambivalence toward Freud was generally of the latter, benign variety. Indeed, if any vestigial Oedipal conflict colored Fromm's feelings toward Freud, it was harnessed creatively in a lifelong intellectual dialogue that combined clear, incisive criticism free of idolatrous fixation with deep respect bordering on veneration. No one—not even Freud—deserves more than this.

Freud scholarship will be immeasurably impoverished if Fromm's critical and historical reflections on Freud's philosophy of history, his character, and his strengths and weaknesses as a clinician and founder of a mass movement are forgotten or ignored. And humanistic and existential psychology would be greatly enriched if it assimilated the spirit of Fromm's existentialism and acquired some of the scholarly rigor that he brought to bear on the human condition and the obstacles to optimal living in an alienated, cybernetic society. Social psychologists, sociologists, political theorists, political psychologists, and psychohistorians would all do well to reexamine Fromm's concept of the authoritarian character and to reevaluate his studies of social character and his theory of social filters with an eye to future research. Finally, laypeople, academics, and mental health practitioners should heed Fromm's warning about our burgeoning ecological crisis and the crisis of reason—and, increasingly, of will—that evidently lies behind it.

As a writer, a clinician, and a simple human being, Fromm touched and transformed the lives of many people. So even if his ideas are not heeded in future, there is no reason to imagine that Fromm lived in vain. The record of his life bears witness to his courage, industry, and ambition; his wit, wisdom, and compassion; and the sorrow, anger, and joy he experienced and embraced. Even when a certain arrogance, insecurity, and dogmatism occasionally come to light, there is very little evidence of callousness, complacency, evasiveness, or hypocrisy in Fromm's life and work. People who live this way have lived well—or as well as can be expected in a mad and ailing world.

Notes

1. The Man and His Work

1. John Gedo (1984) uses the term *loyal opposition* in a decidedly different sense.
2. This book does not examine Fromm's political interests and activities in any depth. Those interested in this dimension should consult the complete bibliography of Fromm's works in Funk (1982).
3. For a more upbeat assessment of Sachs and Reik, see Alexander, Eisenstein, and Grotjahn (1966).
4. Perhaps an analogous shift took place in 1957, when Fromm started to write increasingly in Spanish (Funk, 1984, p. 112).
5. Gerald Sykes (1962) is one critic who tends to construe "Americanization" positively. He compares Fromm to Walter Lippmann, a thoughtful popularizer capable of making complex ideas readily intelligible in the interests of furthering enlightenment and public debate.

2. Freudo-Marxism and Matriarchal Theory

1. Otto Fenichel's "The Drive to Amass Wealth" (1938), which has received considerable attention from some left-wing Freudians, is actually a somewhat derivative treatment of ideas found earlier in this piece of Fromm's, but Fenichel does not cite it.
2. For more on the idea of a "collective psyche," see Chapter 4.
3. Except toward the end of his life, when disappointment colored his perceptions, Reich repeatedly asserted his reverence for Freud, which was no doubt quite sincere. Still, egocentric elements crept into the Reich's self-styled role as Freud's prodigal son and his attempts to revive consideration of the "actual neuroses." An anecdote related by Dr. Ivan Illich illustrates this beautifully. Fromm once confessed to Illich that while in his late twenties he was a staunch adherent of Reich's for several months when emerging doubts and misgivings made personal contact between Reich and him problematic. Still, in retrospect, Fromm noted, and despite whatever strengths or shortcomings

he possessed, Reich had an absolutely uncanny ability to convince people that he was the only man alive who knew what it is like to *really* experience orgasm.

4. In rough translation, the Latin term *patria potestas* means "father right." As Engels pointed out in *The Origins of Private Property, the Family, and the State* (1884), in Roman law the notion of *patria potestas* rendered a man's wife and children his personal property, to dispose of as he wished—by death if need be.

3. Fromm's Clinical Contributions

1. The etiological theories of Alfred Adler and, more recently, American psychiatrists Eric Berne and Jay Haley focus preeminently on the will to power expressed in clinical symptomatology. This problem, though important in certain kinds of cases, is generally only one component in a complicated dynamic structure that underlies the manifest symptom.

2. For a brief but illuminating discussion of Abraham's and Ferenczi's ideas, see Fromm ([1932b] 1970a).

3. Fairbairn's relatively belated emphasis on the regressive lure of symbiotic fusion distinguishes his kind of object-relations theory from that of Melanie Klein, for example. Klein's work, though replete with conjectures about fantasies of the breast and the maternal imago, is influenced by Freud's notion of the death instinct, which, ironically, was formulated to circumvent the necessity of positing a primary regressive urge toward symbiotic fusion with the mother in the first place. For more on this point, see Chapter 8.

4. As Ellenberger points out (1970, p. 732), Jung broke with a close disciple, Swiss psychiatrist Hans Trub, over this issue, as Trub's views on psychotherapy became increasingly influenced by Buber's philosophical anthropology.

5. In a letter to me, dated June 14, 1984, Ashley Montagu, a great admirer of Fromm's, voiced similar misgivings. Though sympathetic to Fromm's central contention that malignant destructiveness is a peculiarly human phenomenon that tends to increase rather than decrease with the march of civilization, he found *The Anatomy of Human Destructiveness* deficient in "the very necessary criticism of Lorenz and Ardrey's appeals to evidence from the animal world," implying that Fromm failed to make a really compelling case for his theory on ethological grounds.

4. Fromm's Existentialism

1. The doctrine of the *felix culpa,* though not central to many varieties of Christian theology, suffused popular Christian piety for many centuries and is beautifully expressed in the traditional prayer for Holy Saturday, when the paschal candle is lit: "Oh truly necessary sin of Adam, which the death of Christ has blotted out. Oh happy fault, which merited so great a redeemer." As a result of Gnostic and Neo-Platonic influences, the Kabbalah, unlike

rabbinic Judaic texts, also contains references to the Fall as a necessary prelude to redemption and a scheme of universal or cosmic regeneration.

5. Studies in Social Character

1. See also the remarks on Erikson in Fromm and Maccoby (1970, p. 15).
2. Thomas and Zanecki's study (1918) of the attitudes and aspirations of Polish peasants included a detailed survey of living conditions and stylistic idiosyncrasies in literary productions (e.g., letters, diaries) but made no attempt to distinguish between their manifest and latent content. Notwithstanding some interesting parallels, Fromm refers to their work only once (Fromm and Maccoby, 1970, p. 149).
3. Georg Lind of the University of Konstantz made a similar point about the psychometric paradigm in a thought-provoking paper in 1988.
4. Here, for the most part, I am referring to the use of personality assessment measures in the clinical setting. However, Lamiell (1981) and Rorer and Widiger (1983) have raised similar objections regarding personality research today, arguing that statistical correlations between various traits elicited in mainstream methodology refer purely to people in the aggregate, and that no valid inferences concerning individual differences or personality structure can really be made on that basis. David Bakan made the same point quite forcefully in 1966.
5. As Sanford pointed out (1956), the idea that Horkheimer and Adorno et al. may not have designed instruments to detect left-wing authoritarianism does not invalidate whatever else they actually did achieve. However, the tendency to minimize or overlook Fromm's contributions and the problems he raised continues. A recent (and very stimulating) attempt to apply the F-scale to high school populations in Germany and the United States tends to overlook the problem of left-wing authoritarianism (Lederer, 1983, p. 45) and to attribute the central inspiration for Adorno's methodology to sources other than Fromm (ibid., chaps. 1 and 2).
6. Fromm and Maccoby initially refrained from naming the village they studied, but the location of their research is now common knowledge. This historic study spawned a rich and rewarding literature on the theory and practice of psychoanalytic social psychology and the psychology of work in the *Revista de psicoanalisis, psiquiatria y psicologia* from 1969 to 1975. Besides Fromm and Maccoby, Alejandro Cordova, Salvador Millan, Sonia Millan-Gojman, and Rolando Weissmann figure prominently. Others who contributed to this fascinating journal founded by Fromm include Henry Ey, Ivan Illich, Harold Searles, and Anthony Storr.
7. In addition to the work of Fromm, I am indebted here to Dr. Jeffrey Wollock for his ideas on the psychology of work in the traditionalist milieu.
8. These features of nineteenth-century capitalism and its effects on individual and social character were depicted with wit, irony, and pathos by critics as diverse as Charles Dickens, John Ruskin, and George Bernard Shaw.
9. In *Escape from Freedom* (1941, chap. 6) Fromm alludes to Hitler's "crude

popularization of Darwinism" but fails to remark on the prevalence of social Darwinism in middle-class ideologies of the nineteenth and early twentieth centuries, such as the eugenics movement, and the many strains of racism that were institutionally and conceptually sanctioned in the burgeoning sciences of psychology, sociology, and anthropology as imperialism extended its global reach (Harris, 1968, chap. 5).

10. Although I would hesitate to characterize this passage as "antipsychiatry," it is hardly a glowing endorsement. For more in this vein, see Fromm (1955b, chap. 5, secs. 2c[i] and 3).

11. Harry Guntrip (1968, p. 48) dwelt briefly on the schizoid character of contemporary life and the way it is apparently reflected in existential philosophy. Michael Maccoby (1976, chap. 7) perceptively discusses many of the pressures conducive to a rupture between head and heart in the business milieu.

6. Consensus, Conformity, and False Consciousness

1. Rabbinic commentary states that after the Flood, God made a covenant with Noah and his sons that is binding on all humanity. Those who abide by the seven commandments (listed below) are deemed "the righteous among the gentiles," and it is for their sake, presumably, that the Lord does not destroy the world entirely. The covenant entails the prohibition of idolatry, murder, blasphemy, incest, theft; the injunction to establish regular courts of law for the administration of justice; and a prohibition on eating a limb from a living animal (Loewe et al., 1966, pp. 52–55). Following Hermann Cohen, Fromm taught that the Noachite prohibition on blasphemy is merely a negative injunction that limits what one can or cannot *say* to or about God; that is, it does not include or imply any positive prescription as to what one should (or should not) believe. According to Cohen and Fromm, one could fulfill the terms of the Noachite covenant and be an agnostic or an atheist (Fromm, 1966, pp. 41–43). This interpretation is not widely accepted, however.

2. In emphasizing the similarities between Hebrew and Stoic universalism, I am following Hugo de Groot (Grotius) and John Selden, who interpreted the Noachite Commandments as early adumbrations of "natural law" (Baeck, 1961, p. 199; Fromm, 1966, pp. 42–43). Nevertheless, although the parallels are real and important, the religious/metaphysical frameworks within which these two universalisms were articulated preclude straightforward equivalence. The Jews insisted—and continue to insist, for the most part—on the radical transcendence of the Creator, who is not "in" nature, but gives the law as a gift and a covenant. Stoic religiosity, by contrast, which gave rise to the idea of natural law, stressed the immanence of the divine in nature and tends to culminate in a kind of materialistic pantheism. One of the biggest problems in medieval philosophy—Jewish, Arab, and Christian—was how to reconcile the Stoic-Aristotelian emphasis on immanence and "natural reason" with the contrary emphasis on radical transcendence and revelation found in scripture.

3. Those familiar with the Rorschach test will recognize Fromm's distinction between the passive registration of external actualities, and generative apper-

ception enriched by affect, imagination, and unconscious fantasy. It is speculation, perhaps, but Fromm would probably have regarded an average or "normal" Rorschach protocol, which evinces adequate form, low color and movement responses, and/or muted depressive affect, as symptomatic of the chronic, low-grade schizoid orientation patterned by prevailing social conditions; as evidence of a "socially patterned defect." His close friend and collaborator Ernst Schachtel certainly did (Schachtel, 1959, chap. 10; 1966).

4. As Fromm himself pointed out, for example, the prestige that science enjoys in our culture, which often borders on frank superstition, gave Milgram's operatives an enormous amount of social leverage they would not have enjoyed in another milieu (Fromm, 1973, pp. 70–76). Culture, not biology, is at issue here, and the specific forms of cultural authority cannot be reduced to a series of instinctual responses to external stimuli.

7. Appraisals of Fromm by Psychologists and Psychiatrists

1. To the best of my knowledge, the manuscript Mullahy referred to was never printed in its entirety. Chapter 7, section 1 of *The Forgotten Language* (Fromm, 1951) may represent an abbreviated version.
2. For a more recent—and in some respects more penetrating—analysis of the theoretical differences and complementarities between Fromm and Sullivan, see Greenberg and Mitchell (1983).
3. In a sympathetic discussion of Fromm, Laurence Stone (1986) mistakenly claims that Fromm's thinking was really closer to existentialism and humanist psychology than to psychoanalysis.
4. This was also Horney's view.
5. The 1978 edition devoted five and a half pages to Fromm, four to Horney, and twenty-one to Sullivan.

8. Fromm's Contribution to the History of Psychoanalysis

1. For a more extended discussion of this point, see Fromm (1964, chap. 6).
2. By "living substance," Freud, whom Fromm is paraphrasing here, apparently meant the chemical components and structure of every living cell in the body.
3. Despite Freud's early allegiance to mechanists such as Brücke and Theodor Meynert, vitalistic elements were present in his theory from the outset; a fact not reflected in Fromm's assessment (Ellenberger, 1970; Sulloway, 1979).
4. For example, compare Fromm's essay on little Hans (1970a) with Swales (1986).
5. Not surprisingly, Fromm endorsed the work of historians who dispensed with pious clichés about Freud. In a letter to R. D. Laing dated December 20, 1969, which Rainer Funk kindly brought to my attention, Fromm informed Laing that he was forwarding a copy of Paul Roazen's recent book, *Brother Animal.* Fromm commented that Roazen's controversial study "lifts the mystery from the personality of Tausk and the circumstances of his suicide. But it also gives some interesting insights into the whole life at the court of Freud. I was somewhat surprised and shocked by the utter coldness with which Freud

dismissed his suicide and stated that he had been a 'danger to the cause'." Fromm said that he was also forwarding an article he had written several years previously on Jones's allegations about Ferenczi and Rank, implying that Roazen's efforts and his own were highly convergent in this regard. The fact that Fromm was shocked by Freud's "utter coldness" indicates that an inextinguishable bit of Freud piety lingered despite his dramatic disillusionment with Freud in the 1930s (e.g., 1935a).

9. Oedipus, Instinct, and the Unconscious in the Fromm-Marcuse Debate

1. For a thorough, thoughtful, and fair-minded review, see Jay (1973, pp. 106–112).

References

Abraham, K. 1924. "A Short Study of the Development of the Libido, Viewed in Light of the Mental Disorders." In *On Character and Libido Development*. New York: W. W. Norton, 1966.

Abrams, M. H., 1971. *Natural Supernaturalism: Tradition and Revolution in Romantic Literature*. New York: W. W. Norton.

Adler, A. 1927. *Understanding Human Nature*. New York: Greenberg.

Adorno, T. 1979. *Negative Dialectics*. New York: Seabury Press.

Adorno, T., et al. 1950. *The Authoritarian Personality*. New York: W. W. Norton.

Alexander, F., S. Eisenstein, and M. Grotjahn. 1966. *Psychoanalytic Pioneers*. New York: W. W. Norton.

Antonovsky, A. 1988. Personal communication to the author. March.

Asch, S. E. 1948. "The Doctrine of Suggestion, Prestige, and Imitation in Social Psychology." *Psychological Review* 55:250–276.

——. 1952. *Social Psychology*. Englewood Cliffs, N.J.: Prentice-Hall. Excerpts quoted by permission of Oxford University Press.

——. 1956. "Studies of Independence and Conformity: I. A Minority of One against a Unanimous Majority." *Psychological Monographs* 70, no. 9.

——. 1988. Personal communication to the author. May 4.

Atwood, G., and R. Stolorow. 1984. *Structures of Subjectivity*. Hillsdale, N.J.: Analytic Press.

Avineri, S. 1968. *The Social and Political Thought of Karl Marx*. London: Cambridge University Press.

——. 1981. *The Making of Modern Zionism*. New York: Basic Books.

Bachofen, J. J. 1973. *Myth, Religion, and Mother Right*, trans. Ralph Manheim. Princeton: Princeton University Press. Partial translation of Bachofen's 1861 work *Mother Right*.

Baeck, L. 1961. *The Essence of Judaism*. New York: Schocken Books.

Bakan, D. 1966. "The Test of Significance in Psychological Research." *Psychological Bulletin* 66:423–437.

Baldry, H. C. 1965. *The Unity of Mankind in Greek Thought*. London: Cambridge University Press.

Bebel, A. 1974. *Woman under Socialism*. New York: Schocken Books.

Becker, E. 1968. *The Structure of Evil*. New York: Free Press.

———. 1973. *The Denial of Death*. New York: Free Press.

Binswanger, L. 1963. *Being in the World: Selected Papers of Ludwig Binswanger*, trans. J. Needleman. New York: Basic Books.

Birnbach, M. 1961. *Neo-Freudian Social Philosophy*. Stanford: Stanford University Press.

Bloch, E. 1961. *Natural Law and Human Dignity*, trans. D. Schmidt. Cambridge, Mass.: MIT Press, 1986.

Boadella, D. 1973. *Wilhelm Reich: The Evolution of His Work*. Chicago: Henry Regnery.

Bonss, W. 1984. "Critical Theory and Empirical Social Research." In E. Fromm, *The Working Class in Weimar Germany*, ed. W. Bonss. Cambridge, Mass.: Harvard University Press.

Bowlby, J. 1978. *Attachment and Loss*. Vol. 1. Harmondsworth: Penguin.

Brett, G. 1965. *Brett's History of Psychology*, ed. R. S. Peters. Cambridge, Mass.: MIT Press.

Briffault, R. 1975. *The Mothers*, abr. G. R. Taylor. New York: Atheneum.

Brown, N. O. 1959. *Life against Death*. Middletown, Conn.: Wesleyan University Press.

———. 1966. *Love's Body*. New York: Random House.

Browning, D. 1975. *Generative Man*. New York: Delta Books.

Buber, M. 1965. *The Knowledge of Man*. New York: Harper & Row.

Burston, D. 1986a. "The Cognitive and Dynamic Unconscious." *Contemporary Psychoanalysis* 22, no. 1: 133–157.

———. 1986b. "Myth, Religion, and Mother Right: Bachofen's Influence on Psychoanalytic Theory." *Contemporary Psychoanalysis* 22, no. 3:666–687.

———. 1988. Review of M. Erdelyi's *Psychoanalysis: Freud's Cognitive Psychology*. *Theoretical and Philosophical Psychology* 7, no. 2:124–129.

———. 1989. "Freud: Clinical Theory and Philosophical Anthropology." Paper presented at the annual meeting of the Canadian Psychological Association, Halifax, Nova Scotia, June 8.

———. 1991. "Freud, the Serpent, and the Sexual Enlightenment of Children." In *Freud and Forbidden Knowledge*, ed. J. Kerr and P. Rudnytsky. New York: New York University Press.

Cassirer, E. 1946. *The Myth of the State*. Reprint, New Haven: Yale University Press, 1979.

Cattier, M. 1971. *The Life and Work of Wilhelm Reich*. New York: Avon Books.

Christie, R., and M. Jahoda, eds. 1954. *The Authoritarian Personality: Continuities in Social Research*. Glencoe, Ill.: Free Press.

Cordova, A. 1990. "El Psicoanalisis de Erich Fromm y lo Religioso." Paper presented at the Primer Congreso Nacional de Psicoanalisis Humanista, Mexico City, March 24.

Danziger, K. 1982. "Towards a Conceptual Framework for a Critical History of Psychology." Manuscript, York University.

————. 1983. "Origins and Basic Principles of Wundt's *Volkerpsychologie.*" *British Journal of Social Psychology* 22:303–313.

Derbez, J. 1981. "Fromm en Mexico: Una resena historica." In *Erich Fromm y el psicoanalisis humanista,* ed. S. Millan and S. Gojman. Mexico City: Siglo xxi editores.

Deutsch, M., and R. Kraus. 1965. *Theories in Social Psychology.* New York: Harper & Row.

Dinnerstein, D. 1976. *The Mermaid and the Minotaur.* New York: Harper & Row.

Dodds, E. R. 1951. *The Greeks and the Irrational.* Berkeley: University of California Press.

Eckardt, M. 1975. "L'Chayim." *Contemporary Psychoanalysis* 11, no. 4:465–470.

————. 1976. "Organizational Schisms in American Psychoanalysis." In *American Psychoanalysis: Origins and Development: The Adolf Meyer Seminars,* ed. J. Quen and E. Carlson. New York: Bruner Mazel, 1978.

————. 1982. "The Theme of Hope in Erich Fromm's Writing." *Contemporary Psychoanalysis* 18, no. 1:141–152.

————. 1983. "The Core Theme of Erich Fromm's Writings and Its Implications for Therapy." *Journal of the American Academy of Psychoanalysis* 11, no. 3:391–399.

————. 1987. Personal communication to the author. April 20.

Edelstein, L. 1966. *The Meaning of Stoicism.* Cambridge, Mass.: Harvard University Press.

Eksteins, M. 1989. *The Rites of Spring: The Great War and the Birth of the Modern Age.* Toronto: Lester, Orpen & Dennys.

Ellenberger, H. 1970. *The Discovery of the Unconscious.* New York: Basic Books.

————. 1976. "Moritz Benedikt." In *Les mouvements de libération mythique (et autres essais sur l'histoire de la psychiatrie).* Montreal: Editions Quinze.

Engels, F. 1884. *The Origins of the Family, Private Property, and the State,* ed. Eleanor B. Leacock, based on a 1944 translation by Alec West. Moscow: Progress Publishers, 1970.

Erdelyi, M. 1985. *Psychoanalysis: Freud's Cognitive Psychology.* New York: W. H. Freeman.

Erikson, E. 1960. "Human Strength and the Cycle of the Generations." In *Insight and Responsibility.* New York: W. W. Norton, 1964.

————. 1961. "Psychological Reality and Historical Actuality." In *Insight and Responsibility.* New York: W. W. Norton, 1964.

Evans, R. 1966. *Dialogue with Erich Fromm.* New York: Harper & Row.

Fairbairn, W. R. D. 1935. "The Sociological Significance of Communism Considered in the Light of Psychoanalysis." *British Journal of Medical Psychology* 15, pt. 3:218–229.

————. 1940. "Schizoid Factors in the Personality." In Fairbairn, 1952.

————. 1941. "A Revised Psychopathology of the Psychoses and Psychoneuroses." In Fairbairn, 1952.

————. 1946. "Object-Relationships and Dynamic Structure." In Fairbairn, 1952.

———. 1951. "A Synopsis of the Development of the Author's Views." In Fairbairn, 1952.

———. 1952. *Psychoanalytic Studies of the Personality.* London: Tavistock.

———. 1956. "A Critical Evaluation of Certain Basic Psycho-Analytical Conceptions." *British Journal for the Philosophy of Science* 7, no. 25.

Fenichel, O. 1945. *The Psychoanalytic Theory of the Neuroses.* New York: W. W. Norton.

Ferenczi, S. 1914. "On the Ontogenesis of the Interest in Money." In *Sex in Psychoanalysis,* trans. Ernest Jones. New York: Dover Publications, 1956.

———. 1924. *Thalassa: A Theory of Genitality.* Reprint, Albany, N.Y.: Psychoanalytic Quarterly, 1938.

———. 1933. "Confusion of Tongues between Adults and the Child." In *Final Contributions to the Problems and Methods of Psychoanalysis.* New York: Basic Books, 1955.

———. 1988. *The Clinical Diary of Sandor Ferenczi,* trans. M. Balint. Cambridge, Mass.: Harvard University Press.

Ferenczi, S., and O. Rank. 1923. *The Development of Psychoanalysis.* Reprint, New York: Dover Publications, 1956.

Feuerbach, L. 1841. *The Essence of Christianity,* trans. George Eliot. New York: Harper & Row, 1957.

Fisher, E. 1979. *Woman's Evolution.* Montreal: McGraw-Hill.

Flugel, J. C. 1946. *Man, Morals, and Society: A Psychoanalytic Study.* London: Hogarth Press.

———. 1964. *One Hundred Years of Psychology.* New York: Basic Books.

Frankl, V. 1955. *The Doctor and the Soul.* New York: Bantam Books.

———. 1959. *Man's Search for Meaning.* New York: Bantam Books.

Freud, S. 1895. *Studies on Hysteria,* with J. Breuer. Vol. 2 of *The Standard Edition of the Complete Psychological Works of Sigmund Freud,* ed. J. Strachey, trans. with A. Freud. 24 vols. London: Hogarth Press and the Institute of Psychoanalysis, 1953–1974. Hereafter cited as *Standard Edition.*

———. 1900. *The Interpretation of Dreams. Standard Edition,* vols. 4, 5.

———. 1901. *Psychopathology of Everyday Life. Standard Edition,* vol. 6.

———. 1905. *Three Essays on the Theory of Sexuality. Standard Edition,* vol. 7.

———. 1905. "Fragment of an Analysis of a Case of Hysteria." *Standard Edition,* vol. 7.

———. 1908. "Civilized Sexual Morality and Modern Nervous Illness." *Standard Edition,* vol. 9.

———. 1912. "The Dynamics of the Transference." *Standard Edition,* vol. 12.

———. 1913. *Totem and Taboo. Standard Edition,* vol. 13.

———. 1914. "On Narcissism." *Standard Edition,* vol. 14.

———. 1915. "Thoughts for the Times on War and Death." *Standard Edition,* vol. 15.

———. 1920. *Beyond the Pleasure Principle. Standard Edition,* vol. 18.

———. 1921. *Group Psychology and the Analysis of the Ego. Standard Edition,* vol. 18.

———. 1925. "Autobiographical Study." *Standard Edition,* vol. 20.

———. 1927. *The Future of an Illusion. Standard Edition*, vol. 27.

———. 1930. *Civilization and Its Discontents. Standard Edition*, vol. 21.

———. 1932. *New Introductory Lectures on Psychoanalysis. Standard Edition*, vol. 22.

———. 1937. "Analysis Terminable and Interminable." *Standard Edition*, vol. 23.

———. 1939. *Moses and Monotheism. Standard Edition*, vol. 23.

———. 1960. *Letters of Sigmund Freud, 1873–1939*, ed. E. Freud, trans. T. Stern and J. Stern. New York: McGraw-Hill.

Fromm, E. 1929. "Psychoanalyse und Soziologie." *Zeitschrift für Psychoanalytische Pädagogik* (Vienna).

———. 1930a. "Die Entwicklung des Christusdogmas." Translated in Fromm, 1963a.

———. 1930b. *The Working Class in Weimar Germany: A Psychological and Sociological Study*, trans. Barbara Weinberger, Cambridge, Mass.: Harvard University Press, 1984.

———. 1932a. "Uber Methode und Aufgabe einer analytischen Sozialpsychologie." Translated in Fromm, 1970a.

———. 1932b. "Die psychoanalytische Charakterologie und ihre Bedeutung für die Sozialpsychologie." Translated in Fromm, 1970a.

———. 1933a. "Robert Briffaults Werk uber das Mutterrecht." *Zeitschrift für Sozialforschung* 2:382–387.

———. 1933b. Review of W. Reich's *Der Einbruch der Sexualmoral. Zeitschrift für Sozialforschung* 2: 119–122.

———. 1934. "Die Sozialpsychologische Bedeutung der Mutterrechtstheorie." Translated in Fromm, 1970a.

———. 1935a. "Die gesellschaftliche Bedingheit der psychoanalytischen Therapie." *Zeitschrift für Sozialforschung* 4, no. 3.

———. 1935b. Review of C. G. Jung's *Werklichkeit der Seele. Zeitschrift für Sozialforschung* 4:284–285.

———. 1936. "Sozialpsychologischer Teil." In *Schriften des Instituts für Sozialforschung*, ed. M. Horkheimer. Paris: Felix Alcan.

———. 1937. "Zum Gefühl des Ohnmacht." *Zeitschrift für Sozialforschung* 6:95–118.

———. 1939a. "Selfishness and Self-Love." *Psychiatry* 2, no. 3:507–524.

———. 1939b. "The Social Philosophy of 'Will Therapy.'" *Psychiatry* 2, no. 1: 229–250.

———. 1941. *Escape from Freedom*. Reprint, New York: Avon Books, 1965.

———. 1943. "Sex and Character." In Fromm, 1963a.

———. 1947. *Man for Himself*. Greenwich, Conn.: Fawcett Premier Books.

———. 1950. *Psychoanalysis and Religion*. Reprint, New York: Bantam Books, 1972.

———. 1951. *The Forgotten Language*. Reprint, New York: Grove Press, 1957.

———. 1955a. "The Human Implications of Instinctivistic Radicalism." *Dissent* 2, no. 4:342–349.

———. 1955b. *The Sane Society*. Greenwich, Conn.: Fawcett Premier Books.

———. 1956a. *The Art of Loving*. Reprint, New York: Bantam Books, 1970.

———. 1956b. "A Counter-Rebuttal to Herbert Marcuse." *Dissent* 3, no. 1:81–83.

———. 1958. "Psychoanalysis—Science or Party Line?" Originally published as "Scientism or Fanaticism?" in *Saturday Review,* June 14, 1958. Under its present title in Fromm, 1963a.

———. 1959a. "On the Dangers and Limitations of Psychology." In Fromm, 1963a.

———. 1959b. *Sigmund Freud's Mission: An Analysis of His Personality and Influence.* Reprint, New York: Harper & Row, 1972.

———. 1960a. "Foreword." in A. S. Neill, *Summerhill: A Radical Approach in Childrearing.* New York: Hart Publishing.

———. 1960b. *Let Man Prevail—A Socialist Manifesto and Program.* New York: Call Association.

———. 1960c. "The Prophetic Concept of Peace." In Fromm, 1963a.

———. 1960d. *Zen Buddhism and Psychoanalysis,* with D. T. Suzuki and R. DeMartino. Reprint, New York: Harper & Row, 1970.

———. 1961a. "Communism and Co-Existence: The Nature of the Totalitarian Threat Today: An Analysis of the 81st Party Manifesto." *Socialist Call* 4:3–11.

———, ed. 1961b. *Marx's Concept of Man.* New York: Frederick Ungar.

———. 1961c. *May Man Prevail? An Inquiry into the Facts and Fictions of Foreign Policy.* Garden City, N.Y.: Doubleday.

———. 1962. *Beyond the Chains of Illusion: My Encounter with Marx and Freud.* New York: Simon and Schuster.

———. 1963a. *The Dogma of Christ.* New York: Holt, Rinehart & Winston.

———. 1963b. "Medicine and the Ethical Problem of Modern Man." In Fromm, 1963a.

———. 1963c. "The Revolutionary Character." In Fromm, 1963a.

———. 1964. *The Heart of Man: Its Genius for Good and Evil,* New York: Harper & Row, 1968.

———, ed. 1965. *Socialist Humanism: An International Symposium.* Garden City, N.Y.: Doubleday.

———. 1966. *You Shall Be as Gods: A Radical Interpretation of the Old Testament and Its Tradition.* Greenwich, Conn.: Fawcett Premier Books.

———. 1968a. "Humanism and Psychoanalysis." Reprinted in *Contemporary Psychoanalysis* 11, no. 40 (1975):396–406.

———. 1968b. *The Revolution of Hope.* Reprint, New York: Harper & Row, 1974.

———. 1970a. *The Crisis of Psychoanalysis: Essays on Freud, Marx, and Social Psychology.* Greenwich, Conn.: Fawcett Premier Books.

———. 1970b. "The Crisis of Psychoanalysis." In Fromm, 1970a.

———. 1970c. "Epilogue." In Fromm, 1970a.

———. 1970d. "Freud's Model of Man and Its Social Determinants." In Fromm, 1970a.

———. 1970e. "Introduction." In A. Schaff, *Marxism and the Human Individual.* New York: McGraw-Hill.

———. 1970f. "Marx's Contribution to Our Knowledge of Man." In Fromm, 1970a.

———. 1970g. "The Significance of the Theory of Mother Right for Today." In Fromm, 1970a.

———. 1973. *The Anatomy of Human Destructiveness.* Greenwich, Conn.: Fawcett Premier Books.

———. 1974. Seminar with analytic candidates in Locarno, Switzerland. Taped by Dr. Bernard Landis. Available at the History of Psychiatry Section, Payne Whitney Clinic, Cornell Medical Center, New York.

———. 1975. "Humanism and Psychoanalysis." *Contemporary Psychoanalysis* 11, no. 4:396–406.

———. 1976. *To Have or to Be?* Reprint, New York: Bantam Books, 1981.

———. 1980. *Greatness and Limitations of Freud's Thought.* New York: Harper & Row.

———. 1981. *On Disobedience and Other Essays.* New York: Seabury Press.

———. 1982. "Postscript." In Funk, 1982.

———. 1986. *For the Love of Life,* with H. J. Schultz. New York: Macmillan.

Fromm, E., and M. Maccoby. 1969. "Conceptos y metodos de la psicologia social psicoanalitica." *Revista de psicoanalisis, psiquiatria y psicologia* 11:3–24.

———. 1970. *Social Character in a Mexican Village: A Sociopsychoanalytic Study.* Englewood Cliffs, N.J.: Prentice-Hall.

Fromm, E., and R. Xirau, eds. 1968. *The Nature of Man.* New York: Macmillan.

Fuller, R. 1986. *Americans and the Unconscious.* New York: Oxford University Press.

Funk, R. 1982. *Erich Fromm: The Courage to Be Human.* New York: Continuum.

———. 1984. *Erich Fromm.* Hamburg: Rowohlt Taschenbuch Verlag.

Gay, P. 1968. *Weimar Culture.* New York: Harper & Row.

Gedo, J. 1984. "On Some Dynamics of Dissidence within Psychoanalysis." In J. Gedo and G. Pollock, *Psychoanalysis,* vol. 1, *The Vital Issues.* New York: International Universities Press.

Gedo, J., and G. Pollack. 1976. *Freud: The Fusion of Science and Humanism.* New York: International Universities Press.

Gossman, L. 1983. *Orpheus Philologus: Bachofen versus Mommsen on the Study of Antiquity.* Philadelphia: American Philosophical Society.

Gould, S. J. 1977. *Ontogeny and Phylogeny.* Cambridge, Mass.: Belknap Press of Harvard University Press.

Green, M. 1988. Personal communication to the author. May 3.

Greenberg, J., and S. Mitchell. 1983. *Object Relations in Psychoanalytic Theory.* Cambridge, Mass.: Harvard University Press.

Greenberg, L., and J. Safran. 1984. "Integrating Affect and Cognition: A Perspective on the Process of Therapeutic Change." *Cognitive Therapy and Research* 8, no. 6:559–578.

Grinstein, A. 1980. *Sigmund Freud's Dreams.* New York: International Universities Press.

Groddeck, G. 1926. *Exploring the Unconscious.* Reprint, London: Vision Press, 1950.

Grosskurth, P. 1986. *Melanie Klein: Her World and Her Work.* New York: Alfred A. Knopf.

Grossman, C., and S. Grossman. 1965. *The Wild Analyst.* New York: Dell Books.

Grotjahn, M. 1968. "The Americanization of Martin Grotjahn." In *The Home of the Learned Man*, ed. J. Kosa. New Haven: Yale College and University Press.

Gruber, H., and J. Voneche, eds. 1977. "Introduction." In *The Essential Piaget*. New York: Harper & Row.

Guntrip, H. 1961. *Personality Structure and Human Interaction*. New York: International Universities Press.

———. 1968. "The Schizoid Personality and the External World." In *Schizoid Phenomena, Object-Relations and the Self*. London: Hogarth Press.

———. 1975. "My Experience of Analysis with Fairbairn and Winnicott." *International Review of Psycho-Analysis* 2:145–156.

Hall C., and G. Lindzey. 1954. "Psychoanalytic Theory and Its Application to the Social Sciences." In *Handbook of Social Psychology* ed. G. Murphy. Cambridge, Mass.: Addison-Wesley.

———. 1957. *Theories of Personality*. London: Wiley.

———. 1978. *Theories of Personality*. 3d ed. New York: Wiley.

Harris, M. 1968. *The Rise of Anthropological Theory*. New York: Columbia University Press.

Hausdorf, D. 1972. *Erich Fromm*. New York: Twayne Publishers.

Heidegger, M. 1927. *Being and Time*. Reprint, New York: Harper & Row, 1962.

Herder, J. G. 1772. "On the Origin of Language." In *On the Origin of Language: Two Essays*, trans. J. Moran and A. Gode. Chicago: University of Chicago Press, 1966.

Heschel, A. J. 1951. *The Sabbath*. Reprint, New York: Farrar, Straus & Giroux, 1986.

Hogenson, G. B. 1983. *Jung's Struggle with Freud*. Notre Dame, Ind.: Notre Dame University Press.

Horkheimer, M. 1972. *Critical Theory*. New York: Seabury Press.

———. 1978. *Dawn and Decline*. New York: Seabury Press.

Horney, K. 1926. "The Flight from Womanhood." In Horney, 1967.

———. 1930. "The Distrust between the Sexes." In Horney, 1967.

———. 1932. "The Dread of Woman." In Horney, 1967.

———. 1967. *Feminine Psychology*. New York: W. W. Norton.

Illich, I. 1972. "The Dawn of Epimethean Man." Paper presented at a symposium in honor of Erich Fromm, Centro Intercultural de Documentacion, no. 75, 227/1–16, Cuernavaca.

Jacoby, R. 1975. *Social Amnesia: A Critique of Contemporary Psychology from Adler to Laing*. Boston: Beacon Press.

———. 1983. *The Repression of Psychoanalysis*. New York: Basic Books.

Jahoda, M., P. Lazarsfeld, and H. Zeisel. 1933. *Die Arbeitslösen von Marienthal. Ein Soziographischer Versuch*. Reprint, Bonn: Allensbach, 1960.

Jay, M. 1973. *The Dialectical Imagination*. Boston: Beacon Press.

Jonas, H. 1963. *The Gnostic Religion*. Boston: Beacon Press.

Jones, E. 1953. *The Life and Work of Sigmund Freud*. New York: Basic Books.

Jung, C. G. 1909. "The Significance of the Father in the Destiny of the Individual." In *The Psychoanalytic Years*. Princeton: Bollingen, 1974.

———. 1913. *Symbols of Transformation*, trans. R. F. C. Hull. New York: Harcourt, Brace & World, 1956.

————. 1914. *On the Nature of the Psyche,* trans. R. F. C. Hull. Princeton: Princeton University Press, 1960.

————. 1926. *Psychological Types or the Psychology of Individuation,* trans. R. F. C. Hull. New York: Harcourt, Brace.

————. 1933. *Modern Man in Search of a Soul,* trans. W. S. Dillard and C. F. Baynes. New York: Harcourt, Brace & World.

————. 1935. *Analytical Psychology: Its Theory and Practice,* ed. R. F. C. Hull. New York: Vintage Books, 1968.

————. 1943. "On the Psychology of the Unconscious." In *Two Essays in Analytical Psychology,* trans. R. F. C. Hull. New York: World Publishing, 1971.

————. 1963. *Memories, Dreams, and Reflections,* trans. R. Winston and C. Winston. New York: Pantheon.

Kalmar, I. 1987. "Lazarus, Steinthal, and Culture." *Journal of the History of Ideas* 48, no. 4:671–690.

Kant, I. 1785. *Groundwork of the Metaphysic of Morals,* trans. H. J. Paton. New York: Harper & Row, 1968.

Kanzer, M., and J. Glenn. 1979. *Freud and His Self-Analysis.* New York: Jason Aronson.

Kardiner, A. 1946. *The Psychological Frontiers of Society.* New York: Columbia University Press.

————. 1977. *My Analysis with Freud.* New York: W. W. Norton.

Kardiner, A., and A. Preble. 1961. *They Studied Man.* New York: World Publishing.

Kernberg, O. 1980. *Internal World and External Reality.* New York: Jason Aronson.

Kerr, J. 1987. Personal communication to the author. July 24.

————. 1988. "Beyond the Pleasure Principle and Back Again: Freud, Jung, and Sabina Spielrein." In *Freud: Appraisals and Reappraisals,* ed. P. Stepansky. Vol. 3. Hillsdale, N.J.: Analytic Press.

————. 1989. "The Core Complex." In *Freud and Forbidden Knowledge,* ed. J. Kerr and P. Rudnytsky. New York: New York University Press.

Kierkegaard, S. 1846. *The Present Age,* trans. A. Dru. New York: Harper Torchbooks, 1962.

Kihlstrom, J. F. 1987. "The Cognitive Unconscious." *Science* 237:1445–52.

Kirscht, J. P., and R. C. Dillehy, eds. 1967. *Dimensions of Authoritarianism: A Review of Research and Theory.* Lexington: University of Kentucky Press.

Kitchen, M. 1975. *Fascism.* London: Macmillan.

Klein, M., and J. Rivière. 1937. *Love, Hate, and Reparation.* Reprint, New York: W. W. Norton, 1964.

Kohlberg, L. 1971. "From Is to Ought." In T. Mishel, *Cognitive Development and Epistemology.* New York: Academic Press.

Kohut, H. 1971. *The Analysis of the Self.* New York: International Universities Press.

————. 1977. *The Restoration of the Self.* New York: International Universities Press.

————. 1984. *How Does Analysis Cure?* Chicago: University of Chicago Press.

Kolakowski, L. 1981. *Main Currents in Marxism.* Vol. 3. New York: Oxford University Press.

Krech, D., and R. Crutchfield. 1948. *Theory and Problems of Social Psychology.* New York: McGraw-Hill.

Kumar, K. 1978. *Prophecy and Progress.* Harmondsworth: Penguin.

Laing, R. D. 1960. *The Divided Self.* Reprint, Harmondsworth: Penguin, 1965.

———. 1967. *The Politics of Experience and the Bird of Paradise.* Harmondsworth: Penguin.

———. 1971. *The Politics of the Family and Other Essays.* New York: Pantheon Books.

Lamiell, J. 1981. "Toward an Idiothetic Psychology of Personality." *American Psychologist* 36:276–289.

———. 1986. "What Is Nomothetic about "Nomothetic" Personality Research?" *Theoretical and Philosophical Psychology* 6, no. 2:97–107.

Landis, B. 1975. "Fromm's Theory of Biophilia-Necrophilia and Its Implications for Clinical Practice." *Contemporary Psychoanalysis* 11, no. 4:418–434.

———. 1981. "Fromm's Approach to Analytic Technique." *Contemporary Psychoanalysis* 17, no. 4:537–551.

Landis, B., and E. Tauber. 1971. *In the Name of Life: Essays in Honor of Erich Fromm.* New York: Holt, Rinehart & Winston.

Leahey, T. H. 1987. *A History of Psychology.* 2d ed. Englewood Cliffs, N.J.: Prentice-Hall.

Lederer, G. 1983. *Jugend und Autoritat.* Darmstadt: Westdeutscher Verlag.

Lenhardt, C. 1976. "The Wanderings of Enlightenment." In *On Critical Theory,* ed. J. O'Neill. New York: Seabury Press.

Levine, N. 1987. "The German Historical School." *Journal of the History of Ideas* 48, no. 3:431–451.

Lind, G. 1988. "The Politics of Scoring Moral Judgment." Address to the International Society for Political Psychology, Secaucus, N.J., July 3.

Loewe, R., et al. 1966. *Studies in Rationalism, Judaism, and Universalism.* New York: Humanities Press.

Lowenthal, L. 1987. *An Unmastered Past.* Berkeley: University of California Press.

Lundin, R. 1972. *Theories and Systems of Psychology.* Toronto: D. C. Heath.

Maccoby, M. 1976. *The Gamesman.* New York: Simon and Schuster.

———. 1983. "Social Character vs. the Productive Ideal." *Praxis International*: 70–83.

———. 1985. Personal communication to the author. May 14.

MacIntyre, A. 1964. "Existentialism." In *Sartre: A Collection of Critical Essays,* ed. M. Warnock. Garden City, N.Y.: Doubleday, 1971.

Makkreel, R. 1975. *Dilthey: Philosopher of the Human Sciences.* Princeton: Princeton University Press.

Malcolm, J. 1981. *Psychoanalysis: The Impossible Profession.* New York: Alfred A. Knopf.

———. 1984. *In the Freud Archives.* New York: Alfred A. Knopf.

Malinowski, B. 1927. *Sex and Repression in Savage Society.* Reprint, New York: Meridian Press, 1955.

Mann, T. 1933. "Freud and the Future." In T. Mann, *Freud, Goethe, and Wagner.* New York: Alfred A. Knopf, 1936.

Manuel, F. E., and F. P. Manuel. 1979. *Utopian Thought in the Western World.* Cambridge, Mass.: Harvard University Press.

Marcuse, H. 1948. "Existentialism: Remarks concerning Jean-Paul Sartre's 'L'Etre et Néant.'" In Marcuse, 1972.

———. 1955. *Eros and Civilization.* Reprint, New York: Vintage Books, 1962. Excerpts quoted by permission.

———. 1956. "A Reply to Erich Fromm." *Dissent* 3, no. 1:79–81.

———. 1972. *Studies in Critical Philosophy.* Boston: Beacon Press.

Marx, K. 1844. "Economic and Philosophic Manuscripts of 1844." In Fromm, 1961b.

———. 1972. *The Grundrisse,* ed. D. McLellan. New York: Harper & Row.

Masson, J. 1984. *The Assault on Truth.* New York: Farrar, Straus & Giroux.

——— ed. 1985. *The Complete Letters of Sigmund Freud to Wilhelm Fliess.* Cambridge, Mass.: Belknap Press of Harvard University Press.

May, R. 1950. *The Meaning of Anxiety.* New York: Ronald Press.

———. 1953. *Man's Search for Meaning.* New York: W. W. Norton.

———. 1967. *Power and Innocence.* New York: W. W. Norton.

Mazlish, B. 1966. *The Riddle of History.* New York: Harper & Row.

McGrath, W. 1986. *Freud's Discovery of Psychoanalysis: The Politics of Hysteria.* Ithaca: Cornell University Press.

McGuire, W., ed. 1971. *The Freud/Jung Letters.* Princeton: Princeton University Press.

McLellan, D. 1977. *The Thought of Karl Marx.* London: Shanghai Printing Press.

Menaker, E. 1982. *Otto Rank: A Rediscovered Legacy.* New York: Columbia University Press.

Milgram, S. 1961. "Nationality and Conformity." *Scientific American,* no. 205: 41–51.

———. 1974. *Obedience to Authority.* New York: Harper & Row. Excerpts quoted by permission of HarperCollins Publishers.

Miller, A. 1986. *Thou Shalt Not Be Aware: Society's Betrayal of the Child.* New York: New American Library.

Millet, J. 1966. "Psychoanalysis in the United States." In Alexander, Eisenstein, and Grotjahn, 1966.

Mills, C. W. 1959. *The Sociological Imagination.* New York: Oxford University Press.

Montagu, A. 1985. Personal communication to the author. April 23.

Moscovici, S. 1985. *The Age of the Crowd: A Historical Treatise on Mass Psychology.* London: Cambridge University Press.

Mullahy, P. 1948. *Oedipus: Myth and Complex,* intro. E. Fromm. New York: Hermitage Press.

Munroe, R. 1955. *Schools of Psychoanalytic Thought.* New York: Dryden Press.

Natterson, J. 1966. "Theodor Reik." In Alexander, Eisenstein, and Grotjahn, 1968.

Nelson, B. 1962. "Sociology and Psychoanalysis on Trial." *Psychoanalysis and the Psychoanalytic Review* 49, no. 2:144–160.

Nietzsche, F. 1871. *The Birth of Tragedy,* trans. F. Gollfing. New York: Anchor/ Doubleday, 1956.

———. 1887. *The Genealogy of Morals,* trans. F. Gollfing. New York: Anchor/ Doubleday, 1956.

Pfeiffer, E., ed. 1966. *Sigmund Freud and Lou Andreas Salome: Letters.* New York: W. W. Norton.

Piaget, J. 1972. *The Child and Reality,* trans. A. Rosin. Harmondsworth: Penguin, 1976.

Polanyi, K. 1944. *The Great Transformation.* Boston: Beacon Press.

———. 1968. *Primitive, Archaic, and Modern Economies,* ed. G. Dalton. Boston: Beacon Press.

Pollack, G. 1976. "Joseph Breuer." In Gedo and Pollack, 1976.

Quinn, S. 1987. *A Mind of Her Own: The Life of Karen Horney.* New York: Summit Books.

Rank, O. 1924. *The Trauma of Birth.* Reprint, New York: Harper & Row, 1979.

———. 1932. *Art and the Artist.* Reprint, New York: Agathon Press, 1976.

———. 1936. *Truth and Reality,* trans. J. Taft. New York: W. W. Norton, 1964.

———. 1941. *Beyond Psychology.* Reprint, New York: Dover Publications, 1970.

Rapaport, D. 1938. *The History of the Concept of Association.* Reprint, New York: International Universities Press, 1974.

Reich, W. 1932a. "The Invasion of Compulsory Sex Morality." In *Sex-Pol Essays,* trans. Lee Baxandall. New York: Vintage Books, 1976.

———. 1932b. *Character Analysis,* trans. T. Wolfe. New York: Orgone Institute Press, 1949.

———. 1934. "Dialectical Materialism and Psychoanalysis." In *Sex-Pol Essays,* trans. Lee Baxandall. New York: Vintage Books, 1976.

———. 1970. *The Mass Psychology of Fascism.* New York: Pocket Books.

———. 1976. *People in Trouble.* New York: Farrar, Straus & Giroux.

———. 1979. *Genitality in the Theory and Therapy of the Neuroses.* New York: Farrar, Straus & Giroux.

Ricoeur, P. 1970. *Freud and Philosophy.* New Haven: Yale University Press.

Riesman, D. 1949. *Individualism Reconsidered and Other Essays.* Reprint, New York: Free Press, 1964.

———. 1950. *The Lonely Crowd.* New Haven: Yale University Press.

———. 1985. Personal communication to the author. July 9.

Roazen, P., ed. 1973. *Sigmund Freud.* Englewood Cliffs, N.J.: Prentice-Hall.

Roazen, P. 1971. *Brother Animal: The Story of Freud and Tausk.* New York: Random House/Vintage.

———. 1974. *Freud and His Followers.* New York: Alfred A. Knopf.

———. 1986. *Freud: Political and Social Thought.* New York: De Capo Press.

———. 1990. *Encountering Freud.* New Brunswick, N.J.: Transaction.

Robinson, P. 1976. *The Sexual Radicals.* London: Temple Smith.

Rorer, L., and T. Widiger. 1983. "Personality Structure and Assessment." *Annual Review of Psychology* 34:431–463.

Rosenthal, E. 1966. "Torah and *Nomos* in Medieval Jewish Philosophy." In Loewe et al., 1966.

Rubins, J. 1978. *Karen Horney: The Gentle Rebel of Psychoanalysis.* New York: Dial Press.

Rudnytsky, P. 1987. *Freud and Oedipus.* New York: Columbia University Press.

Rycroft, C. 1972. *A Critical Dictionary of Psychoanalysis*. London: Penguin.

———. 1981. *The Innocence of Dreams*. Oxford: Oxford University Press.

———. 1985. *Beyond Psychoanalysis*, ed. P. Fuller. Chicago: University of Chicago Press.

Safran, J., and L. Greenberg. 1987. "Affect and the Unconscious: A Cognitive Perspective." In *Theories of Unconscious and Theories of the Self*. Hillsdale, N.J.: Analytic Press.

Sahakian, W. S. 1974. *Systematic Social Psychology*. New York: Chandler.

———. 1984. *History and Systems of Social Psychology*. New York: Hemisphere Publishing.

Sanford, N. 1956. "The Approach of *The Authoritarian Personality*." In F. Greenstein and M. Lerner, eds. *A Source Book for the Study of Personality and Politics*. Chicago: Markham, 1971.

Sapir, A. 1926. "The Unconscious Patterning of Behavior in Society." In *The Unconscious: A Symposium*. New York: Alfred A. Knopf, 1929.

Schacht, R. 1970. *Alienation*. Garden City, N.Y.: Doubleday.

Schachtel, E. 1937. "Zum Begriff und Zur Diagnose der Personlichkeit in den *Personality Tests*." *Zeitschrift für Sozialforschung* 6:597–624.

———. 1959. *Metamorphosis*. New York: Basic Books.

———. 1966. *Experiential Foundations of Rorschach's Test*. New York: Basic Books.

Schaff, A. 1970. *Marxism and the Human Individual*. New York: McGraw-Hill.

Schecter, D. 1973. "On the Emergence of Human Relatedness." In *Interpersonal Explorations in Psychoanalysis*, ed. E. Witenberg. New York: Basic Books.

Schecter, S. 1961. *Aspects of Rabbinic Theology*. New York: Schocken Books.

———. 1971. "Of Human Bonds and Bondage" in Landis and Tauber, 1974.

Scheler, M. 1915. "The Idols of Self-Knowledge." In *Selected Philosophical Essays* trans. D. Lachterman. Evanston: Northwestern University Press, 1973.

———. 1923. "Ordo Amoris." In *Selected Philosophical Essays*. trans. D. Lachterman. Evanston: Northwestern University Press, 1973.

Schopenhauer, A. 1844. "The Life of the Species." In *The Will To Live: Selected Writings of Arthur Schopenhauer*, ed. R. Taylor. New York: Frederick Ungar, 1962.

Schulman, M. 1963. *Moses Hess: Prophet of Zionism*. New York: Thomas Yoseloff.

Schultz, D. 1969. *A History of Modern Psychology*. New York: Academic Press.

Searles, H. F. 1960. *The Non-Human Environment*. New York: International Universities Press.

———. 1965. *Collected Papers on Schizophrenia and Related Subjects*. New York: International Universities Press.

Segal, H. 1964. *Introduction to the Work of Melanie Klein*. New York: Basic Books.

Sherif, M., and C. Sherif. 1948. *An Outline of Social Psychology*. Rev. ed. New York: Harper & Row, 1956.

Shils, E. "Authoritarianism: 'Right' and 'Left.'" In Christie and Jahoda, 1954.

Silva-Garcia, J. 1988. "Erich Fromm in Mexico." In *Symposium Erich Fromm—Life and Work*, Locarno, Switzerland, March 12–14. Tübingen: International Erich Fromm Society.

Simmel, E. 1946. *Anti-Semitism: A Social Disease*. New York: International Universities Press.

Simmel, G. 1908a. "How Is Society Possible?" In *Georg Simmel: On Individuality and Social Forms,* ed. D. Levine. Chicago: University of Chicago Press, 1971.

——. 1908b. "Group Expansion and the Development of Individuality." In *Georg Simmel: On Individuality and Social Forms,* ed. D. Levine. Chicago: University of Chicago Press, 1971.

Spiegel, H. 1987. Personal communication to the author. November 24.

Spiegel, R. 1981. "Tribute to Erich Fromm." *Contemporary Psychoanalysis* 17, no. 4:436–441.

Stam, J. 1980. "Historical Perspective on Linguistic Relativity." In *The Psychology of Language and Thought: Essays in the Theory of Psycholinguistics,* ed. R. Rieber. New York: Plenum Press.

Stepansky, P. 1986. "Feuerbach and Jung as Religious Critics." In *Freud: Appraisals and Reappraisals,* ed. P. Stepansky. Hillsdale, N.J.: Analytic Press.

Stone, L. 1986. *Cognition and Affect: A Developmental Psychology of the Individual.* Buffalo: Prometheus Books.

Sulloway, F. 1979. *Freud: Biologist of the Mind.* New York: Basic Books.

Suttie, I. 1935. *The Origins of Love and Hate.* Reprint, Harmondsworth: Penguin, 1960.

Swales, P. 1982a. *Freud, Johann Weier, and the Status of Seduction: The Role of the Witch in the Conception of Fantasy.* Published privately by the author, 2–6 High St., Haverfordwest, Pembrokeshire, U.K.

——. 1982b. "Freud, Minna Bernays, and the Conquest of Rome." *New American Review* 1, no. 2/3.

——. 1983. *Freud, Martha Bernays, and the Language of Flowers.* Published privately.

——. 1986. "Freud, His Teacher, and the Birth of Psychoanalysis." In Stepansky, 1986.

——. 1987. Personal communication to the author. July 7.

Sykes, G. 1962. *The Saving Remnant.* New York: Harper & Row.

Thomas, W. I., and F. Zanecki. 1918. *The Polish Peasant in Europe and America.* Boston: Badger.

Thompson, C. 1950. *Psychoanalysis: Evolution and Development.* New York: Grove Press.

——. 1964. *Interpersonal Psychoanalysis: Collected Papers,* ed. Maurice Green. New York: Basic Books.

Thompson, E. P. 1978. *The Poverty of Theory.* New York: Monthly Review Press.

Thompson, M. G. 1987. *The Death of Desire.* New York: New York University Press.

Van Herik, J. 1982. *Freud on Femininity and Faith.* Berkeley: University of California Press.

Wachtel, P. 1986. Personal communication to the author. October 18.

——. 1987. "Are We Prisoners of the Past?" *Tikkun* 2, no. 3:24–27 and 90–92.

Wallace, E. R. 1983. *Freud and Anthropology: A History and Reappraisal.* New York: International Universities Press.

——. 1984. "Freud and Religion: A History and Reappraisal." In *The Psychoanalytic Study of Society,* ed. W. Muensterberger, L. B. Boyer, and S. Grolnick. Hillsdale, N.J.: Analytic Press.

Weber, M. 1904. *The Protestant Ethic and the Spirit of Capitalism*. New York: Charles Scribner's Sons, 1958.

——. 1923. "The Social Psychology of the World Religions." In *From Max Weber: Essays in Sociology*, ed. H. Gerth and C. W. Mills. New York: Oxford University Press, 1980.

Weiss, H. 1936. "Die 'Enquête Ouvrière' von Karl Marx." *Zeitschrift für Sozialforschung* 5:75–98.

Wellmer, A. 1974. *Critical Theory of Society*. New York: Seabury Press.

Whorf, B. 1956. *Language, Thought, and Reality*. New York: Basic Books.

Wilhelm, K. 1966. "The Idea of Humanity in Judaism." In Loewe et al., 1966.

Wittels, F. 1939. "The Neo-Adlerians." *American Journal of Sociology* 14, no. 3:433–445.

Wolman, B. 1960. *Contemporary Theories and Systems in Psychology*. New York: Harper & Row.

Wolstein, B. 1981. "A Historical Note on Erich Fromm: 1955." *Contemporary Psychoanalysis* 17, no. 4:481–485.

Wundt, W. 1912. *Elements of Folk Psychology: Outlines of a Developmental History of Mankind*, trans. E. Schaub. London: Allen & Unwin, 1916.

Wyss, D. 1973. *Psychoanalytic Schools from the Beginning to the present*. New York: Jason Aronson.

Xirau, R. 1971. "Erich Fromm: What Is Man's Struggle?" In Landis and Tauber, 1971.

Index